ACROSS THE AISLE

Opposition in Canadian Politics

How do parties with official opposition status influence Canadian politics? *Across the Aisle* is an innovative examination of the theory and practice of opposition in Canada, both in Parliament and in provincial legislatures. Extending from the pre-Confederation era to the present day, it focuses on whether Canada has developed a coherent tradition of parliamentary opposition.

David E. Smith argues that Canada has in fact failed to develop such a tradition. He investigates several possible reasons for this failure, including the long dominance of the Liberal party, which arrested the tradition of viewing the opposition as an alternative government; periods of minority government induced by the proliferation of parties; the role of the news media, which have largely displaced Parliament as a forum for commentary on government policy; and, finally, the increasing popularity of calls for direct action in politics.

Readers of *Across the Aisle* will gain a renewed understanding of official opposition that goes beyond Stornoway and shadow cabinets, illuminating both the historical evolution and recent developments of opposition politics in Canada.

DAVID E. SMITH, FRSC, is the author of *The People's House of Commons* (winner of the Donner Prize for the best public policy book by a Canadian), *Federalism and the Constitution of Canada*, and many books on Canadian politics. He is currently Distinguished Visiting Professor in the Department of Politics and Public Administration at Ryerson University.

Across the Aisle

Opposition in Canadian Politics

DAVID E. SMITH

UNIVERSITY OF TORONTO PRESS
Toronto Buffalo London

© University of Toronto Press 2013
Toronto Buffalo London
www.utppublishing.com
Printed in Canada

ISBN 978-1-4426-4736-7 (cloth)
ISBN 978-1-4426-1547-2 (paper)

Printed on acid-free, 100% post-consumer recycled paper with vegetable-based inks.

Library and Archives Canada Cataloguing in Publication

Smith, David E., 1936–
Across the aisle: opposition in Canadian politics / David E. Smith.

Includes bibliographical references and index.
ISBN 978-1-4426-4736-7 (bound). – ISBN 978-1-4426-1547-2 (pbk.)

1. Opposition (Political science) – Canada. 2. Canada. Parliament – Powers
and duties. 3. Representative government and representation – Canada.
4. Canada – Politics and government. I. Title.

JL167.S65 2013   328.71'0769   C2013-900572-2

This book has been published with the help of a grant from the Canadian
Federation for the Humanities and Social Sciences, through the Awards to
Scholarly Publications Program, using funds provided by the Social Sciences
and Humanities Research Council of Canada.

University of Toronto Press acknowledges the financial assistance to its publishing program of the Canada Council for the Arts and the Ontario Arts Council.

University of Toronto Press acknowledges the financial support of the
Government of Canada through the Canada Book Fund for its publishing
activities.

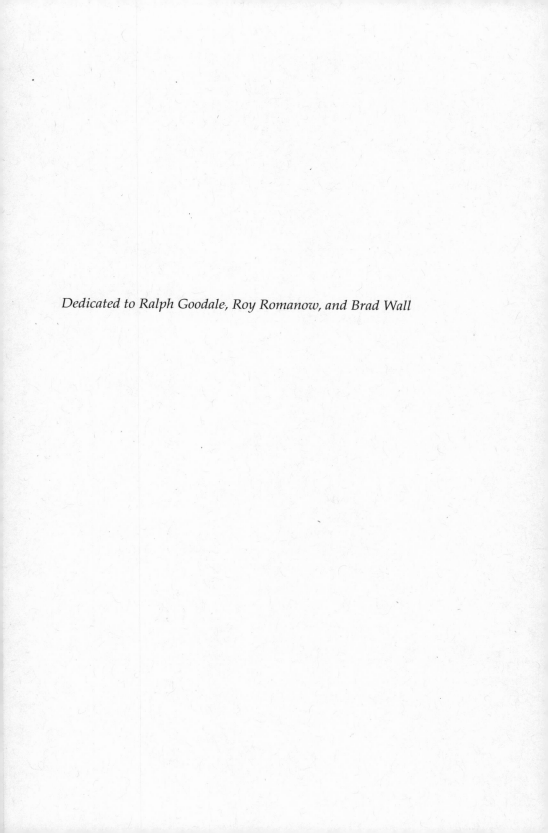

Dedicated to Ralph Goodale, Roy Romanow, and Brad Wall

Contents

viii   Contents

Preface

To say that the public is disillusioned with Parliament is to state a commonplace. Claims of a democratic deficit, verified by forms of democratic audit, are by now a familiar topic in discussions of Canadian politics. Critics claim that strict party discipline in the House of Commons, coupled with an electoral system that awards everything – which is to say, the single seat in contention in each constituency – to the candidate who wins the most but not necessarily a majority of votes cast, has distorted and suppressed representation of public opinion. It is also said that prime ministerial domination (or worse) of cabinet, public service, and Parliament has increased the gravity of the democratic deficiency. What is to be done to right what appears to be a serious imbalance in the arrangement and practice of Canadian political institutions?

This is too large a question to be answered in a single book. Instead, this study examines the evolution and present condition of the political corrective to concentrated power that the system already provides – legislative opposition. Like its Westminster exemplar, Canada's Parliament (and its provincial legislatures, with occasional variations) is divided into government and opposition. In the United Kingdom, the adjective 'loyal' by tradition describes the principal opposition; in Canada, where for nearly a century more than one party has sat opposite the government, the practice has been to use the word 'official.' The important point about the arrangement that for the purpose of this discussion is the one found in the House of Commons is that notwithstanding there being two sides, a sense of oneness holds them together. While it is true that each Member of Parliament is equal because each is elected by voters in a single constituency, it is also the case that voters go to the polls aware that their collective action will normally determine who will form the government. The situation is more complicated than that, but for the moment and from the perspective of this study, opposition appears almost by default: it is not the government, but it is the 'other.' One might say, with political scientist Jean Blondel, that 'the notion of opposition is, so to speak, parasitic on ideas of government.'[1] However phrased, it is the thesis of this book that government and opposition are parts of a shared community – Parliament – but that developments in Canadian politics over the past two decades have undermined that common bond.

In 1922, William Irvine, prairie radical and Labour MP, described the official opposition as 'the politically unemployed.'[2] From Irvine's point of view, all members of mainstream parties were apologists for the capitalist system and therefore interchangeable. Still, his remark demonstrates a truth about the parliamentary system – if not of the human condition – which is, that there are rivals ready to fill one's shoes; or, to vary the metaphor, who stand in the wings, or, again, who wait for their turn at bat. The common point of the metaphorical occupations, as of Parliament, is that they are closed shops: you are in the cast, or on the team, or a member of the House. Outsiders do not participate. Under the Canadian constitution, there is no constituent power outside of Parliament. That exclusionary principle confers – or did at one time – monopoly authority on opposition in the Commons.

Today, however, there are competitors everywhere: the media, social movements, electronic technologies, and more. It is to this last – the 'more' – on which the core parts of this study focus. To be precise, they examine the development of parliamentary opposition from Confederation to the present, using as backdrop the changing character and characteristics of the political parties and the party system. As well, they examine challenges for parliamentary opposition whose sources lie beyond the walls of the House of Commons. To this end, the book's nine chapters are divided among four parts: Part One, the Introduction, takes as its theme the title of its single chapter: 'Opposition: "Somebody Has to Do It"'; Part Two sets out a four-chapter chronology of parliamentary opposition in Canada; Part Three considers challenges for parliamentary opposition under three headings: 'Opposition, More or Less,' 'Opposition in the Federation,' and 'Whither Parliamentary Opposition?'; and Part Four presents a conclusion that analyses 'The Problem of Parliamentary Opposition Today.'

As a guide to the argument that follows, it may be useful to elaborate the chronology mentioned in the previous paragraph. Chapter 2 traces the introduction of the two-party system and the appearance of a formalized parliamentary opposition between 1867 and the end of Union government at the conclusion of the First World War. Chapter 3 examines, first, the Liberal 'ascendancy' that emerged to the Speaker's right in the 1920s and that continued for more than three decades; and second, the fragmentation of opposition that followed upon the arrival of third parties and that remains a feature of Canadian politics. Chapter 4, which begins at the end of the Liberal ascendancy (1957), takes as its theme the alternation between minority and majority governments and the effect this serial shift in power up to 1993 had upon an opposition that was itself undergoing transformation. A sub-theme is the institutionalization of political parties – for instance, the introduction of the concept of 'recognizing' a parliamentary party, and the political separation that arose between, on the one hand, the traditional and cooperating parties inside the House and, on the other, the new, electorally competitive parties, Reform and the Bloc Québécois, outside.[3] Chapter 5 brings the chronology to the outcome of the federal election of 2011, which has resulted in a dramatically reconstituted opposition: the New Democratic Party is now the official opposition; the Liberal party for the first time in the country's history is neither in government nor in official opposition; and of equal significance, the governing party (the Conservative Party of Canada) has devalued legislative opposition, whose status was long derived by tradition from Parliament and the unwritten constitution, and has devalued it for that very reason – because it was not elected.

Of course, in a parliamentary system neither is the government 'elected': a theory simply stated but whose practice appears increasingly difficult to grasp. More than that, the implications of the proposition that governments are elected need to be studied. Among these are the following: government cannot be changed without an election; the accountability of governments 'elected by the people' rather than made in the House and legitimized by the Sovereign's representative is directed *away from* rather than toward Parliament, with separation rather than fusion of executive and legislature the consequence; institutional accommodation of regional and cultural diversity (a concern of prime ministers since John A. Macdonald) is displaced by a preoccupation with permanent campaigning – combat at the polls continues into the House; and, most important from the perspective of this book, the function of opposition in Parliament is doubly denied: 'unelected,' it is disqualified from replacing the government, nor may it legitimately delay or thwart the people's mandate conferred at the election on the government. Consociational democracy, achieved through the conventions of federalism and the conduct of Parliament, declines; contested democracy, which posits the legitimacy of the people in contrast to that of Parliament, rises.

While the subject of this book is parliamentary opposition, the discussion that follows is about something more – the transformation of Canadian politics. As the early chapters make clear, there was a time when the purpose of constituency organizations was to serve the interests of the party in Parliament. Later chapters show a reversal in that relationship: electronic technology has compressed time and space, thereby exposing the parliamentary party to rapidly changing allegiances and loyalties outside of Parliament. It is an open question whether Parliament remains, as it once did, the indisputable centre of Canadian political life.

In 2011, a series of democratic revolutions rocked the Arab world. In each country, as people took to the streets, invariably the first question heard was, 'Who will rule?' In times of political uncertainty in Canada, the answer is deceptively easy: it is the official opposition in Parliament. None the less, there is a degree of false clarity to that response. Opposition in Parliament comes in the guise of political parties, although unlike at Westminster there have for a long time been several of them; and the parties in Parliament by no means exhaust the legislative definition of opposition, because unlike the United Kingdom, Canada is a federation. As will be seen in the chapters that follow, opposition – even when it is limited to legislative opposition – may be unexpectedly complex in its composition.

I have dedicated this book to Ralph Goodale, Roy Romanow, and Brad Wall, the first, a friend, the second, an academic colleague, and the last, a former student. Members of different political parties, each has sat in opposition and in government, although only one in Parliament. In a half-century's study of federal and provincial politics, I have met many people from a number of political parties. Canadians often express disillusionment with their elected politicians, yet I have generally found legislators to be energetic and conscientious. Some might have been more articulate tribunes of their constituents than others, but in that respect the range of talents they displayed was of a piece with the range of qualities found among the people they represented. On balance, Canadians should think twice about the cynicism they so freely express and the criticism they so freely direct at legislators. The three men to whom I have dedicated this book are admirable representatives of both their electors and their calling, whether that is found in government or opposition.

Several individuals have expressed interest in this project. I wish to acknowledge the support I have received from James Bowden, David Brock, John Courtney, Nathan Elliott, Nicholas MacDonald, Doug Richardson, Charles Robert, Roy Romanow, Duff Spafford, and John Whyte. I would like to thank the Johnson–Shoyama Graduate School of Public Policy, University of Regina, for generously providing me with an office and the solitude necessary for the completion of this book. As well, I wish to express my gratitude to the staffs of the following institutions for help given during the course of my research: the Saskatchewan Legislative Library, the Murray Memorial Library, University of Saskatchewan, the Dr John Archer Library, University of Regina, the Diefenbaker Canada Centre, the Saskatchewan Archives Board, and the University of Saskatchewan Archives.

As on former occasions, Ursula Acton has provided great assistance in preparing the manuscript for electronic submission to the press and in compiling the index to the book. Once again, I wish to thank Matthew Kudelka for his expert editorial guidance. I am indebted to both of them for their help.

Regina, March 2012

PART ONE

Introduction

1 Opposition: 'Somebody Has to Do It'

Frank Quennell, 2010, Saskatchewan Minister of Justice, 2003–7;
Opposition justice critic, 2007–11

The House of Commons is Canada's premier institution for the authoritative expression of electoral opinion and for approval of public policy formulated in response to that opinion. This statement oversimplifies the relationship that exists between government and the public service on the one hand and opposition parties on the other. Still, it directs attention to where it has traditionally been paid – Parliament and, more particularly, its lower chamber. The reason for concentration and continuity is simply stated: under the Canadian constitution there is no constituent power outside of Parliament or, in a province, the legislature. Instruments of direct democracy – initiative, referendum, and plebiscite – exist but are rarely used and, in any case, are no more than advice to constituted authority.[1] The one qualification to the primacy of Parliament is the guarantees found in the Canadian Charter of Rights and Freedoms. Even here, Section 33 allows Parliament (or a legislature) to declare that for a period of five years, but subject to renewal, an 'Act or provision thereof shall operate notwithstanding a provision included section 2 or sections 7 to 15 of this Charter.' By declaring this exception the clause affirms the principle of Parliament's supremacy, although governments have been loath to invoke it for fear of the criticism this would elicit.

Arguably, this last phrase might be viewed as a terminological sleight of hand. If there is a commonplace opinion of Parliament today, it is that Parliament is not in practice supreme. Instead, that distinction rests with the executive, that is, cabinet or, as some critics would maintain, the prime minister alone. This fate, invariably viewed as an index to Parliament's decline, is ascribed to a variety of sources, among which the most frequently cited are inflexible party discipline, a professional bureaucracy uninterested in the opinions of the people's representatives, and echelons of political staff whose presence distances ministers and especially the first minister from members of their own party but, most significantly for the purposes of this discussion, from members of Parliament as well.

Where the politics of Parliament were once treated as high, they are now viewed as low – in two respects. Not only are politicians said to be distrusted, and therefore what they say and do suspect in the mind of the general public, but Parliament's politics have ceased to be seen as important as they once were. The development of extra-parliamentary mechanisms to deal with federal–provincial issues, for example first ministers' meetings, has long been interpreted as an intrusion on Parliament's constitutional primacy. More recently, the same criticism has been advanced of courts whose interpretation of rights guaranteed under the Charter trespasses on Parliament's traditional terrain.[2] But these encroachments, if that is what they are, are familiar only because of the high visibility of the politicians and judges who participate in them. In their effect upon Parliament, they are not alone.

Interests, be they social, cultural, environmental, or economic, have proliferated at a rapid rate, as have the media through which they are expressed. In twenty-first-century Canada, it would be untrue to suggest that there are now politics without walls. None the less, the rigid distinction once drawn between politics inside and outside Parliament has ceased to exist. Where in the 1830s and 1840s, opposition expressed through extra-parliamentary activity – Papineau and Mackenzie in the Canadas, the Chartists in Great Britain – was labelled radical, hostile, and assured to be ineffective, this is no longer the case. Parliament's purpose is to generate (and occasionally force, through closure) agreement on policy by using the procedure of successive readings, committee examination of bills, and voting in two chambers (but only one in the provinces). Parliamentary debate is a great leveller of conflicting interests as well as a calming influence on intense feeling. The product achieved through inter-party compromise and, more typically, intra-party discipline is public policy deemed in the interests of the nation. The difference between past and present is that while Parliament remains master of the general interest, it now confronts a niche world ever more characterized by technical and professional knowledge, on the one hand, and a broadened definition and acceptance of minority rights, on the other. Accompanied by a proliferation of interested 'publics,' these developments exist in uneasy tension with a political tradition whose fundamental proposition is rule by the majority.

Political parties and governmental institutions have yet to accommodate the challenges these changes present. Their failure contributes to the sense of political malaise that is a stock subject for journalistic commentary and that is reflected in, among other features of modern politics, a decline in voter turnout, particularly among the young, static party membership except for leadership campaigns, cynicism regularly expressed to pollsters for politicians as a group and for political parties, and increasing public (and academic) confusion about both the content and operation of the constitution. To the diminished capacity of the House of Commons to frame and influence debate must be added a growing sense of citizen impotence.

For almost two centuries the central concern of government in Canada has been to protect Parliament (and the colonial legislatures that preceded it) from influences that would compromise its independence, whether from the Crown above or the people below. In other words, it was a concern that was essentially negative in conception; and that is still discernible in the broad claims advanced for parliamentary privilege over statute law and – from the opposite direction – in ever-expanding structures of political accountability, officers of Parliament being an example, with the restrictive implications such 'agents' pose for the independence of their 'principal.' Once a citadel that demanded deference, Parliament is now a target of complaint, its debates characterized as hyperbolic and polarized, its behaviour described in 2008 by a prime minister (no less), as 'dysfunctional.'[3] Public lamentation and irritation have produced demands – usually from outside of Parliament – for reform: for example, to change the electoral system; to reduce party discipline, thereby increasing the independence of individual members; and to limit the prime minister's monopoly of advice to the Governor General regarding the exercise of prerogative power. Missing from this list and from virtually any other analysis of Canadian parliamentary affairs is reference to opposition, that is, the official opposition and, because of Canada's long history of third parties, other opposition parties. In a Westminster-styled parliamentary system where opposition has a role to play that is equivalent in importance to that of the government (some scholars have argued it is *more* important[4]), the omission is puzzling.

Indeed, government and opposition are all that there is in the parliamentary system. There is no place for independents, not because they are constitutionally prohibited but because it is electorally impractical to send them there. In the words of Phineas Finn, the Irish MP with a seat at Westminster, in Anthony Trollope's classic political novel of the same name: 'If you choose to make Parliament a profession ... you can have no right even to think of independence.'[5] Writing a century later of British (but it could as well be said of Canadian) politics, R.M. Punnett made the compelling yet often unacknowledged point that in the parliamentary system government faces an 'office-seeking Opposition.'[6]

Several ramifications for the conduct of politics flow from that observation. First, in a parliamentary democracy opposition has to be in Parliament. This does not exclude, but is vitally different from, extra-parliamentary opposition, as found, for instance, in the media, or in the form of unions, or interest groups generally. Second, because the purpose of opposition is to oppose the government and not just its policies, it must be prepared to assume power when a government resigns.[7] In reality, opposition is less about *becoming* the government than it is about *being* an 'alternative Government.'[8] The prospect of alternation in power is an incentive for Canadian parliamentarians to think in single-party rather than coalition terms. In addition, it provides compelling reason for party discipline, since it is discipline that 'consolidate[s] the forces ... of the Opposition in the House of Commons.'[9] Third, parliamentary opposition is loyal opposition. Here is a phrase whose literal construction bears close scrutiny. The opposition is loyal because it accepts the constitution (the rules of the political game). For that reason, when a government resigns it knows that it will be treated, in opposition, in a manner that will permit it in the future to return to power. If that were not the expectation, then peaceful succession, which Canadians take for granted because they, unlike much of humanity, know nothing else, would not be the routine practice it is. One vital consequence of this silent understanding is that there is no reason for the Crown to enter parliamentary politics: the 'who' of 'who will govern?' is taken care of. Punnett says it best: 'The existence of the Leader of the Opposition is an essential part of the neutrality of the Monarch.'[10] With politicians on both sides of the aisle loyal, the Crown may (and should) remain above the political fray. If Canada is a 'peaceable kingdom' where order and good government reign, then much is owed for that condition to the quality of opposition those in power face.

Government and opposition are locked in a continuing contest. Election returns have consequences as unpredictable for opposition as they are for government, although it is to the latter that media, academic, and public commentary is more often directed. (The results of the 2011 federal election are an exception to that generalization, since among its unexpected outcomes was the displacement of the Liberal by the New Democratic Party as official opposition.) Appreciation of the link between the two (forged anew at each general election) is a casualty of this selective attention and impedes the larger understanding of the operation of Parliament.

In Canada, where coalition governments at the federal level are exceedingly rare, one party (the winners) gets to form the government, while the other party or parties (the losers) find themselves in opposition, because 'someone has to do it.' On occasion, election returns may belie the sense of finality implicit in such a comment: in 1987, the provincial Liberals in New Brunswick swept every seat. Thus there was no opposition: what to do? Or, following the 1982 provincial election in Alberta, four members to the Speaker's left faced the government, two from the New Democratic Party and two Independents, one of the latter the Leader of the Official Opposition in the previous legislature. How to determine who was to form the official opposition? Analysis of these and other conundrums with a provincial provenance will be found in chapter 7, 'Opposition in the Federation.' The reason for that inclusion is that while the primary topic of this book is government and opposition in Parliament, provincial experience and precedents cannot be, nor are they, ignored in federal practice. Another reason to adopt a broad perspective lies in the traditional federated structure of most Canadian political parties. Notwithstanding theories of federalism that elevate the principles of independence and coordination, parliamentary parties in Canada are not jurisdictionally hermetic. The history and practice of the Reform Party and the Bloc Québécois are exceptions that challenge that generalization, thereby complicating electoral politics and, more relevant to the present thesis, the conduct of opposition in Parliament.

The number of parties to the Speaker's left affects the relationship between government and opposition in multiple ways. For the moment, the aspect that requires emphasis is the following: the counterpart to responsible government – where government must maintain support of the House of Commons (and thus indirectly of the people) – is responsible opposition, which means acting in the constitutional manner set out above. It does not, and cannot, since it is the duty of opposition to replace the government, signify taking responsibility for government policy. Seldom has this 'rule of opposition' been stated so succinctly as it was early in 1957 by soon-to-be cabinet minister Pierre Sevigny to his party leader John Diefenbaker: 'We should then severely criticize the Government for their careless actions being at the same time *most careful* to avoid telling them what we would have done in the same circumstances.'[11] In this conception of parliamentary power and the roles it assigns, there is no place for the constitutional innovations advocated three decades later by Preston Manning, founder of the Reform Party. Rather than as a forum where ins and outs replace one another, Manning promoted the House as a marketplace in which support was mobilized 'to force [ideas] higher and higher on the political agenda' and 'to build and maintain coalitions across regional and party lines.'[12] While a case may be made, as some critics have done, to moderate the Canadian practice of inflexible party discipline, there is a significant difference between that proposition and standing ready to build coalitions, Congress-like, on myriad and unspecified policy questions. Nor is there any constitutional rationale for Mr Manning's suggestion (in response to so-called activist courts) that the House establish 'a judicial review committee to ensure the primacy of the elected representatives of the people of Canada,'[13] or for Mr Layton's condition in 2011 that NDP support for Canada's mission in Libya be contingent upon 'parliamentarians [having] a surveillance and oversight role.'[14]

The import for Parliament of a perspective that views its primary cleavage as legislature-versus-executive rather than government-versus-opposition is open to debate. There is one codicil, however, to that general statement: were it to be implemented, the House of Commons could not carry out its task of exacting supreme responsibility from the government. The terms of constitutional engagement would shift: 'If a congress cannot go through the (often hollow) motions of holding the executive 'accountable' on a daily basis, it can nevertheless resist the will of the executive far more effectively – and even impose its own.'[15] A striking if attenuated example of the House performing its duty, against a background of conflicting views of the role of opposition, is the defeat in 1979 of the government led by Joe Clark. The partisan alliances and misalliances that led to that outcome are for later discussion. For the moment the point deserving emphasis is that the issue was of long gestation but had at its root intra- and extra-parliamentary tension within the Progressive Conservative Party. The dethronement of John Diefenbaker as leader in 1967 has been the subject of extensive comment, usually in the context of making party leaders more accountable to rank-and-file party members. Less prominent has been the subject of inter-generational differences of opinion on the conduct of parliamentary opposition that were emerging in the early 1960s. Within a few years a similar debate would be heard in the Liberal Party, this time over participatory democracy, but the Liberals were in power and that, along with different personalities as leaders (different from Mr Diefenbaker, in any case), made all the difference.

In 1964, Thomas van Dusen, Diefenbaker's executive assistant, wrote to Joe Clark, then National President of the Progressive Conservative Student Federation, setting forth (as instructed by the leader of the opposition) a political and, as it transpired, prescient homily on the subject of opposition:

> The testing ground of Government and Opposition is, of course, Parliament. Governments can be created outside of Parliament; but they are destroyed in Parliament.
>
> The function of the Opposition is to throw into relief the weakness of Government policy and the incapacity of the Government in the execution of its policies.
>
> Governments are brought down through their incapacity to carry out their programs … There is no obligation upon an opposition to propose alternative theories since it is the Government's duty to govern and that of the Opposition to oppose.[16]

In a reply to Van Dusen but whose message was intended for Diefenbaker, the future prime minister urged the former prime minister to recognize the changing nature of politics:

> [M]y [Clark's] concern is with the effect which the performance of this proper and essential role of criticism has upon what we have learned to call our 'Party image.' I think it is recognized that modern communications have ended that era … Today, in contrast, we are involved in a perpetual campaign, in which the events of every day determine Party allegiance. My fear is, that if we perform only the traditional Opposition role of criticism, we will assume a negative aspect which no two-month campaign can dispel … It is one especially destructive of our endeavours to attract young Canadians, whose inclinations are to look forward.[17]

The taut personal relationship between Clark and Diefenbaker preceded and succeeded, but also infected, Robert Stanfield's time as leader of the opposition (1967–76). As Norman Ward observed on Stanfield's retirement: 'I do not envy you that particular record which makes you … the only party leader in our history to have had his predecessor in the Commons all the way. It can't have been easy.'[18] This was an assessment that Stanfield himself appeared to share: 'I hope,' he publicly said in 1977 about the Clark government's policy on national unity, '[that Diefenbaker] will stop sticking a knife into Mr. Clark.' Diefenbaker denied the allegation that he 'represented [his] party's viewpoint. I don't know exactly what it is, but I do say that I don't represent it.'[19] Several factors contributed to this acrimony, among them heightened concern about policies that increasingly touched on sensitive, and largely new, issues – language, minorities, and personal morality, for instance. Each generated vocal and sustained extra-parliamentary opinion, which, over time and due in important part to the communications revolution, government and opposition experienced difficulty in accommodating. What was political and what was accepted as legitimately political, as opposed to personal, was changing in ways that challenged the traditional understanding of Parliament's place in the politics of the nation.

With its bureaucracy, patronage, and constitutional pre-eminence in the control of public expenditure, government possesses some instruments to defend itself against change, albeit not always successfully. The opposition is less fortunate. At one time, an opposition would travel the country (or province) in search of ideas, understanding problems and developing new policy solutions. The new era of instant messaging and frequent swings in public opinion has complicated and redefined the traditional role of parliamentary oppositions. Now they seek to avoid being 'locked in' to most positions because of the incessant swirl of changing ideas and reactions. Thus, holding a government to account and advancing alternative ideas have become less important objectives than appearing to be responsive to public sentiment. One consequence of this change in behaviour is the absence of coherence between policies in any particular period or within a single policy area over time.

The difference in opinion about opposition strategy, evident in the correspondence between leading Progressive Conservatives in the early 1960s, deserves attention for two reasons. First, Clark's concern about the 'negative' effects on 'young Canadians' of the 'traditional Opposition role' signalled the tenor of criticism to come, revealing as it did a political life outside, as well as inside, the House, where the former was about more than electoral organization. Nor was that criticism to remain unique to the party on the opposition benches. In a short time those opposite, on the government benches, would feel the sting as well. Indeed, by the millennium political deference had so declined and intra-party criticism so risen as to indict a current prime minister (Jean Chrétien). Opposition from outside of Parliament but from within the governing party achieved an object – forcing the resignation of a party leader and prime minister – that opposition from across the aisle had never succeeded in accomplishing.

Parliament's adversary culture and the undeviating party discipline it demanded attracted mounting complaint, although still largely from the outside. When Bob Rae, later an architect in Ontario politics of an inter-party accord that would see the NDP sustain a Liberal government in power, but in 1978 freshly elected to Parliament, sought guidance on behaviour from a parliamentary elder, John Diefenbaker counselled: 'Remember [when you ask a question] … go for the throat every time.'[20] This was followed, Rae recalled, by the Chief's now inevitable coda denigrating Tory leaders: 'The only person around here who thinks question period is about asking questions and getting answers is Bob Stanfield.'

A second reason for noting the evolving dichotomy in opinion about the opposition's principal task is that it confounded interpretation of the role itself, not least by opposition leaders. If Diefenbaker and his loyalists to a man (and this includes Ellen Fairclough, Canada's first female cabinet minister, who once championed parliamentary opposition because it 'provides a group of men [sic] who have concentrated their energies and their powers on preparing themselves for the day when they will be called upon to [form] the government'[21]) paid primary attention to Parliament, and if Clark, to his lasting regret, did not, Stanfield became a casualty of conflicting views of how an opposition leader should behave. On the one hand, on the day (15 November 1967) he entered the Commons (a former premier of Nova Scotia chosen by national convention as party leader two months earlier, he had sought and won his seat in a by-election), he told reporters that he would consider it 'my patriotic duty' to oust the Liberal government [led by Lester B. Pearson].[22] But on the other hand, three months later, after the Pearson government was defeated in the House on third reading of an excise tax bill and an election seemed inevitable, the prime minister arranged for Stanfield to meet the governor of the Bank of Canada, Louis Raminsky, at which time he was informed of the seriousness of the dollar situation and the deleterious effect the government's resignation would have on the markets: 'Those in charge felt I ought to know,' Stanfield later admitted. 'The briefing was so convincing,' it was reported, 'that he declined to make an all-out attempt to bring down the administration.'[23] Instead, a motion stating that the House did not consider the defeat a non-confidence vote was subsequently carried with the support of Social Credit members, who had originally voted against the excise bill. Stanfield's decision was considered by key Tories, such as party strategist and former Diefenbaker cabinet minister, Gordon Churchill, a 'capitulation' in that it amounted to a 'surrender' of opposition 'freedom.'[24]

Leaders of Canadian political parties, just like the citizens they claim to speak for, demonstrate an array of qualities. Diefenbaker and Clark (or Stanfield) appeared to be polar opposites in their personal interpretation of how to act as leader of the opposition – or, for that matter, as prime minister. George McIlraith, a Liberal who sat in the Commons without interruption between 1940 and 1972, and then in the Senate until 1983, disputed the view often heard that Diefenbaker was a great parliamentarian. On the contrary, said McIlraith, Diefenbaker 'did not have an understanding or appreciation of the role of prime minister. [Instead], he tended to spend all his time seeking to destroy the opposition.'[25] In this bellicose passion he had predecessors, Arthur Meighen being one: 'When you have a man [or 'enemy,' he said in the same speech] under your hammer never be tempted into doubtful ground and give him a chance to diverge.'[26] Diefenbaker and Meighen not only sounded alike but, according to Chubby Power, looked alike: 'Possibly because he also is an admirer of Meighen, John Diefenbaker seems to have adopted his oratorical gesticulation. John stands up straight, with both hands on his hips, but he makes the grave mistake of sometimes shaking his head, a mistake Meighen never in my recollection made.'[27] Compare that focus with what the biographer of another Tory leader, John Bracken, labels as Bracken's 'non-adventurous approach to opposition.'[28] That euphemistic description, whose meaning might suggest a parallel personality to Robert Stanfield's – described by *his* biographer, Geoffrey Stevens, as 'quiet, direct, unassuming, and unpretentious to a fault' – confirms the range of characteristics found in leaders on both sides of the aisle. [29]

That the individuals named in the previous paragraph were all Conservatives, Progressive or otherwise, should not be deemed significant; nor (perhaps) that Bracken and Stanfield were former provincial premiers. On this latter point, the movement of politicians between federal and provincial governments is a subject for discussion in chapter 7, although in recent decades the frequency of the shift is more prominent in opposition than in government ranks of the Commons. If, in discussion of opposition in Canada, there are more leaders of the Conservative or Progressive Conservative Party than of the Liberal, it is because there have been more of them. Liberal prime minsters have been long-lived and have faced a succession of (official) opposition leaders: King, six, Trudeau, four, and Chrétien, seven. Notwithstanding that there have been fewer Liberal leaders, the range of leadership styles is broad, from wily King, to Augustan St Laurent, to supercilious Trudeau, to straight-talking Chrétien ('Parliament is not a mutual admiration society').[30] Absent from this list is Lester Pearson, whose personality was the ob-verse of Diefenbaker's whichever side of the chamber he sat. 'What drew so many people to Pearson,' writes his biographer, John English, 'were those qualities that seemed to make him not a politician.'[31] Unlike Pearson, Diefenbaker was not a leader to see two sides to a question – he had 'views.' Whether Pearson's broad-minded perspective, perhaps arising as some have suggested from his earlier career as a diplomat, was debilitating to him as a political leader, and whether (if true) that debilitation was more of a handicap in opposition than in government, are important questions that will be considered later in this book.

Individual personality may influence leadership capability – a con-tribution seldom alluded to, however, in the sparse literature on gov-ernment–opposition relations in Parliament. The personal enmity between King and Meighen, and between Pearson and Diefenbaker, is a familiar topic in discussions of the periods when those pairs held of-fice, but beyond the unpleasantness their mutual dislike generated in the House, it is unclear how it affected the conduct of either govern-ment or opposition.[32] There are a dozen or more references to 'leader of the opposition' in R. MacGregor Dawson's *Government of Canada*, long the standard text on Canadian government, but the individuals who held that post are largely absent.[33] This is unexpected, for parliamen-tary politics is closely identified with personalities. It is as if there is theory on the one hand and politics on the other. What is missing is a sense of correct proportion between the two. Norman Ward suggested one explanation for this: 'I don't think it ever occurred to Dawson that a student of the House of Commons … should actually watch it a great deal. You worked from the record, which you then could cite.'[34]

Paradoxically, a literate analysis of the resulting problem is found in a debate of more than sixty years ago, precipitated by a Report of the American Political Science Association's Committee on Political Parties. Titled 'Toward a More Responsible Two-Party System,' the report ar-gues forcefully for an effective opposition party on the premise that 'the fundamental requirement of accountability is a two-party system in

which the opposition party acts as the critic of the party in power.'
Putting to one side the question of whether responsible government is
achievable where there are more than two parties – a proposition that
Canadian experience would seem to support – the Report generated
strong debate in the pages of the *American Political Science Review* but no
measurable change in the conduct of politics in Congress. The reason
why is made clear in a critique written by Austin Ranney that depended
heavily on the views of A. Lawrence Lowell of a half-century earlier:
'Unified, disciplined and responsible parties are appropriate *only* to a
government which seeks to locate full public power in the hands of
popular majorities … British [or Canadian] parties are an integral part
of a governmental system aimed at quite different goals than those the
American system seeks to realize.' Ranney maintains that 'the British
system is about majority rule and the American system about minority
rights'; criticizes the committee for concealing the contrast and for re-
fusing to say what happens when 'a party minority cannot "conscientiously" agree' with the majority; and concludes that at Westminster [or
Ottawa] there is 'full power of government' on one side of the House,
and, by implication, full power of opposition on the other.[35]

The debate in the APSR highlighted the importance in Parliament of
what was absent in Congress – the clarity of focused opposition within
the walls of the legislature – which is as common in the former as it is
rare in the latter. In the theory of parliamentary politics, there is no opportunity to fulfil a promise, such as Joe Clark pledged before he became prime minister: 'to make Parliament his master' and to put
Parliament 'back into the hands of ordinary MPs.'[36] That this remains a
perennial ambition of inexperienced politicians, provincial as well as
federal, may be gauged by the pledge of the new premier of Alberta in
2011, to reform Question Period and give her opponents a more substantial input into decision making. Nor is there any possibility of realizing
Preston Manning's ambition that in debate 'participants [will be] free to
alter their positions in the light of what is being said … This freedom …
is almost entirely missing from the Canadian House of Commons due to
the constrictions of excessive party discipline.'[37] For the opposition the
value of free speech is not to defeat government – governments as a rule
do not lose debates – but to give it 'the chance of influencing public
opinion outside the House against the Government.'[38] This is the reason
why political scientist John Wilson strenuously maintained that 'opposition is really more important than government – especially in a parliamentary system.'[39] That importance lies in what Wilson called the

opposition's 'nuisance' value: 'to make the government fear for its life over the longer term.' In short, its primary job is to harass. Stanley Knowles, long-time master of the House and its procedures, shared that sentiment: 'We are called obstructionists, time-wasters, and so on ... Posterity will [I submit] continue to bless the pertinacity of those to Mr. Speaker's left who do their job the best they can.'[40]

The temporal reference in Wilson's comment bears examination, for the tempo of parliamentary debate is different from, among other examples, instantaneous messaging, or organized street demonstrations, or even a model parliament. For an opposition in Parliament that is united behind its leader, the preferred strategy is slow and steady criticism of government – tortoise and hedgehog not hare and fox the faunal metaphors. The clash of government and opposition over issues that are matters of immediate debate – the subjects of daily media focus – diverts attention from the continuity of parliamentary politics in Canada, as demonstrated by long periods of single-party government – Conservatives in the nineteenth century, Liberals in the twentieth; long careers of party leaders in office – Macdonald, King, and Trudeau; and the constancy of issues – relations with the United States and (at one time) Great Britain, relations between English and French Canada, and the tariff. The succession of minority governments of the last decade and the proliferation of parties in Parliament in the decade before that one may alter the immediate tone of debate, but the sense of permanency remains. The continuation of opposition personnel is one explanation – Ralph Goodale, Jack Layton, and between 1990 and 2011, Gilles Duceppe, are prominent examples. Party identification notwithstanding, Members of Parliament have much in common, beginning with the fact that they are all members of the same club and they all entered it the same way. Indeed, election expense and party finance legislation have helped equalize career chances for politicians to an extent rarely experienced by ordinary Canadians. Uninterrupted tenure in power is a venerable source for criticism of government voiced by opposition and public alike. 'Never Have So Many Been In So Long' was Eugene Forsey's summation in May 1957 of the Liberal reign, begun in 1935, then drawing to a close.[41] He was not the first nor was he alone in passing this judgment. 'Most of us,' echoed Stanley Knowles, 'have the feeling that the interval between changes [in government] in this country is becoming a bit longer than is reasonable.'[42]

In concert with the multimedia revolution that exposes MPs generally (and opposition members, without the resources of government to

shield them, especially) to public pressure, reforms intended to empower the individual MP (for instance, election finance legislation
and research budgets for opposition parties) work in a manner that
may undermine the sense of common purpose that members of the
Commons used to experience. The speed of politics and of changes in
public opinion, along with the growth in the prominence of constituency concerns for the average member, discourage and impede association across the aisle. An example, thanks to air travel, is how infrequently
during a session MPs today stay in Ottawa over the weekend and thus
socialize, as they once did (sometimes across party lines). Although the
observation was made of legislative politics in Ontario, the assessment
applies with equal weight to Parliament: 'It [the change just described]
is a reflection of the professionalization of the legislature, which is erod-
ing the clubbishness of Queen's Park.'[43] A variation on this theme, now
raised to a 'law' ('The Iron Law of Emulation') is to be found in Daniel
Patrick Moynihan's 'principle [that] organizations in conflict become
like one another.'[44] Moynihan says nothing about the law's applicability to parties on either side of the aisle in the lower chamber of a
Westminster-styled parliament. Still, it is worth reflecting whether, and
to what extent, reforms intended to help improve the condition of opposition have contributed as well to the adversary culture of which the
'loyal opposition' is now so visibly a part.

As important as they may be to the conduct of parliamentary government – and they provide a crucial guide for the discussion of opposition
in this book – none the less, there is an exhausted quality to the traditional descriptions of opposition in Canada's parliamentary system.
Debate, criticism, scrutiny – opposition in Ottawa does all of these,
some better than others and some better at some times than at other
times. Yet to say this and no more would be to leave unsaid what is a
vital part of the opposition's role in Canadian politics, its contribution
to maintaining the federation. There is more here at issue than the electoral fortunes of the opposition – regional concentration of party support, for instance. At issue as well is opposition in the context of a
bicameral parliament in which the upper chamber, the Senate of Canada,
is widely depicted as flawed both as a voice of the provinces or regions
and as a check on the lower house. Senators are appointed by governor-
in-council on the advice of the prime minister. They are a continuing
(and gratuitous) reminder to the opposition of the government's power.
Since senators may hold their appointment until seventy-five years of
age, the Senate, unlike the Commons, is a continuous body. It has no

'life' (however else jesters might use that term), in the sense that Parliament (i.e., the House of Commons) has of a maximum of five years. As a result, partisan control of one chamber does not necessarily signify partisan control of the other chamber. Even when they are domi-nated by different parties, the Senate by convention uses its powers, which except for appropriations are equal to those of the Commons, judiciously. Senators recognize that it is not their duty, where the will of the people is clear, to reject legislation coming from the lower house. Of course, between those extremes there is wide scope for differences of opinion and partisan strategies.

Despite the fact that for the past ninety years, representatives of what Canadians call minor or third or protest parties have sat continuously in the Commons but only a minuscule number holding those partisan persuasions have been appointed to the Senate, and despite also the fact that the major one (as measured by longevity) of those minor par-ties, the Co-operative Commonwealth Federation, later the New Democratic Party (CCF/NDP), has consistently opposed an upper chamber on socialist principle and has advocated its abolition, the rela-tionship between the Senate and the opposition in the Commons re-mains largely unexplored. This despite the additional fact that some minor parties in Parliament have existed for years or even decades as major parties in some provinces (Saskatchewan and the CCF/NDP, Alberta and Social Credit). That dichotomy has permitted such parties to divide (federal versus provincial entities) in their support for, among other questions, the National Energy Policy, the Constitution Act, 1982 (which includes during the negotiations that preceded it), and the Meech Lake Accord, 1987. Among the unexamined consequences of in-troducing an elected Senate into Parliament is the influence this inno-vation would have on the conduct of opposition in the lower house. Australian example is often cited in discussions of Senate reform in Canada. It would be useful on such occasions to examine intra-party relations between the two elected chambers of the Australian parlia-ment with the object of determining the effect these exert on the con-duct of opposition in Canberra.[45]

Whether or not one accepts the critics' claim that the Senate of Canada lacks legitimacy because it is appointed, the Senate remains one cham-ber in a bicameral parliament. For that reason the relationship between the two houses deserves scrutiny. This point relates to the manner in which upper-house behaviour affects the conduct of opposition in the lower house. A cardinal rule governs that relationship: the Senate shall not, except in rare instances, thwart the legislative will of the Commons by rejecting a bill. (Delaying its passage is another matter.) How is the behaviour of the opposition in the Commons affected by knowledge of that 'convention'? And, for that matter, by a second piece of knowledge: because of the (generally long) partisan career path of senators versus the comparatively high turnover of members of the House at each general election, the weight of legislative experience resides in the Senate. This offers one explanation for the following comment on 'the deplorable state of critical debate and scrutiny in the Commons itself':

> Never has the Commons opposition been so divided, so weak and so totally ineffective. Never has the legislation and oversight role been so sloppy and maladroit. We sat in the Senate and saw legislation coming across that hadn't been properly scrutinized by the Commons, by either members on our side or by the opposition ... Never, in effect, have the checks and balances in parliament taken such a holiday.[46]

It is not immediately clear what the reference to checks and balances implies. It *is* clear, however, that from the viewpoint of this former senator (Jerry Grafstein), a signal role of the Senate is to do what the opposition in the Commons ought to be doing better: improving poorly drafted legislation. Since the provinces do not have upper chambers (five once did), a discussion of the effect of upper chambers on legislative opposition in the provinces is moot, although it does raise the question whether opposition in the provinces is essentially different from that in Ottawa as a consequence.

The influence of the upper house, the experience of long periods of one-party domination of government, and the proliferation of third parties, each, it will be argued, has a distinctive influence on the conduct of opposition in Parliament. Another Canadian political practice that should be added to that list is the use of conventions to select political party leaders. It is worth noting that the first such convention was called by the Liberals – then in opposition – after that party, led by Sir Wilfrid Laurier, had split over the formation of a Union government committed to introduce military conscription in 1917. Among those who supported Union were western farmers, many of whom had voted Liberal before 1914 but who became disillusioned with traditional party allegiances after 1917. By 1920, the farmers provided the basis for what was to become the first 'third party,' the Progressives. Thereafter, third parties, always across the aisle, became the way of parliamentary politics. Yet, and of equal importance, the farmers' revolt was confined within the parliamentary dimension. The explanation for the successful channelling of this unrest lies in the leadership skills of Mackenzie King, the choice of the Liberals in 1919. Unlike that of Canadian party leaders before him, King's authority derived not from the caucus but from a convention of members of the party outside Parliament. It was Meighen's view that this Liberal invention '*compelled* the Conservatives to follow the same method when in Opposition.'[47] Indeed, King had been defeated as a candidate in the general elections of 1911 and 1917. The convention proved the penultimate step to the Commons, a by-election victory (in King's case, in Prince, P.E.I.) the final step. Although the Liberal, King, blazed this political trail, others, including later Progressive Conservative leaders, such as Stanfield and Mulroney, followed it. This separation of authority of the parliamentary party, on the one hand, from on the other, its leader, and the effect that separation exerted on the conduct of opposition in Parliament provided context for another opposition-inspired innovation, the leadership review, inspired in the late 1960s by a faction of the Progressive Conservative party anxious to remove John Diefenbaker from his front row Commons seat opposite the prime minister.

PART TWO

Parliamentary Opposition

2 From Coalition to Coalition, 1867–1920

'The struggle for responsible government' was at one time a venerable theme in Canadian high school history classes. From four decades' experience teaching university students in Canadian politics courses as well as observing the education of children and grandchildren, I may confidently assert that knowledge of that achievement – Canada's undisputed contribution to the history of parliamentary government in the Empire and Commonwealth – no longer holds the prominence it once did in the school curriculum. Even in that golden age, understanding of the concept was limited. It seldom went beyond pronouncements that representatives of the Crown, in whose name legislation was passed, normally did not act on their own but rather on advice of individuals (ministers) who sat in the elected chamber and who had its support. That, of course, is the essential principle of the concept, and those who know this and nothing else know more about the subject than those who know everything else but this. None the less, there is more to achieving the practice of responsible government than declaring the principle, a discovery that J.E. Hodgetts demonstrated in *Pioneer Public Service: An Administrative History of the United Canadas, 1841–1867*.[1] Structures promote clarity of decision making and in turn accountability, and without those structures responsible government is unachievable or, at the very least, inadequately realized. Hodgetts's contribution was to demonstrate the central importance of that truth.

The fundamental point to note is that responsible government structured not only the forces of government but also those of the opposition. Its achievement set the stage for a continuing struggle between the two within the legislature. The subject of this book takes one half of that dialectic, opposition; the subject of this chapter the emergence and development of opposition in Parliament during the period from Confederation to the end of the First World War. In 1917, the Conservative party, led by Sir Robert Borden, then prime minister, with a large number of Liberals, but not their leader Sir Wilfrid Laurier and his loyalists, joined in a Union government to prosecute the war to its conclusion. By the next general election, in 1921, the two-party system and its architectural reflection, the serried ranks of Liberals to one side of Mr Speaker and Conservatives to the other, had ceased to exist, thereby confounding a half-century's experience of government and opposition in Canada.

Before there was the federation of Canada, there were the colonies of British North America, three of which (Canada, Nova Scotia, and New Brunswick) united in 1867 in a federation of four provinces. Responsible government had been secured in each of the colonies in the 1840s. The events associated with those achievements are not relevant to the discussion, but the constitutional arrangement and the theory (separation of powers) that preceded responsible government are. The relevance of that past to the twenty-first century lies in the charge heard today that instead of responsible there is irresponsible government, in the form of engorged and inadequately checked prime ministerial power. Long voiced, this critique has grown increasingly audible, and malleable. In 2008 and 2009, controversy surrounded the Governor General's exercise of prerogative power to prorogue Parliament and, more particularly, the extent of her discretion in this action, as opposed to unreservedly following the advice of the prime minister. Again, the details of these events are for the moment not relevant, but will be examined in chapter 6, 'Opposition, More or Less.' One matter that does call for attention is the advocacy now being made for a set of 'checks and balances' to limit prime ministerial power.[2] Part of this advocacy takes the form of calls to codify the conventions that have enveloped the use of prerogative powers, but part of it calls for the setting up of barriers, for instance, that would require legislative supermajorities to sanction the use of executive authority. Such innovations have at their base a rationale closer to the one that sustained colonial politics before the achievement of responsible government. More than that, this rationale makes slight provision for the presence of opposition as it has operated in Parliament for the past 160 years.

The taproot of the constitution that preceded the introduction of responsible government was the Glorious Revolution of 1688, in which Parliament, having vanquished Charles Stuart, the Pretender, and having invited William and Mary to ascend the throne, emerged as the pre-eminent partner in its relationship with the sovereign. 'Relationship' was the apposite word because at the end of the seventeenth century the constitution was a mixture of coequal parts (Crown, aristocracy, and Commons) whose balance was a prerequisite for order. M.J.C. Vile, the authority on the post-revolutionary settlement, anatomized the new arrangement as follows: 'The principle of "harmony" was now the dominant one in the British system of government.'[3] A century and a half after the Glorious Revolution, in a debate in the Parliament of United Canada, Louis-Joseph Papineau showed that he was familiar with the Settlement of 1688, when he spoke of 'the three elements work[ing] well together with a preponderance of the democratic element.'[4] From the perspective of the present century, the association of balance of powers with the British Constitution strikes the observer as foreign. Strange or not, that alignment of powers and that principle made the journey across the Atlantic and found expression – some critics of the Act said distortion – in the Constitution Act, 1791, which created Upper and Lower Canada and gave representative assemblies to each, along with separate nominated legislative and executive councils. The appeal of 'the principle of harmony' had a long life in the New World. Half a century after its arrival, Robert Baldwin, co-father with Louis LaFontaine of responsible government, still used this language although with an evolving purpose in mind – to achieve harmony within the elected assembly:

> That in order to preserve that harmony between the different branches of the [now united] Provincial Parliament, which is essential to the happy conduct of public affairs, the principal [sic] of such subordinate officers, the advisers of the representative of the Sovereign, and constituting as such the Provincial administration under him ... ought always to be men possessed of public confidence, whose opinions and policy harmonizing with those of the representatives of the people, would afford a guarantee etc.[5]

What has a history of Canada's penultimate constitution to do with the subject of opposition? A great deal, for the function of opposition today is to replace the purpose of separation of powers of two centuries ago. A preoccupation of colonial legislatures before the grant of responsible government was to exclude officers of government, as well as members of the judiciary:

> In Upper Canada ... judges could [until 1838] run for election to the Lower House ... In Lower Canada, however, judges were not welcome ... When

a judge was a candidate, [a legislative committee] reported: (i) the liberty of the electors was constrained, (ii) the dignity of a judge is exposed, and (iii) the confidence of the administration of justice is diminished when a judge presents himself. Two sessions later, An Act for declaring Judges to be disabled and disqualifying them, from being elected, or from Sitting and Voting in the House of Assembly was passed ... on March 21, 1811.[6]

Much of the debate in the Canadas into the 1840s, as earlier in the United Kingdom, focused on excluding those whose presence was thought to compromise the independence of the chamber.

Part of the concern stemmed from possibility of the Crown exerting influence through place holders. Eventually, in 1843, by means of An Act for better securing the Independence of the Legislative Assembly of this Province,[7] a long list of functionaries, officers, contractors, and even translators were disqualified, while 'members of the Executive Council ... upon accepting from the Crown any office of profit were to resign but could be re-elected.' This latter requirement continued in federal and provincial law until the 1930s.[8] Efforts to address the above-noted concern were of long lineage in the United Kingdom and fundamental to the conduct of parliamentary government. Macaulay, for instance,

> pointed out that important conditions for the development of opposition were secured by the provisions in the revolutionary settlement guaranteeing the tenure of judges and regulating treason trials. Previously the Crown could eliminate opponents 'by means of ... brow-beating judges.' Since the enactment of these provisions, 'no statesman, while engaged in constitutional opposition to a Government, has had the axe before his eyes.'[9]

Separation of powers, it was maintained, would promote constitutional harmony through a policy of exclusion. The political armature in that arrangement was found in the independence of legislature (Parliament) from executive (the Crown). By the end of the eighteenth century, however, just as Canada was receiving its Constitutional Act, 1791, the British constitution was in 'the process of reformulation,' with 'the balance ... now ... in a great degree in the House of Commons.' This evolution had occurred for two reasons: first, the House had come to 'possess nearly the whole of legislative authority,' a result that the expanded franchise in the Reform Bill of 1832 permanently sealed; and second, within the House 'were to be found ministers with ... influence over "government members," and members who were dependent upon aristocratic support, as well as independent members.'[10] The influence of the Crown was no longer to be checked by expelling its agents from the legislature but rather by requiring the presence of the Crown's advisers in the House (thus the modern convention that ministers must have, or must quickly secure, seats in the chamber). Parliamentary harmony now depended upon what went on in the Commons and, most especially, what went on between supporters of the Crown (the government) and opponents of those supporters – but not of the Crown (opposition).

Few transformations in the practice of parliamentary government have been as significant as this, nor have any adhered more scrupulously to the British custom of change through convention rather than statute law. But if the way of the political future was clear in the mother country early in the nineteenth century – government versus opposition – in the colonies along the St Lawrence there were still unique hurdles to scale before that vantage might be attained: they were dependencies of an Empire and, with the creation of United Canada in 1840, there was a very un-English sense of a divided society. These two factors complicated and prolonged the constitutional transformation in Canada. On the one hand, to legislative–executive tensions that separation promoted were added colonial–imperial ones, with the result, as noted by John Beverley Robinson, that 'the business of the house is not conducted by anyone as representing the Government.'[11] The constitutional arrangements introduced in 1791 made assembly members suspicious of the actions and motives of the governor and his appointees in the executive and legislative councils. Whatever the theory, harmony was an absent feature of the politics of the day. To colonial sensitivities were added, in Lower Canada, the division between English and French inhabitants. There, because the disparity in numbers between the two groups was so marked, French-speaking members of the Assembly were assured what amounted to a permanent majority.

Desire by the colonists for control of local affairs, resentment at power exercised by a privileged elite whose patron was the British governor, and bad feeling between the French and English in Lower Canada set the stage for the struggle of responsible government, an event whose details are outside the focus of this book, except to repeat the claim, already made, that the achievement of 'responsible government' created as well the concept of a 'responsible opposition.' It took more than a decade for understanding of this constitutional principle to become clear. In the interval, search for a mechanism by which to achieve the same end turned on occasion to creation of an elected upper chamber. The point of this reference is that, today, opposition in the lower chamber and the structure of the upper chamber are not seen as matters having much in common. Certainly, responsible government, with the function that principle assigns the opposition, is seldom viewed as an alternative to an elected Senate. On the contrary, in Canada, reform of the Senate is generally discussed in terms of 'improved' representation rather than greater responsibility on the part of the executive. This was not always the case, however, as witness the observation in 1853 by Henry John Boulton, member for Norfolk in the Legislative Assembly of United Canada:

> Our present position is exactly that described by [Montesquieu and Jefferson] – that the leader of the government for the time being was all but absolute, and that nothing was safe from his interference, that the judiciary could be interfered with at any moment, and that no constitutional check existed to protect from spoliation the most sacred rights of property ... The Upper House ought to possess powers equal to those of the other branch of the Legislature.[12]

Boulton's prescription lies in the realm of 'what might have been.' After the late 1840s, the checks on government rested in the first instance – and for a long time solely, until the rise of officers of Parliament as 'a new element of separation of powers' – with opposition within the elected chamber.[13] The narrowing of the political forum that this transformation represented and the shift in attention accompanying it in the middle of the nineteenth century remained constant for decades to come. The telecommunications revolution and growing doubts about the political relevance of elected legislatures – two causes of the 'democratic deficit' discussed in chapter 6 – constitute an unprecedented challenge to the second 'political settlement,' one that has survived more than a century and a half.

In the two decades that separated the grant of the principle of responsible government and the enactment of Canadian federation, parliamentary democracy in British North America matured, albeit in circumstances different from those found in the mother country. Notwithstanding that after 1840, Upper and Lower Canada were united in one colony, Canada, with a single set of political institutions, the two halves remained fragmented by language, religion, and law. Unity came to depend upon cooperation between the leaders of political parties emerging in those sections east and west of the Ottawa River. As O'Brien noted in his study of pre-Confederation parliamentary procedure: 'The first case of a central

Canadian government resigning due to loss of confidence in the lower house occurred in ... 1848, [when] the Sherwood government was defeated on an amendment moved by Robert Baldwin to the Address in Reply to the Speech from the Throne ... Following the resignation ... the Great Ministry of Baldwin and LaFontaine took office.'[14] There are many reasons for accepting the claim that the Great Ministry represents 'the foundation of modern Canada.'[15] Foremost among them are its legislative achievements, and foremost among these was the Rebellion Losses Bill, intended to indemnify persons in Lower Canada who had suffered property damage as a result of the 1837 Rebellion. Explosive criticism from Tories, who believed the rebels would profit from the terms of the bill, led to riots and to the destruction of the legislative building by fire, but did not prevent the governor, Lord Elgin, from signing the measure on the advice of his ministry. That assent is customarily treated as a (perhaps *the*) cornerstone of parliamentary democracy in Canada and as an important advance on the road to colonial self-rule. It is that, and it is also an interpretation that gives prominence to the executive. Here is further evidence that history is not so much unkind to opposition as that it pays opposition scant attention – an oversight that was not overcome after Confederation, when in place of an imperial officer and, later, revolving ministries there was now one man in charge who appeared for decades to have almost a monopoly on the office of prime minister.

The events of 1849 in Montreal were not the finest moment for opposition in the Canadian system of responsible government. There is no shortage of reasons to explain the failure: the principle of responsible government was new; the political parties on whom the practice depended were raw; the British model was inimitable: between 1841 and 1858, for example, Conservative and Whig prime ministers, in the persons of Peel, Russell, and Palmerston, took turns on the government benches at Westminster; in Canada opposition had learned to act irresponsibly because it held 'no hope of office and no means to call governments to account';[16] and, most of all, the imperative of dualism – composed of language, religion, and region – which had revealed itself a conundrum to opposition intent on acting as an alternative government. The two decades after 1848 saw as features of Canadian politics coalitions and double-headed ministries, a peripatetic capital, and procedural innovations such as, on occasion, resort to a double-majority in the adoption of culturally sensitive bills – denominational rights in regard to education a pre-eminent example. Supporters of coalition government in Parliament in the twenty-first century would be advised to study the period before 1867, when short-lived governments – usually coalitions – and short-lived oppositions were the rule. In the decade and a half before 1867, the lifespan of individual governments declined, while the number of ministries and elections rose. In the sad words of a high school civics text of seventy years ago, then on the curriculum of four western and two Atlantic provinces: 'Political affairs in Canada [in the 1860s] were in a very bad way.'[17] And, from a contemporary Nova Scotian perspective, the situation was not much better: 'Partizan [sic] spirit [had] rent these [British North American] Provinces asunder ... Heaven only knows where this state of things is to end.'[18]

With Confederation, the 'state of things' changed dramatically. This is not an allusion to the proliferation of jurisdictions that the federal system introduced. As important as these would be to the future of the country, it would be tautological to attribute the change to the structures of federalism. The reference is to the arrival of one-party government under the leadership of one man for twenty of the next twenty-four years. Nothing of this kind had occurred in the colonies of British North America, and nothing suggested at the time of Union that it would happen now (or that long periods of single-party rule under a single leader would become a repeated feature of politics at the centre or in the provinces). By contrast, between Confederation and 1891, the year Macdonald died, there were in the United Kingdom five Conservative administrations (two led by Disraeli, two by Salisbury, one by Derby) and three Liberal (all led by Gladstone). The key reason for the difference lay in the territorial expansion of Canada, from four provinces at the outset to seven by 1873. Macdonald, besides being a master tactician in the House, was unsparing in his labours as party chieftain outside. He understood that control of the chamber depended on control of party organization in the constituencies; and Conservatives who made it to Parliament as MPs knew how they got there and where their loyalty should lie. Male suffrage, with controversial exceptions, was the rule in Canada from Confederation onward. This was not the case in the United Kingdom, where the franchise for males was successively extended through the last part of the century. The resulting contrast in relationship between intra- and extra-parliamentary parties had important implications for the organization and conduct of politics in Canada and the United Kingdom.

British parties originated in Parliament, and the governments they formed looked in the first instance to Parliament to sustain them. It was not until the election of 1867 that a prime minister (in this case, Gladstone) took advantage of newly built railways to travel outside of London in a campaign. While it is proper to speak of political alignments, such as Tories and Reformers, in pre-Confederation Canada, party organization as understood after 1867 was synonymous with activity outside of Parliament in constituencies of great diversity extending over several thousand kilometres. A national political party, in its extra-parliamentary (electoral) guise, had necessarily to accommodate diversity too. From the beginning, a leader in Canada, whether his party formed the government or opposition, found it necessary to succeed outside as much as inside the Commons.[19] The measure of the first success is seats, of the second support in the House. John A. Macdonald set the bar for both. He won a clear majority of seats and votes in five of the seven elections he fought (no subsequent prime minister would match this record), as well as more seats than the Liberals won in 1872. In the chamber, he was a 'House of Commons man' who understood and loved Parliament. This affection permeated his relationship with the party, the cabinet, the caucus, the press, the provincial parties, and the public. No one who succeeded him in office expressed similar feelings so consistently. Laurier, who is often treated as the Liberal counterpart in assessments of early great prime ministers, shared much with Macdonald, but not in this respect. Laurier was an intellectual admirer of Parliament, but much more the remote orator and executive who left the House to others. In contrast, Macdonald left nothing, or almost nothing, to the discretion of others.[20] Such intensity was an irritant to his ministers and supporters and proved a far greater obstacle to the development of a parliamentary opposition in Canada.

Sir Richard Cartwright, a Conservative supporter of Macdonald before and after Confederation, and then a Liberal after 1869 and minister of finance in the Mackenzie government after 1874, said of the two:

> [They] stood almost at the very opposite poles in every way. Politically speaking, Sir John attended to the one thing needful and let the rest take care of itself. He thoroughly understood that the mass of the people paid no sort of attention to the details of public affairs except perhaps at election time, and that under ordinary conditions no party could hope to win in such a country as Canada unless they possessed a complete and vigorous organization and kept it steadily at work.
>
> Sir John paid little enough attention to the proper work of the several departments over which he at various times presided, and in many instances the public interests suffered grievously thereby. But he never neglected his work as leader and he took most excellent care to keep on the best terms with his supporters.[21]

Wilfrid Laurier, third (after Mackenzie and Edward Blake) Liberal leader of the opposition (1887–96), and the first to become prime minister following long seasoning across the aisle, said of Mackenzie that 'we never had a better debater in the House; a grand man on his legs … [but] he had not the imagination nor the breadth of view required to lead a party and a country; he gave to the details of a department the time that have should have gone to planning and overseeing the general conduct of the administration.'[22]

Mackenzie's problems of perspective, whether on administration or on party, proved in time to be unique neither to him nor to his period in office. Of longer-term significance, indeed until the end of the century, was another obstacle whose origin rested with Macdonald. More particularly, it rested in his dominance of political events before Confederation and in his long tenure afterward. Taking the pre-1867 years first, it was Cartwright's opinion that 'the manner in which Confederation had been brought about [saw] Macdonald … succeed in weeding the ranks of his opponents of nearly every prominent politician of any training … The remainder, including Mr. Mackenzie himself, could hardly be said to have had any such training at all.'[23] Macdonald's strategy was to use a first minister's monopoly of patronage appointments (a premeditated tactic, as Donald Creighton in his biography of Macdonald makes clear in a chapter with the revealing title 'The Humiliation of George Brown'), and in doing so he 'ruin[ed] … the great Liberal party Brown had been labouring to create ever since the autumn of 1857.'[24]

The explanation for the Liberals' weak launch in national politics is more varied than Macdonald's strategy alone. That is to say, there was more than Tory cunning that thwarted them. The Conservatives brought to the new Parliament their pre-Confederation coalition of interests, now united behind the single Tory banner. The Liberals took some decades to learn and then master the formula for national electoral success. The preliminary test, to agree on a leader, proved inauspicious. George Brown had been expected to lead the Liberals in the House, but at a time when it was possible to hold a seat both in the Ontario (or Quebec) legislature and in the Commons, he was defeated provincially and federally in 1867. In consequence, Edward Blake, who did win a provincial and a federal seat in 1867, was treated until 1871 as leader. For the next two years the position was vacant, a situation Cartwright phrased more elegantly: 'Practically, in 1873, the leadership of the Opposition might have been said to have been in a commission, of whom Mr. Mackenzie was one, the others consisting of Mr. Blake, Mr. Holton and Mr. Dorion.'[25] Later (between 1880 and 1887), Blake again acted as leader of the opposition. But, mercurial and impatient, he was, in O.D. Skelton's words, 'not a man to fight uphill battles,' and by his own admission, he 'prefer[red] to be a private.'[26] Temperament and personality thus made him (until Stéphane Dion more than a century later) the first leader of the Liberal party not to become prime minister.

The system of dual premiership, which had marked the Union, disappeared with Confederation; in Skelton's apposite remark, 'the prime minister was really first.'[27] That was a situation Macdonald devoutly sought, but it also met the condition set down in the Reform Convention's resolution passed on the eve of Confederation:

> And while this convention is thoroughly satisfied that the Reform party has acted in the best interests of the country by sustaining the Government until the Confederation measure was secured, it deems it an imperative duty to declare that the temporary alliance between the Reform and Conservative parties should now cease, and that no Government will be satisfactory to the people of Upper Canada which is formed and maintained by a coalition of public men holding opposite political principles.[28]

Of the many ramifications that flowed from this change, the one most germane to this discussion has to do with the influence it exerted on opposition. Parliament no longer featured serial alliances that temporarily bound the interests of Canada East and Canada West. Rather there was one party in government led by one leader. Clarity to the right of Mr Speaker demanded similar purity to his left, if opposition was in time to replace government. This second enterprise took longer and proved more difficult to achieve than the first, and not only because of the disproportionate resources available to government rather than to opposition.

In the first Parliament there was no Liberal party – in the singular – but rather congeries of provincial Liberal eminences, including Dorion from Quebec and Albert Smith from New Brunswick. In the absence of a 'force,' such as Macdonald, in their ranks, but confronted by the temporizing of Blake, the opposition did not choose a leader until the eve of the expected election of 1872. It was then that a caucus committee took the initiative and agreed he should come from Ontario. Blake, their first choice, declined, and Mackenzie, under pressure, accepted. The Pacific scandal, the forced retirement of Macdonald, and Lord

Dufferin's summoning of Mackenzie, after just eight months as leader
and slightly over a year after the conclusion of balloting in the 1872
election, saw the only Liberal government between 1867 and 1896
come to power.

In his *Reminiscences*, Cartwright suggests that the unfolding of events
was less precise than this account might imply. In answer to the question, 'Was it not rather a surprise that Lord Dufferin should have sent
for Mr. Mackenzie?,' Cartwright replied that 'in a certain sense it was.
It could hardly be said that Mr. Mackenzie was the recognized leader of
the Opposition, though he was the leader of the Ontario section, which
was by far the largest.'[29] At issue is not whether caucus selection of the
leader was legitimate. Until selection by delegate conventions became
the norm after the First World War, leadership lay within the gift of
caucus: in 1887, the Liberal caucus offered leadership of the party to
Wilfrid Laurier, after Edward Blake had stepped down for a second
time from the post. Nor is the role of the Governor General question-
able. It was indisputably his or her task then, as it is today, to select as
advisers those who have the support of the Commons. The part of
Cartwright's reply that demands attention is the phrase 'recognized
leader of the Opposition.' Recognized by whom and in what form?

The answers to these questions depend upon when they are asked. In
the nineteenth century when there were only two parties, even if less
self-disciplined than today, the leader of the opposition had of necessity
to be the individual whose party did not form the government. Since at
this time selection of the leader rested with the parliamentary caucus,
there was no possibility, as occurred much later, of a division in loyalties between those who looked to a leader whose support lay in caucus
and those who looked to a leader chosen by a convention composed in
the main of extra-parliamentary supporters. In the absence of statute
law touching on the office of leader of the opposition, which was first to
appear in 1905,[30] 'recognition' could only be measured by the behaviour of caucus members. One index was where MPs stood when called
upon to declare their allegiance. According to Norman Ward,

> Mackenzie and Macdonald were on opposing sides in thirty substantive
> divisions during 1867–8, and an analysis of the lists reveals these significant
> facts: thirty-five M.P.'s did not once oppose Macdonald in the thirty div-
> isions; twenty-four opposed him only once; and a further thirty-two op-
> posed from two to five times. The corresponding figures for Mackenzie's
> supporters are fifteen, eleven, and twenty-one. Macdonald, that is, had a

clear majority of the total membership of the House, who either supported him, or refrained from voting against him, in at least twenty-five of the thirty divisions.[31]

In the nineteenth century, divisions mattered, as far as appearances were concerned, a belief Macdonald cryptically supported in answer to the following question put by his secretary, Sir Joseph Pope: 'Why were there so few divisions when the Conservatives were in opposition?' The reply: 'I saw no advantage in publishing to the world every morning that we numbered only a handful.'[32]

Macdonald proved to be first of several (but not all) Canadian prime ministers who were masters of the executive. Indeed, it was his long-standing taunt that Mackenzie was 'the leader of the Puritan party,' in the sense that like that party in the Long Parliament, he 'sought to cut down the Executive power.'[33] As leader of the opposition between 1873 and 1878, Macdonald continued this line of attack, depicting the Liberals in power as small-minded in matters of territorial and economic expansion, even though they were committed to promoting national status through constitutional advances, such as legislation to establish a Supreme Court. He exploited discord between Mackenzie and Blake over these issues, successfully, as the results of the 1878 election illustrated. As was to happen in the Conservative and Progressive Conservative parties from the late 1930s through to the mid-1950s, electoral defeat served as justification to replace the leader. Laurier, one of five Liberal MPs who pressed Mackenzie to retire, put it unequivocally: 'We have been defeated; you have been defeated; it is only human nature that a defeated army should seek another general.'[34] The following day, Skelton recounts, Mackenzie addressed the House: 'I yesterday determined to withdraw from my position as leader of the Opposition, and from this time forth I will speak and act for no person but myself.' The simplicity and speed of this exit from the positions of leader of the opposition and of the Liberal party is in sharp contrast to that of Mr Diefenbaker's exit from comparable positions eight-and-a-half decades later.

The Liberal interregnum, from 1873 until 1878, produced important legislative and policy initiatives, but from the perspective of affecting government–opposition relationships, it scarcely made an impact. When Mackenzie stepped down as leader of the opposition in 1880, the caucus chose Blake as his replacement, a position he held for seven unmemorable years. On the government side of the House, Macdonald resumed his parliamentary pre-eminence, a status he retained until his death in 1891. As regards political personalities in the House, the signal change occurred in 1887, when, after asking Blake for his advice, the Liberal caucus chose Laurier, who for a decade had been playing the French-lieutenant role, to succeed him. Nine more years would elapse, during which Macdonald would die and a succession of four Conservative prime ministers in five years would follow; only then, with the Tories in great disarray, did Laurier lead the Liberals to power, a position they would occupy for fifteen years.

The first three decades of Canada's parliamentary history afford little insight into the theory and practice of opposition. For ninety years after 1921, third parties provided a sustained, varied, and vigorous dimension to the country's political landscape. In the fifty years before then (and after Confederation), there were two, and only two, political parties that contested successive national elections. (The election of 1896 was exceptional in that short-lived third parties won 10 per cent of the vote, thus distorting the results for the other parties: the Liberals, for instance, won fewer votes than they had in 1891 and fewer votes than the Conservatives in 1896, yet gained twenty-seven seats.) Post-Confederation experience introduced a parliamentary pattern to become familiar – long periods of one-party government dominated by a commanding leader facing an opposition challenged by problems of organization and leadership. In contrast to British political parties, the roots and loyalties of Canadian parties are extra-parliamentary. Perhaps this was inevitable in a country where, because of the strength of local and regional sentiments, federation was the only option. Alternation in power depended less upon mastery of policy or procedure, as important as these might on occasion be, than it did on voters' perception that leaders were responsive to public opinion. Not all opinion, but that which was capable of arousing strong feeling. Not uniformly across the country, but where sectional or regional feeling was intense. The election of 1896 dramatically illustrated that dictum, for whatever position the two parties took on the tariff or on relations with the United States or the Empire, the issue that dominated the campaign, that set the parties and their leaders apart, and that influenced the parties' electoral fortunes for decades to come was the Manitoba School Question.

At issue were denominational rights for Roman Catholics as regards education. The details of the Question are usually discussed from the perspective of the constitution and federalism.[35] For a study of parliamentary opposition in Canada, however, the focus is different: it is on leadership. When the Conservative federal government (using power it possessed under Section 93 of the Constitution Act, 1867) introduced a bill to restore educational rights granted Roman Catholics in the Manitoba Act (1870), and which the courts found that provincial legislation had infringed, the Liberal party now under a Roman Catholic, bilingual leader from Quebec exploited an opportunity foreign to the theory of parliamentary opposition at Westminster but at the core of the founding of the federation. This was not the first occasion when the Protestant–Roman Catholic, French–English, and Quebec–Canada cleavage of Canada's Union revealed itself – a decade before there had been the execution of Louis Riel; nor would it be the last – yet to be experienced was the tension of official bilingualism; but this time there was a new factor: a leader with the capacity and insight to interpret the controversy as an issue of federalism, to be precise, as an issue of provincial rights. Laurier did not introduce provincial rights as a cause in Canadian politics – that distinction is customarily awarded to Oliver Mowat, premier of Ontario (1872–96) – but he divined its usefulness to the leader of a federal party.

Donald Creighton's account of these events is representative of interpretations that elevate the importance of leadership, in this instance from the opposition side of the Commons:

> Led by Laurier, the Liberals blocked [the legislation] with a sustained filibuster, and before the remedial bill could be passed, the seventh Parliament expired by the effluxion of time ... The Conservatives were never united in support of Tupper's straightforward stand [to uphold confessional schools and federal authority] ... Laurier enjoyed a distinct advantage. He could, and did, remain evasive and non-committal throughout the entire controversy. At no point did the Liberal Party commit itself to a frank advocacy of provincial autonomy in education ... The main difference between the two parties was that one was politically vulnerable and the other was not.[36]

The dualism of the United Canadas – French–English relations under another name – had been mastered through coalition government or through variations on the theme of institutional duplication. In the federation, dualism was accommodated within the structure of the Conservative and Liberal parties, which in this era dominated provincial as well as federal politics. With the political thrust now vertical as well as horizontal, harmony depended upon the skills of redress possessed by the leader in government or in opposition. As events surrounding Union government two decades later were to show, such feats of reconciliation had their limits.

But before then, a series of controversies involving federal and provincial jurisdictions, language of instruction (i.e., instruction permissi-
ble in a language other than English), and support for denominational
schools roiled debate in Parliament and relations between and within
the political parties. The Laurier government's Autonomy Bills of 1905,
to create the provinces of Alberta and Saskatchewan, perpetuated in
modified form the publicly supported separate school system already
established in the Territories. The Conservatives, now in opposition,
adopted Laurier's stance of the previous decade and pressed for an
amendment to ensure 'full powers of Provincial self-government.'
(Retention by Parliament of the new provinces' natural resources was a
further part of the grievance.) But not all Tories shared this view; when
the vote came, thirteen of their number, most of them from Quebec,
broke with their leader. Also, according to Borden's biographer, 'a
month later, while debate on the autonomy bills continued, the school
question was submitted to the Ontario electorate in [two] by-elections
… But to no avail. The defeats broke the spirit of the Opposition.'[37]
(Parenthetically, the influence of by-elections on opposition behaviour
in Canada is worth more interest than it usually receives, as would be
the consequences of adopting a proportional representation electoral
system that makes no provision for by-elections.) Borden's belief that
notwithstanding race and religion, Canadians should all be 'content to
be Canadians,' presaged another (former) opposition leader's philoso-
phy on bilingualism some seventy years later. A resolution, introduced
by the Trudeau government in 1973 (6 June), reaffirming support for
the 1969 Official Languages Act, won approval in the House of
Commons, except for sixteen Progressive Conservative members (all
but two from western Canada), led by Mr Diefenbaker and in defiance
of pressure from their leader, Mr Stanfield. Mr Diefenbaker defended
his action on the grounds that Borden would in all likelihood have
echoed, that he 'had fought all his life to bring equality to Canadians of
every ethnic origin.'[38]

A pre-war conflict that extended into the war period concerned
Ontario's Regulation 17, which limited school instruction in the French
language. By 1916, resolutions condemning this policy were being heat-
edly debated not only in the legislature of Quebec and in the Senate of
Canada, but in the House, too, where, says Creighton, 'the Liberal
members from the western provinces and Ontario protested that this
resolution was ill-timed, out of place, and dangerously provocative; but
Laurier was adamant.'[39] The 1916 battle was a harbinger of the more

divisive debate over conscription to come the following year; unlike in 1916, when Laurier's threat to resign brought dissenting Liberals on-side, in 1917, a majority of Liberal Members of Parliament failed to come to the aid of their leader.

The tragedy of the Commons today, say some observers, lies in its vulnerability to such encroachers as the media, interest groups, social movements, and courts. Yet as this discussion illustrates, trespassers are neither new nor impartial in the effects of their actions. For exam-ple, controversies over minority rights, over provincial rights, over the compact theory of Confederation – all of these have singular implica-tions for the work of the opposition in the Commons.[40] First, they all demand a response from the opposition, as would be expected on any issue – the tariff, say – but all of them also require something more: an articulated commitment to a conception of Canada. Where, in the mat-ter of language, for instance, does the opposition (regardless of party allegiance) stand? Is it for cultural (that is, dualistic) federalism, or does it stand behind territorial federalism? If opposition in a system of re-sponsible government is loyal, that is, constitutional, opposition, how can it then be opposed to a matter so fundamental as the government's interpretation of Canada? Yet that conception is confounded by another complication: dependency upon another power, Great Britain up to the 1940s and the United States afterward. The chronology may not be as precise as that statement suggests, but the complications from depen-dency are. This is particularly true of the imperial relationship. The ten-sion between centralism and decentralism in domestic affairs had its counterpart in external affairs. In consequence, a second part of the op-position's conception of Canada demanded that it take a position on the degree of autonomy required in relations with others.

Before the First World War the specific issue that signified this prob-lem was Canada's commitment to imperial defence. The Borden gov-ernment said that commitment should take the form of a gift of three ships to the Royal Navy, and introduced legislation to this effect; the Liberals replied that Canada should establish its own navy. In face of a two-week Liberal filibuster but with the help of a new closure rule (Sir Ivor Jennings once remarked that 'it is easier for a government to stop criticism than to answer it'[41]), the government, in 1913, carried its bill in the Commons. In the Senate, where the Liberals held a majority and conducted another filibuster, it failed. Neither the details nor the virtues of the parties' contrasting positions are of interest here. What needs to be addressed is that on the Naval Bill, as on language and educational matters earlier, opposition was not confined to debate in the Commons. Indeed, on these types of issues, the opposition speaks to the electorate as much as it does to the House. Rather, the upper chamber and (on the schools matter) some provincial legislatures were enlisted in the attack. Nor was this a phenomenon only of the early twentieth century, although Laurier's Quebec roots melded with his commitment to Canada's British parliamentary traditions, and Borden's sense of destiny to lead Canada as a full, not just a colonial, participant in imperial affairs, gave these events enduring as well as immediate significance. Still, the sequence established then – of filibuster, closure, Senate and/or provincial legislative activity – repeated later in controversies over culture, the economy, and foreign relations, such as debate on the pipeline in 1956, the flag in 1964, and the Canada–United States Free Trade Agreement in 1988, suggests an episodic pattern linked to events that are deemed to challenge Canadian independence or security. In this chronology the absence of reference to the three decades after 1920 calls for notice. Those are the years the next chapter calls the time of 'Liberal ascendancy.' They are also a period of extremely weak opposition, particularly on the part of the other major party, the Conservatives.

The author of closure was Arthur Meighen, a Conservative back-bencher in 1912–13, but later holder of several portfolios under Borden and, from July 1920 until December 1921 (and again, June to September 1926), prime minister. Described as an 'incomparable parliamentarian' by Eugene Forsey and the individual to whom he dedicated his book, *Freedom and Order*,[42] Meighen was also the primary author of the War Measures Act, the Military Service Act (which imposed conscription), the Wartime Elections Act, and the Military Voters Act. (Actions taken under the last two statutes were cited in 1920 as reasons for creating Canada's second officer of Parliament, the Chief Electoral Officer.) It is simplistic to say, but no less true, that these Acts, which more than any other guided Canada's wartime policies and government, were universally condemned in Quebec.[43] Nor were they welcome elsewhere. The prairies, for instance, were hit hard by wartime requisitions of manpower and horsepower; and pressure from the organized farmers as they broke free of traditional party allegiances proved an important destabilizing influence in the immediate post-war years. Still, Meighen's identification with policies so repugnant to Quebeckers and their leaders, such as Laurier and the more voluble and nationalist Henri Bourassa, caused a rift between the Conservative party and Quebec voters that would continue for decades.

Laurier declined to join the Union government because he personally – and, he was confident, Quebeckers generally – would not accept military conscription. The split between Laurier Liberals and Liberal Unionists fractured the party and made a mockery of partisan loyalties. It was to reunite the party that a policy convention, eventually called for November 1919, became with Laurier's death the country's first leadership convention. Whatever had been the intent, Canada's only experiment at governing through a union of parliamentary parties did not include the leader of the opposition. The Liberal convention selected Mackenzie King as its new leader, and he became leader of the opposition once he secured a seat in the Commons. But that was in the future. For the moment, the past, that is, the conclusion of Union government and the transition to a new Conservative leader, must be summarized.

In 1901, Borden had been selected party leader and, thus, leader of the opposition by the Conservative caucus composed of Tory MPs and senators. In 1920, the same process was employed, but this time a Conservative leader was in power and his successor would necessarily be prime minister. In recognition of the changed circumstance and the unusual complexion of the caucus, '"a unique method" for selecting the new leader' was agreed upon: 'The selection ultimately is to be made by Sir Robert ... Each member of Parliament supporting the late government is to indicate by letter his first and second choices and his reasons therefor [sic]. Sir Robert is to sift them out.'[44] This was, his biographer says, 'plainly an advisory procedure. Borden still would name his own successor.'[45] Which is what he did, first proposing to the Governor General the name of Sir Thomas White, who subsequently declined the invitation to form a government, and then that of Arthur Meighen, who accepted. The explanation for the priority is that, in the opinion of James Calder, master tactician of party organization (Liberal as well as Conservative), 'Meighen "could not gain any ground" for the new [post-Unionist] party in Quebec.'[46] This was a prediction of unusual accuracy. Except for three months in 1926 (under Meighen) and five years (1930–5) under R.B. Bennett, the Tories did not again form a government until John Diefenbaker led them back to power in 1957. The golden age of Conservative opposition was set to begin.

3 The Liberal Ascendancy, 1921–1956

Margaret MacMillan opens her acclaimed book, *Paris 1919*, with the observation that 'for six months in 1919, Paris was the capital of the world ... [She] was at once the world's government, its court of appeal and its parliament.'[1] All of which is true and deserving of study. Yet the same year, remarkable events in Canada were destined to guarantee that country a political future unlike its past. Laurier died unexpectedly in February 1919, and the party's policy convention, already called for August, was handed the additional task of selecting a new chief, one who would also be leader of the opposition and the man to take the party into the next federal election. In July, a farmers' candidate won a provincial by-election in Alberta and the organized farmers (the United Farmers of Alberta) decided to run candidates in the next provincial election. In October, the United Farmers of Ontario ran candidates for the first time in a provincial election and emerged to form the government, although without a majority of seats in the legislature. Three federal by-elections that fall, in Saskatchewan, New Brunswick, and Ontario, saw agrarian candidates immediately triumph where no attempt had been made before. More than that, in Parliament Canada's farmers committed themselves to independent political action.

The centre block of the Parliament buildings had been destroyed by fire in 1916. For the next four years the House of Commons sat in the semicircular auditorium of the Victoria Memorial Museum. (The Senate sat in the natural history museum's former geological department). The whole life of the Union government was spent in that aisle-less chamber. For the only time in Canadian history the House structurally resembled the National Assembly in Paris, with Conservatives and Liberal Unionists at one end of the arc of seats and Laurier Liberals at the other. Between those partisan concentrations sat eleven farmers' representatives, some who supported the government, some of whom opposed it, and some of whom retained their individuality as Liberal Unionists. When the House met for the first time in February 1920 in the reconstructed but unfinished new centre block, the farmers caucused under the leadership of T.A. Crerar (founding president of the United Grain Growers in Winnipeg and minister of agriculture from 1917 to 1919, in the Borden government) and 'formally constituted themselves the "National Progressive Party."'[2]

There were long-term and short-term reasons for the farmers' unrest. Prominent among the first was the protective tariff, long associated with Conservative governments. The Laurier government had sought to moderate the tariff through a reciprocity agreement with the United States but had gone down to defeat in 1911. Of first-order importance among the short-term reasons was regulation of agrarian manpower during the war imposed by a government of Conservatives and Liberals, whose decision to coalesce disparaged in the farmers' mind the concept of partisan loyalty. Unrest in the cities accompanied unrest in the countryside. During June and July 1919, the Winnipeg General Strike occupied the attention of the public and government alike, in part because of the breadth of labour disruptions in Manitoba's capital and in part because of associations being made in the press and Parliament with recent events in Russia. Between April and June 1919, more than 4,000 Canadian troops returned from Siberia, where they had been sent the previous year as part of a multinational strategy to quell the Russian Revolution. Arthur Meighen, serving as acting minister of justice because the minister, Charles Doherty, was in Paris with Borden at the Peace Conference, went to Winnipeg, took a dark view of what was happening there, and soon afterward introduced into the House an amendment to the Criminal Code (ultimately Section 98) that defined as 'unlawful' associations whose purpose was 'to bring about any governmental, industrial or economic change in Canada' by force or violence.[3] Although Meighen's biographer declared the comment 'irrelevant' in the context of debate on the amendment, opposition Liberals said of its author that 'if there exists in some quarters of the country a feeling of distrust of Parliament and Parliamentary institutions ... the Acting Minister of Justice is one of those who are largely responsible for it.'[4]

The accuracy of the attribution is beyond the scope of this discussion. What is not in doubt is the substance of the comment and its relevance to the discussion of parliamentary opposition. Beginning in the post-war era, but continuing with episodic degrees of strength thereafter, a distrust of parliamentary processes became evident where none had existed before. Figuratively, it might be said that Canadian parliamentary institutions were cast in the Westminster mould. The reproduction was not perfect, but no one before the war had suggested that the original and its imitation were in any way fundamentally flawed. Passage of the Parliament Act, 1910, which reduced the House of Lords' power to obstruct to that of a suspensive veto only, and the introduction of closure in 1913 in order to limit debate in the Canadian Commons, may not have been welcome by those immediately affected. Still, the larger institution was not suspect. Quite the reverse – Parliament at Westminster remained for many the greatest legislative assembly in the world. And, in light of the demands of war successfully met and the transformation of the British party structure (Liberals in decline and Labour on the rise) accommodated, it was also among the most adaptable.

At the outset, the principal messenger of distrust, but not its agent, was the Progressive movement, whose raison d'être lay in its members being neither Liberals nor Conservatives. When the Progressives' moment came, in the returns of the 1921 election, which gave them sixty-five seats to the Conservatives' fifty and the Liberals' 116, in a House of 235, they declined to embrace it. Several reasons are customarily offered for this decision, among them inexperience, lack of internal cohesion, and the possibility of achieving more in the way of public policy through cooperating with the Liberals rather than opposing them. Crerar's biographer, J.E. Rea, offers a variation on that explanation but from an opposite perspective: 'It may be that the Liberals feared the result if the Progressives became the Official Opposition, since that might ... build in a structural rigidity that might thwart any future union.'[5] According to E.C. Drury, the United Farmers of Ontario premier following the provincial election in 1919, King sought (through Drury) but did not pursue (because of opposition from within the Progressives) cooperation with the farmers.[6] Another possibility, offered by Crerar himself, might have been drawn from a text on parliamentary practice: 'If we become the Official Opposition we are expected to oppose. If we fail to do that and support the government when it is right, Meighen, whether he occupied the position of Official Opposition or not, would come to be so regarded in the country.'[7]

'When it is right': the phrase says volumes about the Progressives and their negative assumptions about parliamentary government. It should also have served as a warning about the confusion that would ensue when the Progressives had to decide which side was in the 'right,' and whom they should therefore support, in the constitutional crisis of 1926. 'There is, or should be, more to Parliament than adversarial politics': this is an evergreen homily first heard in the 1920s, repeated sixty years later by Preston Manning, but not uncritically echoed in the interval by all opposition leaders. Public policy might be judged good or bad, legal or illegal, constitutional or unconstitutional. 'Right or wrong,' however, introduces a standard outside the judgment of Parliament. It foreshadows another – external – standard of a later date, when Joe Clark told John Diefenbaker that, for the good of the party and country, young Tories believed he should step down as leader. To this piece of intelligence Diefenbaker replied: 'You are a credit to your teachers.'[8] The response is sarcastic yet the inference clear: there is no external 'authority,' decisions of such magnitude are to be made in Parliament by parliamentarians.

It could be said that with the election returns of 1921, the first 'third' party had arrived in Parliament; for since that date there have always been representatives of at least one party, movement, or group, other than the Liberals and Conservatives, on the floor of the House of Commons. These collectives did not constitute recognized political parties, as that term was later defined, because recognition of Canadian political parties in Parliament and law was a slow process. Still, John Courtney, who has studied this matter, notes that in the 1920s, 'separate rooms [were] reserved for each of the parties for the purpose of holding regular meetings' and 'the Commons adopted a procedural change whereby an amendment to the amendment of a main motion would be accepted by the Speaker and voted on independently, a change [he concludes] that was of considerable import to the existent third party and to all subsequent minor parties.'[9] And, it might be added, to the work of opposition in the House of Commons, since as a result of these changes the single-party world of opposition was acknowledged to have passed. Thus Parliament adjusted to the presence of the Progressives; the Progressives, however, proved less adaptable to adjusting to the ways of Parliament. By the end of the 1920s, they had disappeared as a parliamentary force. The explanation of this outcome is usually a combination of the cunning of King, on the one hand, and on the other, confusion among Progressives over their purpose and priorities.

An answer to what went wrong for the Progressives (and why) is found in the work by W.L. Morton, and in the ten-volume 1950s Social

Credit series, of which his book, published in 1950, was the first, and D.C. Masters's history of the Winnipeg general strike, also from 1950, was the second.[10] What the story signifies for the conduct of parliamentary politics has attracted less scrutiny. The Progressives were *in* but never *of* Parliament. They distrusted it and did not understand either its folkways or its procedures. In a brutally critical assessment of his caucus, Crerar went so far, in 1922, as to say that 'it is difficult for a man who ... has had little or no public experience, to adapt himself effectively to the requirements of Parliament. I think ... that the best place for our group is on the side lines.'[11] Such a sense of inferior place never plagued the Co-operative Commonwealth Federation (CCF), whose lineage had Progressive associations. For instance, J.S. Woodsworth, elected in 1921 as a Labour member for Winnipeg Centre, looked to and received Progressive support in the House. Some Progressive MPs joined him and William Irvine in 1924 in the 'Ginger Group,' so-called because of their fierce commitment to the concept of group (i.e., economic group) government. In the case of Woodsworth and Irvine, they were 'in Parliament,' the latter said, 'specifically to represent labour.' On their organization, Irvine elaborated: 'The hon. for Centre Winnipeg is the leader of the Labour group – I am the group.'[12] Like the CCF, of which they were to be a founding element, Woodsworth and Irvine saw themselves as belonging to a group whose legitimacy and morality originated in the ballot box and in the authenticity conferred by Parliament. Unlike the Progressives, they demonstrated neither apology nor indecision in the Commons. Command of and respect for legislative procedure earned Woodsworth and his successors as spokesmen of the left a continuing reputation as masters of the House. M.J. Coldwell, Stanley Knowles, and T.C. Douglas approached politics from the perspective of a party whose policies depended for their enactment upon Parliament and for their approval on public support at elections. Also, unlike the Progressives, who, from the margins, decried party discipline, the parliamentary socialists (for that is the most accurate generic term to apply) accepted, even welcomed, it in their quest to implement controversial social and economic policies. Paradoxically, says Kenneth McNaught, 'when the orthodox Progressives began to show their true [anaemic] colours, then the radicals were prepared to reconsider their stand on the subject of party organization.'[13]

Thus, it can be said that the returns for 1921 disguised the variety even as they revealed the extent of non-Liberal and non-Conservative electoral support. This finessing of the outcomes was abetted by the

Progressives' refusal to assume the role of official opposition. As a result, the partisan lines after the contest looked deceptively much as they did before. Except for one vital difference: after the votes were counted the Liberals were in and the Conservatives out of power. The Parliament the election produced was the first in which no party held a majority of the seats. That deficit presented the new prime minister, W.L. Mackenzie King, with a challenge that his predecessors had not faced – the real, as opposed to theoretical and therefore rare, possibility of defeat in the House. At the same time, the election results presented the parties now in opposition with true possibilities of defeating the government, if they were so inclined.

Mackenzie King took the oath as President of the Privy Council on 29 December 1921. Since he became prime minister for the first time as of this date, it would be reasonable to trace the beginning of 'Liberal ascendancy' to this moment. Except, as in so many aspects of his political career, there is another possibility to consider: King had been selected leader of the Liberal party two years before, at its first national leadership convention in August 1919. At this point he became leader of the opposition, thereby replacing, not Laurier, but D.D. McKenzie, who, chosen by caucus and assisted by an advisory committee of thirteen MPs following Laurier's death, had served for six months as Canada's first acting leader of the opposition. Minister of Labour (1909–1911) in the Laurier government, King's strongest recommendation to convention delegates was that he had not deserted Laurier over conscription. Of the four contenders (W.S. Fielding, W.M. Martin, G.P. Graham, and King), only Fielding (age seventy-one) held a seat in the House, and he had abandoned Laurier, a desertion that Quebec delegates refused to forgive. Thus, as well as choosing a national party leader for the first time through means of a convention and lending credence to the idea that the 'party outside parliament should be involved in the task of leadership selection,' in selecting King (age forty-seven), the party had chosen an individual who did not have a seat in the House.[14]

Having won a by-election on Prince Edward Island, King entered the House in October. Yet according to his biographer, he was willing, because he was ignorant of current issues, 'to allow McKenzie and Fielding to carry a large part of the load.'[15] Another authority on leadership has generalized that predisposition of King's to delegate:

Initially, in opposition and in the first years in office, he relied heavily on Fielding's experience and prestige; then, I think, on George Graham's good temper and good humour to ease matters. Later [1930–5], Ian Mackenzie owed his promotion to the role to his mastery of parliamentary procedure, unqualified loyalty to the PM, and zest for parliamentary combat while in opposition.[16]

One consideration that perhaps served as a warning against taking initiative was division within the Liberal ranks over the peace treaties: How nationalistic, how imperialistic, how internationalist (through support for the League of Nations) should Canada be in the post-war period? Echoes of the naval and conscription debates of 1913 and 1917 reverberated in the Liberal caucus under the new and uncertain leader. Meighen, with his talent for acid summary, caught his opponent's dilemma: King, he said, had been 'shifted or tossed or elevated ... to the post of leadership – [the] outside leader of the outside party in this country.'[17]

At this point the wartime government was approaching its end. In July 1920, Meighen succeeded Borden as leader of what was now called the 'National Liberal and Conservative Party.' It was a government with problems, the post-war economic slowdown being one, a second party in opposition another.[18] One satisfaction afforded Meighen, in government and later in opposition, was his contempt for King. Roger Graham, Meighen's biographer and usual defender, saw his pursuit of King in the House as 'so relentless, with such savage, ironic scorn, that [it] embarrassed even his own supporters.'[19] His colleague, Charles Doherty, the minister of justice, took a larger, more strategic but equally disparaging view: 'Mackenzie King is – to us – a tower of strength.'[20] This low estimation of King in the two decades after 1920 is by now a familiar facet of commentary on Canadian politics between the wars (King's opinion of Meighen is less frequently examined). One reason for its strength and longevity lies in the writings of Eugene Forsey, who, fifty years after King and Meighen first confronted each other across the aisle, composed this judgment of King:

> I set about it in a spirit of stern academic objectivity, telling myself that, though Mr. King's behaviour in 1926 was constitutionally inexcusable, he could not have been consistently wrong on such subjects. Evening after evening I went to the Parliamentary Library determined to find evidence of his constitutional good deeds. Evening after evening, within half an hour or less, what I found was fresh evidence of the contrary: either outrages I had forgotten, or new ones I had never heard of, both of which sent me soaring into the dome of the library in a state of incandescence.[21]

More than that, Forsey wrote an exhaustive text on the reserve power of dissolution, the core issue of the constitutional crisis of 1926, in which King, as prime minister, Meighen, now leader of the opposition (because the leader of the Progressives had declined to accept the position), and Viscount Byng, the Governor General, were the principal actors.[22] Forsey's prominence as the country's foremost public constitutional expert for much of the last part of the twentieth century, and his pungent and unwavering criticism of King's (and the Liberals') parliamentary standards, did not cut short the Liberal ascendancy (as the title of an article he wrote in 1957, about the St Laurent and his ministers, phrased it: 'Never Have So Many Been In So Long'[23]), but they conferred on it a reputation that infected both government and opposition. Government, and particularly Mr King's, did not respect Parliament. He was the first prime minister to propose appealing to the people to resolve what was in essence parliamentary conflict or uncertainty. Thus it was King's contribution to raise the people up as a theoretical rival to Parliament, which is to say a rival to the opposition. In practice, nothing really changed – except that in this constitutional universe the opposition now could be depicted as opposed to the people as well as to government. In the thirty-one years the Liberals held power between 1921 and 1957, the only opposition leader to attempt to refute this innovation, in precise, constitutionally coherent fashion, was Arthur Meighen. He, along with Forsey, Roger Graham, and later scholars, such as Peter Russell, by no means vanquished what they viewed as a constitutional heresy.

Whether King was scheming and duplicitous is an open question and in any case beside the point. What is not arguable is that he introduced a third, popular element into parliamentary debate, one still invoked, as in the claim in 2008 that 'gross violations of democratic principles would be involved in [the Governor General's] handing government over to the coalition without getting the approval of the voter.'[24] Also unarguable is that King kept secret his Manichaean concept of authority. Quite the reverse: when in 1920 a replica of the Speaker's Chair at Westminster was presented to the House of Commons in Ottawa, to be installed in the reconstructed chamber, King, as leader of the opposition, summarized (for him) the significance of the occasion:

There are, under British parliamentary institutions, two symbols of authority – the Crown, which speaks of the sovereignty of the King; the Speaker's Chair, which speaks of the sovereignty of the people. That, under the aegis of the British flag, the two sovereignties have blended into one, is not less a tribute to the character and devotion to duty of British rulers, than to the genius of the British peoples in the art and science of government.[25]

During the constitutional crisis of 1926, five days before Meighen assumed office for the second time, King (still prime minister) in a speech later published under the title 'The British Constitution,' elaborated on the heterogeneity of his subject, as he saw it:

It is a strange mystical sort of thing, this British Constitution that we love. It is partly unwritten; it is partly written. It finds its beginnings in the lore of the past; it comes into being in the form of custom and tradition; it is founded upon the common law. It is made up of precedents, of magna chartas [sic]. Of petitions and bills of rights; it is to be found partly in statutes, and partly in the usages and practices of Parliament. It represents the highest achievement of British genius at its best.[26]

The attention that has been devoted to the constitutional crisis of 1926 has done little to further understanding of parliamentary government, especially the role of the opposition. The question – which of the principal actors acted constitutionally and which did not – has long been debated, with inconclusive findings, Forsey notwithstanding. None the less, when measured by academic allies, the prize must be awarded to Byng and Meighen. Yet the whole episode is a diversion from ordinary parliamentary life, although not lacking instruction. As noted in chapter 1, 'the existence of the Leader of the Opposition is an essential part of the neutrality of the Monarch.' The events surrounding the request for dissolution in 1926 (as with the requests for prorogation in 2008 and 2009) illustrate that when opposition seeks, or comes to, the assistance of the Crown, in a controversy that must necessarily involve the government, the customary perspective on the performance of government and opposition disappears. In parliamentary politics there is one prize only – power – and in instances like these the Crown may confer what voters have denied.

By the mid-1920s the Progressives were, in Murray Beck's blunt phrase, 'spent as a national force.'[27] Probably at no other time in Canadian political history have the conventions of parliamentary government proved so determinative of the fate of parties in the House. For the Progressives, independence as a political force was recognized as unachievable (a hard truth corroborated by their failure to have machinery in place to reorganize when the West's representation in the House grew by eleven seats as a result of the redistribution following the 1921 census[28]); for the Conservatives under Meighen, the call of constitutional duty (in the form of an invitation to form a government following Mackenzie King's resignation) could not be denied; and for the Liberals, who sought but were refused a dissolution of the Commons by the Governor General, there was no choice except to resign. That the second Meighen government would last but ninety days and that it would be followed by the third election in five years, the one to give King his first majority, were themselves as much the consequences of the unfolding of constitutional conventions as they were the outcome of adroit or maladroit leadership.

That said, the difference in parliamentary leadership between King and Meighen remained striking. According to Graham, after 1921, 'even more than when he had been Prime Minister the performance of [Meighen's] party in the House was a one-man show.'[29] The Progressives' preference not to see themselves as an alternative government was one explanation, since the weight of opposition rested on the Tories. By contrast, King described the Progressives as 'a people's movement,' liberal and Liberal in sympathy, to be accommodated through policy adjustments and, ultimately, absorbed as an electoral threat.[30] That conciliatory cast of mind was reinforced by the parallel need to reunite Unionist and Laurier Liberals, on the one hand, and to harmonize Quebec and western Liberal differences on economic matters, on the other. It was as if the lens of perception for the Conservatives had been narrowed to Parliament, while for the Liberals it had widened to embrace the party and electorate outside Parliament. Nor can the broadening effect of a leadership convention composed of delegates intended to give weight to party opinion across the country be excluded from the explanation for the Liberals' behaviour. It was a shift in orientation that the Conservatives were soon to follow:

Following the 1926 general election (in which Meighen himself had been defeated in a Manitoba constituency), the Conservative party could not avoid a critical self-examination. How similar, in many ways, its position proved to be that of the Liberal party in 1918–1919! By late 1926 the Conservatives had been in opposition for five years, except for the three-month term of office in 1926 under Meighen; in 1918 the Liberals were entering their seventh year on the Speaker's left. The Conservatives had failed to retain or regain power in three successive elections (1921, 1925 and

1926), the Liberals in two (1911 and 1917). The Conservative parliamentary group was more English-speaking Canadian than the Liberal caucus had been French-speaking, yet both groups were only too aware of the need to correct such imbalances and to appear as truly national political parties.[31]

John Courtney has studied leadership conventions in Canada, including, importantly, reasons for their summoning. For the Conservatives in 1927, there was the influence of the Liberal convention in 1919, but also the Ontario precedent of 1920, when that province's Conservatives used a convention to select a new leader, G. Howard Ferguson. It was that precedent that led the *Toronto Mail and Empire* to pronounce editorially that 'the leadership of the Conservative party ... is not in the gift of any coterie ... but must emanate from an organic body of the party, constituted for [that] purpose.'[32] When the Tories, in convention at Winnipeg, chose a successor to Meighen, it was R.B. Bennett who emerged victorious. Assessments of Mackenzie King and Bennett usually find little in common between the two men, the former a self-styled apostle of national unity, the latter an internationalist and imperialist, if in the last instance appointment to the House of Lords in 1941 is any measure. From the perspective of the subject of this book, and in contrast to the men each succeeded as leader of their respective political parties, there is another similarity of note. King had had three years' parliamentary experience (more than a decade before 1919), and the man who came second at the convention (Fielding) had seventeen years; Bennett, who returned to the House in 1925 after an eight-year absence and who possessed a total of eight years' experience, 'defeated five other men who had served, on average, eleven years in parliament.'[33] (His closest competitor – Guthrie – had served for twenty-seven uninterrupted years.) Thus, unlike Laurier and Borden, King and Bennett were not parliamentary men. Hereafter, and in consequence of the introduction of leadership conventions in the decade following the war, whatever functions the opposition might have, they did not include schooling future prime ministers.

Meighen's principled, or combative, approach to parliamentary debate convinced many Canadians (with Liberal help) that the Conservatives were too British in their sympathies, despite Meighen's controversial proposal in the 1926 campaign that if his government decided to participate in a war it would go to the people in a general election before troops left the country, as well as insufficiently French (no French-speaking Conservative was elected from Quebec in the general elections of 1921,

1925, or 1926). Partly because constitutional issues bulked so large in the 1920s and partly because Meighen prided himself on his constitutional acumen, for much of the time the leader appeared to be the party. Bennett adopted something of a new style, evident in his willingness to seek counsel, particularly from Major-General A.D. McRae, chairman of the organizing committee of the 1927 convention and, after 1929, national director of the Conservative party. If as prime minister Bennett has impressed political historians as a different breed of Conservative from those who had gone before – father of public broadcasting in Canada, of the Canadian Wheat Board, and of an early version of agricultural support payments, among other policy innovations – then some of the credit for change goes to McRae, who less than a year before the 1930 general election advised Bennett, now leader of the opposition, to reject 'the negative-opposition role' in favour of 'an alternative-government image':

> The old political school considered it bad policy for an Opposition to enunciate constructive issues in advance of the campaign … I disclaim any membership in this school … It is now imperative that we take active steps to convince the public of our constructive abilities, and what they may look for if the Conservative Party, under your leadership is given an opportunity to govern the Dominion.[34]

Still, Bennett reprised Meighen's dominating role as prime minister, which is almost a prerogative of all first ministers but also leaders of the opposition; and for a reason that many leaders of opposition before and after have encountered: in the 1935 election (as in 1921) the Tory caucus was decimated. The leader, Bennett (or Meighen), of necessity 'completely overshadowed his caucus.'[35] In such straitened political condition, the leader is obliged to spend much of his time defending the actions and policies of his previous government. The health of the parliamentary and extra-parliamentary parties suffers in consequence of this defensive preoccupation. (A rare dissent from that view, although one that must be granted credence given its source, is by Charles G. 'Chubby' Power, the masterful Liberal strategist, who used his party's years in opposition, from 1930 to 1935, to 'hammer' the parliamentary caucus into 'a useful attacking force.'[36]) Bennett's contribution to policy debate on both sides of the House may have eclipsed Meighen's in quantity and breadth, but when he stepped down in 1938 the Conservative party was still viewed as lukewarm in its sensibility to Quebec while passionate in the cause of English-speaking Canada, Great Britain, and the Empire.

In his impassioned plea against the introduction of closure on the naval bill in 1913, Laurier had maintained that 'there are occasions ... when an opposition or a minority owes it to itself, on account of the strong views it holds upon some public measure, to oppose that measure with all the force at its command.'[37] In the interwar period no 'occasion' of this magnitude arose in House debates, though in 1938 when the King government was accused of withholding information from Parliament, Bennett advanced a strong claim for the opposition as a defender of minority rights.

> I occupy a position in which I am placed by statute, and one of my duties is to do exactly what I am doing, to try to safeguard the liberties of Parliament from encroachment by the Government of the day. That is my duty. It is one of the difficulties of the position which I occupy, and I will discharge that duty whether it be on behalf of a member of the Opposition or of any other party when there is tyrannical exercise of power on the part of the Government by reason of a great majority, enabling the administration to destroy the liberties of this Parliament, which have been secured in the manner we all know.[38]

The Liberals under Mackenzie King returned to power following the general election of 1935. They remained in government (under St Laurent after 1948) until 1957. In that twenty-two-year span, the Conservatives, given the adjective Progressive at the instigation of the former Manitoba premier John Bracken, selected leader by a delegate convention in 1942, had four leaders and three acting leaders. Of this number – Robert Manion (1938–40), Richard Hanson (acting 1940–3), Gordon Graydon (acting 1943–5), John Bracken (1945–8), George Drew (1948–54 and 1955–6), Earl Rowe (acting 1954–5 and 1956), and John Diefenbaker (1956–7) – only the last broke the spell and led the party to power. The others joined Edward Blake in failing to make the transition from leader of the opposition to government. Both Hanson and Manion acted for Bracken, who despite being chosen leader of the party in December 1942 was not elected to the Commons until 1945. Hanson acted as well for Arthur Meighen, who was party leader between November 1941 and December 1942 but who, after resigning from the Senate where he had sat since 1932, unsuccessfully sought a seat in the Commons, being defeated in a by-election in February 1942.

The Liberal ascendancy and the twenty-year period after 1963 (broken only by the interregnum of the Clark government in 1979) during which

Lester Pearson and Pierre Trudeau were prime ministers, provide support for the assertion frequently heard that the Liberals are (or were) Canada's 'natural governing party.' The wilderness of opposition that resulted from this dominance explains the poverty of scholarly examination of parties other than the Liberals,[39] and even they, putting to one side studies of Mackenzie King, have attracted minimal attention. The exception to that generalization is Reginald Whitaker's *The Government Party: Organizing and Financing the Liberal Party of Canada, 1930–58*.[40] The thesis of that work, summarized accurately in its title, illustrates its lack of relevance to this study of opposition, with one qualification. In 1930, the Liberals responded to defeat and confinement to opposition by resorting, as they had in 1919, to a new extra-parliamentary organization, the National Liberal Federation. Until the 'participatory democracy' reorganization carried out by Keith Davey in the 1960s, the Liberals were unabashedly federated in structure. Compare this response to that of the Conservatives after a crushing defeat in 1935, when they won ten fewer seats than in 1921. Bennett's resignation in 1938 was followed by a delegate convention in which R.J. Manion, with more than seventeen years' experience in the House, defeated M.A. MacPherson, who had none. According to Glassford, Manion's victory was explained by 'his popularity with the English-speaking rank and file, his symbolic appeal to Quebec [he was Roman Catholic (Irish) and his wife French-Canadian], and his campaign organization.'[41] His liabilities were great: elected a Liberal-Unionist candidate in 1917, he had been a minister in both of Meighen's governments and in that of Bennett; despite this loyalist background, Meighen and Bennett opposed his selection.

A greater obstacle than this lay in wait: it was Mackenzie King, 'nemesis of the Tory party' and vanquisher of Meighen, Bennett, and (ultimately) Manion.[42] At the war's beginning, the Conservative caucus, with Manion's reluctant agreement, since in his mind oppositions were supposed to oppose, proposed a national government of the 'best brains' in the country.[43] King's experience of intra-party division following coalition government in 1917 guaranteed that this proposal would be unpalatable to him. That Manion and others – for instance, the unnatural allies Mitch Hepburn, Ontario's Liberal premier, and George Drew, that province's Conservative leader of the opposition – also censured the federal government's prosecution of the war presented an opportunity. Despite a political truce agreed to by the prime minister and the leader of the opposition – no contested by-elections, for example – King dissolved Parliament unexpectedly in January 1940, then during the campaign ridiculed Manion's national government proposal. The Liberals won an absolute majority of the vote, the first party to do so since 1917. The CCF had campaigned without J.S. Woodsworth as leader (a pacifist, he refused to follow his caucus members in their support of the declaration of war). It was now led by M.J. Coldwell, who made the King government's use (he said, abuse) of emergency powers a principal plank of the CCF platform. The performance won them only one additional seat, but the issue of concentrated executive power proved a harbinger of a campaign the CCF would mount through the following decade up to the great pipeline debate of 1956. Five months after the election, Manion submitted his resignation to the parliamentary caucus, although he had been selected by a delegate convention (at this time the respective roles and responsibilities of the two entities remained blurred), because, he said, 'a Convention is not a continuing body, the only group who at the moment have any authority to speak for our Party from a federal stand point, are the Conservative members of the House of Commons.'[44] John Diefenbaker later described extra-parliamentary critics as 'an assemblage of the Warwicks,' and in 1967, when the PC convention chose Robert Stanfield to succeed him as leader, Diefenbaker brought John Bracken into his Maple Leaf Gardens box, symbolizing in this act (he said) that 'they did it to John Bracken, and now they are doing it to [me].'[45]

Over the next five years the Conservative party survived in a form of receivership. For the first two-and-a-half years, R.B. Hanson, another former Bennett minister, served, at the request of caucus, as acting leader. Senior party officials discussed but rejected in wartime the idea of calling a leadership convention. Instead, they agreed to invite Arthur Meighen, now a senator, to assume the role of party leader. Meighen tried to convince the agrarian premier of Manitoba since 1922, John Bracken, to take this responsibility. When Bracken declined, prominent Ontario Conservatives, including George Drew, urged Meighen to accept. He agreed, resigned from the Senate, ran (in support of conscription for overseas service and national government), unopposed by a Liberal candidate, in an Ontario seat that had for forty years returned a Conservative, then lost to the CCF candidate. (There were several reasons, superfluous to this discussion, for Meighen's defeat. One that was not, however, was the King government's announcement during the course of the by-election campaign that it would hold a national plebiscite asking the public to release the government from its earlier promise of no overseas conscription. As in 1926, the public and not Parliament was to determine the political course, the first casualty of which was

Meighen and partisan-imposed conscription.) While the extent of covert Liberal support for Meighen's opponent in the by-election was afterward disputed, the consequences of its outcome for the Conservatives were indelible – this was the nadir of Tory fortunes in Parliament.

Yet that parliamentary picture of the party was misleading, for at the end of 1942 another Conservative delegate convention chose the still reluctant John Bracken as its leader. As in 1938, M.A. MacPherson, out of the House, came second. The candidate to come third, and the only one of these three with parliamentary experience and a seat, was John Diefenbaker. Bracken made changing the party's name to Progressive Conservative a condition of his candidacy. In his mind this constituted no cosmetic nomenclature but the first step towards a party that accommodated western Canadian progressive sentiments and policies. A professor of agriculture and then a premier of an essentially non-partisan government, Bracken possessed no talents to be an effective leader of opposition in the Parliament of Canada. As it transpired, he had no opportunity to demonstrate his capabilities in this office until after he sought (for the first time) and won a seat in Manitoba in the general election of 1945. (In the interval and in succession to Arthur Meighen, another acting leader, Ontario MP Gordon Graydon, was selected by a narrow margin over John Diefenbaker.) In 1948 Bracken stepped down as leader for reasons of health; the following year he was defeated when he ran in the general election. In that contest the concentration of PC victories in Ontario and hardly anywhere else grew more pronounced, compared to 1940, while the CCF seat count more than tripled and its popular vote surpassed that of the Progressive Conservatives.

One of the difficulties of analysing the opposition during the period this chapter calls the Liberal ascendancy is that there is so much activity – conflicting ambitions, leaders coming and going, internal dissent about strategy, charges and counter-charges over policies – but so little achieved in the way of developing sustained parliamentary opposition. The consequences of coalition during the First World War preoccupied King and the Liberals for years afterwards. Those same consequences explain his supporting a partisan truce at the beginning of the Second World War, while at the same time rejecting any idea of national government. He liked to say, after the 1940 election, that Canadians had a national government: Liberals elected in all nine provinces, the Conservatives eliminated in three. Partisanship, as manifested for example in appointments to wartime agencies, should be dampened for the duration but not destroyed. King had allies in his truce. Citing a policy established in 1939 not to permit 'political controversy ... over the radio in time of war,' the Canadian Broadcasting Corporation refused to allow the opening session of the Conservative convention of 1942 to be broadcast across the country.[46] Although government critics might claim to see partisan favouritism on the part of the Crown corporation, the situation could have been worse: in 1947, the BBC 'forbade discussion of any matters either currently being debated in parliament or due in the next fortnight to be debated there.'[47]

For the Conservatives, the consequences of coalition in the First World War had less influence on postwar developments than they did for the Liberals (the effect of conscription on Tory support in Quebec being the exception to this). Meighen, Bennett, and Manion all had political roots in this event yet seemed untroubled by the difficulties (and lingering effects) that wartime policies had for farmers and western Canadians, generally, and for French Canadians. It was the opinion of the incomparable Liberal memoirist C.G. 'Chubby' Power, who with his father held the seat of Quebec West (renamed Quebec South) for fifty years after 1902, that Meighen's attacks on King were motivated more by personal than partisan antipathy. When he was not castigating King, '[Meighen] was the Tory advocate, and his job was to justify Tory policy to themselves, not to convert opponents.'[48] That assessment – Meighen as the favourite of caucus and caucus his favourite audience – is given further credence by his continuing influence with the parliamentary party even after he had stepped down as leader. Bennett never commanded such loyalty from his colleagues.[49] In those pre-radio days (free-time radio broadcasts were provided for the first time in the 1940 general election), who were MPs, especially opposition MPs, to address? Was it their opponents across the aisle, the press gallery, or their supporters arrayed behind them? Whatever the academic theory of parliamentary opposition, for the conflicted Progressive Conservatives the last orientation was as necessary as it was explicable.

Notwithstanding the election results of 1949 – Liberals increasing their total by sixty-five seats and the PCs losing twenty-six (with the CCF also down fifteen) – the contrasting trajectory in long-term party fortunes between Liberals (up) and Tories (down) reversed itself after 1948. When the subject is parliamentary parties, votes and seats won at general elections are not necessarily indicative of the strength of the opposed forces in the House. In retrospect, the most significant act the Progressive Conservatives took after the end of the Second World War was to select George Drew, then premier of Ontario, as national party leader in 1948. An index of the importance of the occasion is that unlike the previous three conventions, only one ballot was required to select the party leader. Drew won with 67 per cent of the vote. The same year the Liberals held a delegate convention to select a successor to Mackenzie King. Louis St Laurent, the favourite, won on the first ballot with 69 per cent of the vote. In 1919, King had been one of four candidates, winning on the third ballot with just 51 per cent of the delegate vote. In the 1950s, when each of the old parties replaced its leader, again only a single ballot was required to make the choice, Diefenbaker for the PCs in 1956 and Pearson for the Liberals in 1958.[50]

In his study of the Conservatives, John Williams said that 'with the advent of Drew in the House of Commons, the new leader quickly infused new life into the parliamentary group.'[51] More than that, and more relevant to a study of opposition, Williams, writing at a time when Drew was still in the House as leader, noted an important contrast between 'the wholehearted support' the new leader received from the parliamentary group and 'the pre-Drew days when the Conservatives seemed to wish their leaders the worst of luck.'[52] Now opposition unity was marshalled to support a strategy of obstructing House business rather than criticizing the government. For some, the unity was cosmetic. When he became leader of the opposition, Diefenbaker for one took a contrary view of the role he and his supporters should play: 'Criticism of the Opposition is largely directed toward the electorate, with a view to the next election, or with the aim of influencing government policy through the pressure of public opinion. To merely oppose by criticism is not enough. The role of the Opposition is more complex and more responsible.'[53] On the premise that the sovereignty of the people is delegated to Parliament, and not the executive, the true role of the opposition was to become 'the people's instrument of intelligent criticism.'

If most Canadians were asked to name which politician in their history best fits the description prairie populist, John Diefenbaker's name would confidently be proposed many times over. Although he believed all his life in Parliament's supremacy, he saw elections as confirming or ratifying its decisions. In this perspective he was not unlike legendary CCF parliamentarians, such as M.J. Coldwell and Stanley Knowles. Also, in this he was quite unlike preceding Conservative leaders, and especially Drew, whose manner and appearance earned him the reputation of being a patrician snob. There is no biography of Drew to support or refute that depiction, although Diefenbaker's principal biographer, Denis Smith, confirms that he stood aloof from new and promising PC leaders in the provinces – Robert Stanfield of Nova Scotia, Duff Roblin of Manitoba, and Hugh John Fleming of New Brunswick – men who presumably shared his preference for a less dominant central government. Drew's arrogance towards the government would in time mirror ministerial arrogance towards the opposition. Unlike the cooperative Liberal-Progressive John Bracken, the first premier to be national PC leader, Drew was politically bellicose. It might be said that he was partisan to the core, but that description would not explain his aligning himself and the Ontario Tories with Hepburn's Liberals against the King government in 1940. It was also an opposition different from Meighen's, if only because for the first time in three decades Mackenzie King was no longer prime minister.

The government of Louis St Laurent (1948–57) represented the apotheosis of Liberal ministerialism, which originated in the 1920s but became institutionalized under the National Liberal Federation created when the Liberals were out of power in the early 1930s. Ministers, like James G. Gardiner of Saskatchewan and C.D. Howe of Ontario, were the chiefs of the party in their respective provinces, which resembled fiefdoms, while the office of prime minister became in turn a holding corporation. This is a generalization, to be true, but St Laurent's avuncular personality, so different from King's, permitted ministers an independence they had not previously enjoyed. The distinction between the leadership styles of the two prime ministers during the period of Liberal ascendancy needs to be stressed since it was an important influence on events leading to the Liberal defeat of 1957. In an assessment for the publisher of the manuscript that would become *Mr. Prime Minister, 1867–1964*, Norman Ward commented that 'Mr. St. Laurent was extremely shrewd, and never shrewder than when he saw himself finally as a failure in regard to [his relationships] with Parliament, the party and the public.'[54]

On the opposition side, the strength and clarity of objective of leaders such as Drew, Diefenbaker, and, in the CCF ranks, Coldwell and Knowles proved to be important. The personal animosity between King and his opponents across the aisle had disappeared. Drew might be sarcastic, but he did not have a King on whom to vent his sarcasm; while St Laurent, the first Liberal prime minister not to have sat in opposition or as a backbencher, displayed none of the wiliness of his predecessor. Meighen and, to a certain extent, Bennett had concentrated their energies in the House too often on seeking to destroy King rather than his government. In this tactic they were encouraged by the low esteem in which they permanently held the prime minister.

By the beginning of the 1950s, there was a convergence of opposition men and government circumstance. Unlike after the First World War, this time the party that had formed the government during wartime continued into the (long) postwar period. The exercise of exceptional wartime powers remained after the conflict had ended, and that persistence, evident in 'the annual request for renewal of the Emergency Powers Act [until 1954] provided the opposition parties with an opportunity to repeat their charge that the government had become accustomed to almost dictatorial powers.'[55] Long before the word 'pipeline' was heard – a reference to the great debate in 1956 and the imposition of closure on that debate in order to expedite passage of financial legislation through the House – the mustard seed of concern about the government's subverting the constitution had been planted.[56] Time was the government's enemy, in this particular instance – financing for construction of the natural gas pipeline had to be passed if the agreement with private American developers were to be honoured; but more generally too: 'Since the end of the World War II the typical session has run eight months or more, even when the Government had an overwhelming majority, and there has always been some business left unfinished.'[57] There is no disputing the judgment of William Kilbourn that 'the opposition had brought the government to its knees.' Ultimately, the bill may have passed, but not before its opponents had made 'great political gain and won a kind of moral victory.'[58]

As rare as such David-and-Goliath moments might be in Canadian politics, and as important as this debate was to moulding public opinion leading to the defeat of the Liberals the following year, another, less commented, influence for change occurred at this time. C.D. Howe, 'minister of everything,' had propelled the pipeline bill without regard for the opposition or – more important for the purposes of this discussion – for some of his own colleagues. According to George Nowlan, a prominent Tory frontbencher and witness from across the aisle to the Liberal imbroglio: 'Walter Harris [the Liberal minister of finance] would like to see Howe get a bloody nose out of this.'[59] In short, not just their opponents in the House, and not just the public, thought matters had got out of hand – so did some Liberals. The point needs emphasizing, because the end of Liberal ascendancy in 1957 did not signify transition to a Progressive Conservative variation on the theme of dominance. On the contrary, an all-party attitude embracing a sense of revival emerged, reflected in action more than in articulated policy, to strengthen the legislature in its relations with the government, and to do this through accepted methods, which was to say, through the political parties present in the House of Commons. As election returns would prove, there were to be more parties, more often, in the chamber than at any time in the past.

4 Majorities and Minorities, 1957–1992

The first stage in the chronology of Canadian politics, the period chapter 2 labels 'coalition to coalition,' is characterized by symmetry. It begins and ends in times of partisan uncertainty: at the outset there is no formal opposition with an acknowledged leader and at the conclusion party lines have become blurred and loyalties frayed. Yet between those apparently identical stations on the road of parliamentary politics, party structures in and out of Parliament and on both sides of the House solidified as leaders grew in dominance. While the change of parties in government might be infrequent by British standards, still alternation did occur. The world of Westminster appeared to have been replicated, with adaptation, in Canada's national parliament. By contrast, if there was a prevailing feature of the next stage – the more-than-three-score years of Liberal ascendancy after the First World War – it was the absence of symmetry. In its place the long trajectory of Liberal rule was accompanied by the atrophy of Tory opposition, evident in the accelerated turnover of Conservative leaders. A contemporaneous development, which became a permanent part of parliamentary politics, was the arrival of third parties whose strength, in the first two of nine general elections between 1921 and 1957, made impossible the formation of a government with the support of members of one party alone. Minority government, the term Canadians coined to describe the situation, disappeared after the mid-1920s and did not return until 1957, when on that occasion and in five subsequent elections their formation was again required. As the next chapter will discuss, minority governments reappeared in the first decade of the twenty-first century but for reasons and with consequences for opposition different from those discussed here.

A principal, and perhaps principled, defence of the role of opposition in the parliamentary system is that if they play by the rules, and the government does as well, then at some point (admittedly, perhaps a very distant point) the opposition party will replace the governing party in power. Patience is a parliamentary virtue. In the interval, however, what George Perlin later labelled the 'Tory syndrome' – the development of an opposition mentality fostered by inexperienced and indecisive leadership – might occur. As accurate as that depiction might be of the Progressive Conservative party at the time his book appeared in 1980, it was not applicable to the period following its electoral success in 1957. To begin with, there was a new leader (John Diefenbaker, chosen in 1956) who possessed at the time of his selection more parliamentary experience (seventeen years) than any of his predecessors as prime minister. His short stop as leader of the opposition he had found 'onerous and trying,' he told his brother (an opinion of the office he revised following experience in government: 'It is far less work being leader of the Opposition than Prime Minister').[1] Yet compared to his Conservative predecessors in that position, men like Bennett and Meighen, Diefenbaker's lot had been easy. The most obvious contrast was that the party's electoral expectations were now so great. By 1957, the PCs faced a tired prime minister – sarcastically, during the pipeline debate, St Laurent was nicknamed 'Louis the Silent' – and he was depicted as weak, the pawn of his 'minister of everything,' C.D. Howe.[2] The Liberal era was drawing to a certain close, and with it came, in Eugene Forsey's words, 'our greatest deliverance.'[3]

Dramatic as that statement was, the prediction it embraced had wider consequences than Forsey in all likelihood foresaw. In retrospect and in the context of discussion of opposition in Parliament, the election returns of 1957, which saw the first minority government formed in thirty years, and the returns of 1958, which saw the Progressive Conservatives win the (to then) largest majority in Canadian history, signalled not only the end of the Liberal ascendancy but the beginning of what might be called a new parliamentary mood. Any more precise description would be misleading, for it would imply a break in the evolution of parliamentary attitudes and behaviour that was not immediately apparent, though its cumulative influence on the conduct of opposition in the House of Commons was none the less discernible. After an ignominious spell, opposition acquired stature in large part because of the public interpretation given the pipeline debate, when on four occasions the government had used closure to force through Parliament legislation to construct a natural gas pipeline in northern Ontario. C.E.S. Franks has described the debate as 'perhaps the most important … in parliament's history,' because it 'inaugurated the modern parliamentary age of both obstruction and reform.'[4] According to Denis Smith, 'the Conservative message that Liberal cabinets had usurped the House's powers – and thus, perhaps the country's liberties – struck popular chords.'[5] As much by inference as by assertion, the opposition identified itself with the House of Commons and the country's liberties. Not just an alternative government, or an opponent, opposition stood, if not for the first time then more than in the past, as an ally of the public. As prime minister, in his conflicts with Parliament, Mackenzie King had invoked the supremacy of the people; now members of Parliament, and particularly those in opposition, looked in the same direction. They saw themselves as more than partisan; they had become instruments for communicating the people's will to government, which, recent history had shown, could in its absence become autocratic.

Fifty years later, effort is required to recall the prestige that opposition possessed in parliamentary systems in the post-war period. In Canada, that appreciation took some time to mature. Unlike after the First World War, which saw the Liberal opposition come to power in 1921, after the Second World War there was no change in government for another decade. Indeed, the issues that roused parliamentary emotions in the 1950s originated in government's practice of seeking parliamentary approval to extend emergency powers well into the postwar era. Even before 'the pipeline,' these requests had served as set pieces during which the opposition would cite the 'new despotism' that awaited the country if the renewals continued. On these occasions, academic Cassandras of administrative power, such as Lord Hewart, J.A. Corry, and Ivor Jennings, were regularly invoked to support the prediction.[6] Mr Diefenbaker entered Parliament in 1940, at a time when civil liberties were limited because of wartime restrictions under the Defence of Canada Regulations. In his maiden speech to the House, he defended their temporary curtailment but also asserted Parliament's prerogative to oversee administration of rights. This was the same position he maintained twenty years later when introducing a statutory rather than an entrenched Bill of Rights. The first throne speech of his government, delivered by the Queen to the House of Commons, promised that 'it will be the high purpose of my ministers not only to preserve these qualities [of parliamentary government, justice, authority, and dignity] but to take steps to make both houses of this parliament more effective in the discharge of these responsibilities to the people of Canada.'[7]

If there is an integrating theme to the story of Canada's Parliament in the last half of the twentieth century, when parliamentary majorities ebb and flow (as, in reverse order, do the fortunes of minor parties), it is found in the evolving concern to moderate partisan influence and favouritism in the conduct of elections and to reduce government domination of the work of the House by enhancing the scope of activity open to backbenchers, especially those on the opposition side. From one perspective this is an unexpected assertion. If there is a familiar criticism of Parliament today and for the past two decades, it is that MPs are (and have been) denied that opportunity: 'A central issue of this [2011] election [is] democratic reform ... At the top of the list is more power to the ordinary MP.' The 'list' (here and customarily) includes, among other items, 'more freedom and resources for parliamentary committees,' 'a truly muscular freedom-of-information law,' and 'a sharp restriction in the matters deemed to be issues of "confidence."'[8] Implicit in that critique is a failure to recognize how different the operations of Parliament are today from what they were fifty years ago, or to perceive the effect these changes have had on the conduct, perspectives, and perceptions of parliamentary opposition.

It is useful to specify some of these changes. In the realm of the House, they include (roughly in the chronological order in which they were introduced) emergence of a government House leader, part-time from the late 1940s, with responsibility for a portfolio as well, then full time after 1968; selection of a member of the opposition as chairman of the Public Accounts Committee (1958), the first occupant being Alan Macnaughton, who later became Speaker; introduction of a system of simultaneous translation (1959), thus enabling all members to speak the official language of their choice and to be understood by all members of the House (decades later, the Bloc Québécois demanded rigour in the matter of written French); official designation of an opposition House leader (1963), although there had been a de facto opposition House leader since 1957; payment of an additional allowance to a party leader other than the prime minister or leader of the opposition (1963); definition of a parliamentary political party as one with 'a recognized membership of twelve or more persons in the House of Commons' (1963); recognition of the right of 'a spokesman for each of the parties in opposition to the government' – including at one point, as a result of a Speaker's ruling, Social Credit and Créditiste groups, with five and nine members respectively – to comment briefly to a minister's state-ment on motions to the House (1965); provision of research assistance for officially recognized political parties (1969), and for government party members (1970); payment, in the form of a sessional indemnity, to the House leader of the official opposition (1974), and of 'recognized' third and fourth parties (1980); abolition of appeals on Speaker's rul-ings (1965); limitation on speaking time for individual MPs at Question Period (1964), except for the prime minister and the leader of the official opposition; an all-party business committee formally constituted under the standing order for the purpose of planning the business of the House (1965); election of the Speaker by secret ballot (1986); and com-mittee selection of chairs (2002).[9]

When compared with the perennial plea for less party discipline and by extension for greater independence for individual members, these innovations may be treated as inadequate, even unimportant. This would be a mistake, but explicable: 'One factor which may account for the prev-alence of this pessimistic interpretation is that, overshadowed by the cabinet's immediate responsibility for "affairs of the state," the work of backbenchers and opposition members does not always receive the credit it deserves.'[10] Taken together, the changes after 1957 erected scaffolding that over time gave the House a new, corporate dimension it had hitherto lacked, in part because they 'facilitated communications and negotiations among parties.'[11] Prior to then, the House had been dominated almost exclusively by the front benches and particularly the government front bench. It is the case that the influence of the changes noted in the previous paragraph has not been solely to the benefit of individual members; the distribution of research funds, for instance, rests with party leaders. Even so, before those changes, the idea that the individual member had a part to play in House (as distinct from constituency) affairs other than to cast a vote scarcely existed. More than that, 'parliamentary procedure and tra-dition … had been based on the "non-existence" of political parties, being premised on the notion of individual members acting independently and alone. In the absence of a prescribed minimum number of members that a party had to have, matters tended to be worked out behind the scenes and on an ad hoc basis.'[12] After 1957, the sense of a parliamentary as dis-tinct from a party life did emerge – inchoate and of limited realization as it might be. Still, this explained why a government and later opposition backbencher, Gordon Aiken (MP 1957 through 1965), might write a book with the generic title *The Backbencher* but with the more illuminating sub-title, *The Trials and Tribulations of a Member of Parliament*.[13] In a chapter on 'the mood of the House of Commons,' Aiken explained that a government could not always get what it wanted when it wanted it. On the contrary, it had to recognize that the House 'moves with a fluid temper'; 'it must be coaxed.' It is inconceivable that a book of such subtle perceptiveness would have been written by a member of Parliament before or during the Liberal ascendancy.

Students of Parliament invariably mention that it was in Canada in 1905 that the leader of the opposition was first accorded statutory recognition and awarded a salary.[14] True, it is significant; still, that historical first needs to be interpreted with caution, for the Act says nothing about how and when an opposition leader emerges. The limitations of the law in the matter of the conduct of parliamentary politics were demonstrated decades later when, after a long intra-party struggle involving parliamentary and extra-parliamentary wings of the Progressive Conservative Party to replace John Diefenbaker as leader, Robert Stanfield was chosen as his successor. The question then arose as to what form succession to leader of the opposition would take. The following long letter from the then Speaker of the House, Lucien Lamoureux, sets down in detail the transfer of power in what must be considered an office of constitutional importance. An important aside in this particular incident, one that is relevant to the general theme of the establishment of a corporate dimension to the House, relates to the emergence of the Speaker as an ally of the members. The first 'post-pipeline' Speaker was Roland Michener, who, as a House reporter observed, 'was determined to restore the Speakership to its independence from government diktat.' Of Lucien Lamoureux, his successor, the same commentator noted that after sitting as a backbencher for four years he held the Speakership another nine. The result was enormous respect from both sides of the aisle.[15] The Speaker's letter is written to Norman Ward, an authority on Canadian government and politics. In acknowledging its receipt, Ward confessed that 'I had, to my discredit, never before thought of several issues raised by Stanfield's position':

> Thank you for your letter of September 21st [1967] in which you raise various inquiries as to the procedures followed on the assumption of the office of Leader of the Opposition ...
>
> As you no doubt know, the office of the Leader of the Opposition is not established by an act of Parliament in Canada, but is recognized by statute. Section 42 of the Senate and House of Commons Act (chapter 249), as amended, provides for payment of a sessional indemnity and annual allowance 'to the member occupying the recognized position of leader of

the opposition in the House of Commons.' The standing orders of the House of Commons also recognize the special position of the Leader of the Opposition, notably by exempting him from the time limits normally applied to speakers.

I find also that the position in Canada is somewhat different from that in the United Kingdom, in that in England there is an Act of Parliament known as the Minister of the Crown Act, 1937, which provides that in case of doubt the Speaker may decide which Member of the House should occupy the position of Leader of the Opposition, and that his decision is final. The United Kingdom Speaker has never been called upon to use his discretion under the Act.

To turn now to your specific inquiries:

1. At precisely what point does Mr. Diefenbaker relinquish the office?
   In the past, information as to the name of the member occupying the recognized position of the Leader of the Opposition has been conveyed to the Clerk of the House of Commons by a letter signed by the Whip of the principal party in opposition to the government, and presumably reflecting the view of the caucus of that party. In the case of Mr. Diefenbaker, advice was received by the Speaker from the Party Leader, Mr. Stanfield, that the Progressive Conservative Parliamentary Caucus had appointed the Honourable Michael Starr to the position of Leader of the Opposition. This was confirmed in writing by the party Whip to the Clerk of the House. The former Leader of the Opposition is assumed to have relinquished his office from the moment the new appointment became effective.

2. At precisely what point does Mr. Stanfield assume it? Is there any hiatus between the two? Ie. Is the office temporarily vacant?
   On the assumption that Mr. Stanfield is elected to Parliament, he will commence his duties as Leader of the Opposition upon receipt of advice from him, confirmed by letter from the Whip of his party, that he will take office from a stated date. There is no hiatus between Mr. Diefenbaker and Mr. Stanfield in that the Honourable Michael Starr is the actual Leader of the Opposition in the interim.

3. How does Mr. Diefenbaker resign? Ie. Does he sign some instrument, and if so to whom is it addressed?
   As far as the Speaker of the House of Commons is concerned, there is no resignation by Mr. Diefenbaker, and he signs no instrument addressed either to the Speaker or to any other officers of the House of Commons. What internal arrangements are made in the party is something about which I have no knowledge.

4. How does Mr. Stanfield assume the office? Does he sign any instrument to qualify him to start receiving the Leader of the Opposition's stipend as such? Does he take any kind of oath except as an M.P.?
   Mr. Stanfield assumes the office according to the procedure outlined in the answer to your first question. He signs no instrument qualifying him to begin receiving the salary. On receipt of the letter from the Whip the Clerk advises the Chief Treasury Officer of the House of Commons of the effective date.
   The Leader of the Opposition does not take any oaths except as a Member of Parliament.
5. Through whom are the arrangements made through which Mr. Diefenbaker vacates the premises he has occupied as Leader, and Mr. Stanfield moves in? Is all this governed by custom, or are there established rules?
   In the case of Mr. Diefenbaker and Mr. Stanfield the procedure has been, as far as I know, that Mr. Diefenbaker and Mr. Stanfield have arrived at mutually satisfactory arrangements whereby Mr. Diefenbaker vacated the space allocated to the Leader of the Opposition on a day agreed upon. Until such time as Mr. Stanfield is elected to the House of Commons, this space is at the disposal of the Honourable Mr. Starr in his capacity as Leader of the Opposition and, presumably, if and when Mr. Stanfield is elected and we are officially notified of his selection by the caucus as Leader of the opposition further arrangements will be made between Mr. Stanfield and Mr. Starr, subject to the Speaker's approval.[16]

In this letter and in the examples given above of changes to Commons procedure after 1957, there is considerable overlap between recognition of political parties, on the one hand, and the work and life of the House, on the other. This is inevitable since nearly every MP is a member of a political party. If there are exceptions, they are exceptions that prove the rule. Independents do not get elected, and sitting members who desert their party to sit as Independents do not get re-elected as Independents. The interweaving of Parliament and party is unavoidable in discussion of the House, and we would be confounding understanding of Parliament's operations were we to avoid it. Today, the fact remains that members lead a double life, one that is parliamentary in dimension and another that is party. Still, it is a mistake to discount the first as only an extension of the second. Despite the criticism heard – more today than half a century ago – about the domination that members experience at the hands of party leaders and, most of all, at those of the prime minister and the staff of the prime minister's office, there is a semi-autonomous sphere for the individual MP on Parliament Hill.

Where at one time party and leader dominated the parliamentary stage, with the member assigned a small supporting part, after 1957 and particularly in the 1960s and 1970s, the House assumed a role separate from that determined only by officialdom. In the unattractive language of the time, it became 'institutionalized.' More work, because of the volume and complexity of legislation, had to be done, and it could only be accomplished through assigning duties and responsibilities that had little to do with direct electoral calculations. The world of House leaders, standing committees, and revised procedures, among other innovations, had arrived. The moderated partisanship that this organization entailed appeared elsewhere as well. After a century of electoral boundaries being drawn by partisans in the House, and in fulfilment of a 1957 campaign promise to 'bring government back in touch with the people,' the Diefenbaker government in 1962 introduced but failed to carry through Parliament a bill for the creation of non-partisan commissions to readjust electoral boundaries after each decennial census; this initiative the Pearson government resurrected and Parliament adopted in 1964. Individual opposition members were no longer at the mercy of vindictive (majority) government members. (The 1952 Redistribution Bill, the product of a parliamentary committee, was 'received with horror by the opposition.' Three Saskatchewan seats, all rural, had to be removed. In the end, 'John Diefenbaker's seat of Lake Centre was dismembered to become parts of adjacent constituencies.' For the member from Lake Centre, this was 'a form of political assassination planned and perpetrated by [Jimmy] Gardiner [for twenty years Saskatchewan's 'minister' in the King and St Laurent governments] and the Saskatchewan Liberal machine.'[17]) The same year, 1964, saw the Pearson government establish 'an advisory committee to the Secretary of State,' whose work led in 1973 to passage of the Election Expenses Act. Among its provisions were restrictions on spending by parties and candidates, reimbursement of a portion of expenses of parties and candidates, and a sliding scale of tax credits to taxpayers who donated to registered parties and to candidates. The implications of this legislation for the conduct of elections in Canada have been broad and deep. For the purposes of this discussion, however, its signal importance lies in establishing the principle of what Leslie Seidle has described as 'a degree of financial equality ... among candidates and political parties.'[18]

Fairness in establishing the rules of the parliamentary game, a guarantee of minimal equality of condition in electoral contests, and promotion of public engagement – these characterized the altered political values of the last forty years of the twentieth century in Canada. Their origin lay, at one extreme, in a heightened appreciation of rights (a key moment in Canada being the debate over Mr Diefenbaker's Bill of Rights, 1960), and, at the other, in a series of scandals during the years of the Pearson government that impugned (fairly or otherwise) the political morality of the period. There was as well the undeniable influence of a succession of minority governments. According to Seidle, 'the final shape of C-203 [the Election Expenses Act] was influenced by amendments proposed by Conservative and New Democratic Party MPs.' David Lewis, leader of the NDP, argued that 'the vast improvements in the present bill cannot be due to anything but the fact that the government is not a majority government, that it had to pay attention to opposition parties and their views on this matter.' Conservative MPs proposed eighty amendments, thirty-four of which were incorporated into the Act. For the NDP, the respective numbers were fifty-two and six. Even the Liberal House leader, Allan MacEachen, introduced thirty-two amendments.[19]

Significantly in a discussion of minor parties, Seidle notes that 'the Social Credit Party made no impact upon the Election Expenses Act.' Nor on any other policy, it might be said. As a regional movement it attracted some scholarly attention; as a party in Parliament it garnered almost none. In the mid-1950s, a report composed by the research department of the Progressive Conservative party of Canada sought to remedy this deficiency, although its conclusion offered little enlightenment: 'The story of Social Credit at the federal level is largely a pale shadow of developments in the province of Alberta.' In short, it was a standard-bearer for 'the doctrines of Major Douglas,' 'the evil growth of supranational government,' and 'peculiar monetary theories and remedies.' Social Crediters in Ottawa 'waited for reinforcements which never came.'[20] Although a negligible influence on policy – certainly when compared to the CCF/NDP – as one in a constellation of groups that composed the minority parliaments of 1957, 1962, 1963, 1965, and 1972 (which would fragment further after Real Caouette split from Social Credit ranks to form the Créditistes in 1963), Social Credit's 'strength,' said Gordon Aiken, '[lay] in small numbers.'[21] Unencumbered by the need to reconcile its policy objectives with its parliamentary preferences, since it had no policy allies in the House, Social Credit's role as an opposition party was to maintain the element of uncertainty that prevailed during the twenty years between the end of the Liberal ascendancy and its own demise, the last of its MPs being elected in 1979.[22] In this function, if in nothing else, it provided a harbinger of the Bloc after 1990.

Compared to the past, and in contrast to what is currently decried as hyper-partisanship in Parliament, the decades after 1957 witnessed a concerted effort to promote both cross-partisan and non-partisan behaviour.[23] Yet this was the same period when traditional limits on political activity by public servants were removed and when collective bargaining in the federal public service was introduced. No longer viewed as a 'servant of the Crown,' the public service became 'an institution with its own rights and responsibilities.'[24] More than at any time in the past, the boundaries that separated the political from the non-political, and acceptable from unacceptable behaviour in politics, shifted. Part of the explanation for these changing attitudes, as well as a reflection of them, is to be found in the proliferation of officers of Parliament. The relationship between officers of Parliament and parliamentary opposition is examined in chapter 6, 'Opposition, More or Less.' What calls for attention here is that until 1970, when the Commissioner of Official Languages was appointed, the only officers of Parliament were the Auditor General of Canada (1878) and the Chief Electoral Officer (1920). (Information and Privacy Commissioners were appointed in the 1980s, and Ethics officers for the two Houses of Parliament in the 1990s.) The uniqueness of these positions, and their attraction for proponents, has been in their purported independence. The accuracy of that depiction – and, if accurate, its implication for the performance of the tasks of opposition – is a subject for later analysis. As early as 1970, Pierre Trudeau perceived a contradiction between the function of officers – in this specific instance, that of the Auditor General – and the function of opposition. At issue was whether, as Trudeau phrased it, the then Auditor General, Maxwell Henderson, was 'infringing on the rights of the opposition who perhaps don't fulfill that function very well.'[25]

This harsh but blanket judgment was of a piece with the prime minister's equally low assessment of Members of Parliament as 'nobodies' when off the Hill. None the less, and presumably without a gift for foreknowledge, Trudeau was drawing attention to a conundrum: What is it that officers do that cannot be done by Members of Parliament? And when they do it, to what extent do their efforts undermine elected politicians?

The latent ambiguity in the functions of these parliamentary offices, for that is the common patrimony of both opposition and officers, arises out of the different policy concerns of the period after 1960. Identity questions, such as language, religion, race, gender, and, later, sexual orientation demanded of politicians advocacy and protection. Articulated in a vocabulary of rights, the debates they engendered did not fit easily or usefully into the traditional adversarial relationship of government and opposition. Nor for that matter did other issues, such as national unity or reform of the criminal law as it dealt with, for instance, the death penalty and abortion. On the contrary, and to an extent not seen before, these issues caused as much intra-party as inter-party tension, with especially debilitating effects on opposition parties. No longer was it the black and white of the familiar parliamentary alignment, but lengthening shades of melding grey.

The paramount (and early) example of partisan damage, and especially damage to opposition, that such policies might cause was bilingualism and biculturalism (B and B), first as a subject of study by the Royal Commission of that name, appointed in 1963, and then as a statute of constitutional importance, the Officials Languages Act, 1969. The partisan victim was the Progressive Conservative party. As a topic both of research and of law, bilingualism and biculturalism was an initiative of the Liberals and – extraordinarily so – it appeared first as a proposal of Lester Pearson when he was opposition leader. While J.W. Pickersgill was neither dispassionate nor disinterested in his judgments, still his backroom and frontbench party experience confer authority on his opinion that 'Pearson was to prove more effective as leader of the Opposition than any other leader in this century except Mackenzie King.'[26] Support for that view he found in the capacity of both leaders to recognize and use political talent. An outstanding example of Pearson's acuity was the employment in the office of the opposition leader of Allan MacEachen (MP 1953–8 and 1962–79, then Senator) for his already evident skill at parliamentary tactics. George Nowlan, minister in the Diefenbaker government from 1957 through 1963, corroborated Pickersgill's estimation:

Sensing the mood of Quebec, Pearson had called for a commission to review the 'bicultural and bilingual situation of our country.' His speech was drafted by Pearson's 'indispensable adviser on Quebec,' Maurice Lamontagne [a Laval University professor, later an economic adviser in the Privy Council Office, and after 1957 adviser to Pearson as leader of the opposition], and strongly endorsed by André Laurendeau, the influential editor of Le Devoir. Pearson's articulation of Quebec's vision of Confederation did not appeal to most of the Anglophone members of the Progressive Conservative party and it put the Quebec conservatives in an impossible position.[27]

The terms of reference of the B and B Commission, appointed by the Pearson government in 1963, spoke of two founding peoples – English and French – a description that made Canada foreign to those who lacked this paternity, a large proportion of whom lived in western Canada and who, after the Diefenbaker sweep of 1958, were PC supporters. The concept of Canada as a country made up of two nations, whose languages received privileged status under the Official Languages Act, raised objection not only among Tories but also from some supporters, although not leaders, of the recently formed New Democratic Party.[28] By the time the official languages legislation came before the House, Pierre Trudeau, another Pearson protégé (brought to Ottawa, along with Gérard Pelletier and Jean Marchand, to blunt rising Quebec nationalism spawned by the Quiet Revolution), was prime minister and Robert Stanfield had replaced John Diefenbaker as leader of the opposition. Ever a thorn in his successor's side, Diefenbaker and other PC caucus members did not hide their disagreement (and partisan disloyalty) over Stanfield's support for the proposed Act. Even though Stanfield 'patiently … talked out the problems of national unity with the hard liners,' and even though 'the other parties … hoping to display some national unity on the matter, would not insist on a recorded vote,' when the big moment came, 'seven western Conservatives stood up rebelliously to force a recorded vote. [They] were joined by ten others, including former leader John Diefenbaker.'[29] Stanfield's agony over language policy, this time in the constituencies and not in caucus, continued when, to keep faith with the party's position on bilingualism, he refused to sign the nomination papers of a candidate who opposed the policy. The requirement for the leader's signature to make a nomination official, a product of the 1974 law discussed earlier, became a feature of the electoral expenses regime. In theory at least, it should have strengthened the hand of each leader but especially those of the opposition parties, who historically face dissent leading to splits more often than does the governing party.[30]

B and B, official languages legislation, provision of French immersion for public servants and for children whose mother tongue was not French, the protection of minority rights (in Manitoba, for example) – the ripples of language in aid of promoting national unity spread across Canadian politics and society after 1960. One measure of support for that cause could be found in the thinning of opposition to initiatives taken in its promotion. First ministers' agreement, minus that of René Lévesque of Quebec, on the contents of what became the Constitution Act, 1982, won the support of nearly all members of the parliamentary parties (246 MPs in favour and 17 PCs, 5 Liberals, and 2 New Democrats opposed). The Meech Lake Accord, consisting of amendments to the constitution, was a prime ministerial initiative of Brian Mulroney to meet the conditions Quebec required to be met before it would sign the 1982 Act. Once again, 'the two opposition leaders in the House of Commons, the Liberals' John Turner and the NDP's Ed Broadbent, were quick to praise the accord.'[31] (In an instance of the exception proving the rule, Audrey McLaughlin, MP for Yukon and newly arrived in Ottawa, was given 'a rare dispensation from Ed Broadbent to vote against the party's pro-Meech Lake stance,' because she had campaigned against the Accord on the grounds that it was bad for women and Aboriginal Canadians.[32]) When the Meech Lake Accord failed to achieve required unanimity of legislative support, discussions among first ministers followed. This time the resulting agreement (the Charlottetown Accord) was placed before the Canadian people in a referendum, which also failed to secure requisite (this time, public) support. For their part, says constitutional scholar Peter Russell, 'the three major parties in the federal Parliament – the Conservatives, the Liberals, and NDP – got together to form a "yes" committee headed not by active politicians but by retired political leaders and distinguished citizens from all parts of the country. This official, multi-partisan "yes" committee anchored the organization of the "yes" campaign.'[33]

These much analysed events need no further discussion here, except to note that partisan unity on behalf of national unity concealed deep and lasting disunity within the opposition parties. The Constitution Act, 1982, caused a rift between the West and central Canada and between provincial and federal jurisdictions. This was most evident in the New Democratic Party. Although the Trudeau government commanded a majority, patriation of the constitution unilaterally or even with a portion of provincial support required allies, the most useful of which sat in Parliament. Despite public dissent from four Saskatchewan NDP members, as well as from Grant Notley, leader of the opposition in Alberta, and despite silence from the NDP leader of the opposition in Manitoba, Howard Pawley, Ed Broadbent committed his party – whose caucus numbered thirty-two, twenty-six from the four western provinces – to support the federal government. His most articulate opponent was Allan Blakeney of Saskatchewan, leader of the only NDP government in the country:

Blakeney, determined to maintain control of his province's resource revenues, launched an all-out attack on the Constitution [the background to that determination was the confiscatory, in western eyes, National Energy Policy of a few years earlier]. Much of his ire was directed against a Charter of Rights that would, in effect, give more power to an appointed judiciary and reduce the power of elected politicians. In other words, he trusted politicians more than judges. It was on this issue that Stephen Lewis and his father David Lewis had their first major political dispute: Stephen agreed with Blakeney, David supported Ed, as did Tommy Douglas and Stanley Knowles.[34]

'I was disappointed [said Blakeney] that Ed Broadbent supported [Trudeau].' None the less, in his memoirs two decades later, the provincial leader paid tribute to his federal counterpart for 'acting [in opposition, it needs to be stressed] as advocate for the Saskatchewan government' in securing a new Section 92A of the Constitution Act, 1867, to clarify provincial taxation powers over natural resources.[35]

The unity debate presented a quandary for the opposition in Parliament: the debate was about federalism, but Parliament, adapted from a unitary system, had not been designed to deal with matters of federalism. The negotiations leading to the Constitution Act, 1982, and events surrounding its passage illustrate the challenges the unity question presented the parliamentary opposition. None the less, C.E.S. Franks concludes that

Parliament was enormously influential in determining the final outcome ... Obstruction by the opposition was essential in forcing a stubborn, wilful government to adhere to what the Supreme Court determined to be constitutional conventions [of provincial support for change] ... Both the strategy and the tactics of the Progressive Conservatives ... had a great deal to do with internal party politics ... The approach they took, of insisting that the role of the provinces be recognized and that due process be observed, was a safe one which enabled them to stand on a matter of principle without committing themselves to a matter of substance.[36]

It might be said that for the NDP the tension caused by the constitutional wars was vertical or inter-jurisdictional, a dimension of opposition normally neglected in theoretical discussions of the topic since the bulk of the literature originates in the United Kingdom, a non-federal system. For the Liberals, the most public, although not exclusive, tension was and has remained horizontal or intra-jurisdictional. John Turner's support for Meech Lake as leader of the opposition was purchased at a terrible cost: the irreparable division of the party, beginning with more than one-quarter of the forty-member Liberal caucus voting against the Accord in 1987. More than that, there was extra-parliamentary opposition as well, the most intimidating being that of Pierre Trudeau, who, with like-thinking Liberals, saw the terms of the Accord as a refutation of their pan-Canadian view of Canadian federalism. It is not necessary to view John Turner's support for the Accord as the first (fatal) step leading the Liberals to third-party standing following the 2011 election in order to appreciate the problem for an opposition of reconciling national and party unity.[37] There is no doubt that part of the problem is the government itself, which exploits – as Mulroney was adroit at doing through domination of the legislative timetable – the discomfort of its parliamentary opponents. A further example, again in the form of an 'all-party resolution,' this one promoting agreement between the Manitoba government and the province's francophone minority, caused grief for both the Liberals ('[Turner] seemed to suggest the protection of official language minorities was not a matter for federal leadership') and the NDP, which formed the Manitoba government and which viewed the involvement of the federal government on the issue as 'counterproductive.'[38] It needs saying, of course, that the national unity riddle is a challenge for government too, not only in producing workable policy but also in maintaining unity within the government caucus. The emergence of the Bloc Québécois, under the leadership of Lucien Bouchard, a former cabinet minister in the Mulroney government, is testament to the potential to create opposition through governmental fission. At the same time – and for the first time in Canadian politics – a 'non-federalist alternative' sat across the aisle. Never again, in Chantal Hébert's words, would Quebec's federalist MPs 'acquire legitimacy by default,' as had happened in 1982, and 'then use that legitimacy to undermine the National Assembly.'[39]

The attention paid to the subject of national unity demands an explanation since in the nearly four decades this chapter examines there were numerous other bills and debates in the House. Two reasons may be offered. First, the problem of national unity entered public and political consciousness while the Diefenbaker government was in power – and it did not go away. In 1958, the Tories won fifty of Quebec's seventy-five seats, the largest number for them since 1882 and the first double-digit win since 1930. The Quiet Revolution is usually identified as beginning with the victory of the provincial Liberals under Jean Lesage in 1960. Three years later the B and B commission was appointed. From that moment until the end of the century and into the next, the subject of national unity remains ever-present. The analogy may be less than perfect, but during those years Quebec became Canada's Ireland, in the sense that the difficulties appeared intractable to resolution through policy (echoes of Gladstone, Home Rule for Ireland, and the division of the Liberal party in Great Britain) and – more directly relevant to the subject of this book – in the sense that policies intended to alleviate the problem, the Meech Lake Accord for example, had fissiparous consequences for the parties in Canada's Parliament. Second, the spectre of national disunity and the quest to avoid that fate led the parliamentary parties to suppress their customary adversarial relationship in favour of partisan unity. This is not the customary behaviour of government and opposition in peacetime, although it might be argued that there is an emergency dimension to the unresolved unity conundrum. The invocation by the Trudeau government of the War Measures Act in 1970, to combat the violence associated with the activities of the Front de libération du Québec, is one illustration of this (the unknown consequence of Quebec's separation from Canada is another). In 1970, in a House of 264, T.C. Douglas, then leader of the NDP, and fifteen of his followers refused to support imposition of the Act; after the fact, Robert Stanfield, PC leader at the time, and Eric Nielsen, later that party's House leader, said they had erred and were ashamed of their support of the government. Substitute legislation in the form of a Public Order Act swiftly followed. This time a single Progressive Conservative member (David MacDonald) voted nay and 196 voted yea.

Unlike the Liberal ascendancy examined in the previous chapter, the nearly four decades of Canadian politics under consideration here are marked by no single overarching partisan theme. Instead, there are majority governments – the Diefenbaker sweep of 1958, the Trudeaumania (Liberal) phenomenon in 1968, and the Mulroney tidal wave of 1984 – and minority governments, six to be exact: 1957, 1962, 1963, 1965, 1972, and 1979. All minorities are not the same, however, as C.E.S. Franks has helpfully noted:

> The 1957 election was a step towards the Conservatives' ascendancy; that of 1962 a step toward their downfall. The 1979 election, was seen as by many Conservatives as comparable to that of 1957, and Prime Minister Clark in particular was prepared for a short parliament and a quick election. But the Clark government was soon found wanting by both the House and the electorate, and its life ended quickly and ignominiously.

The three longer-lived minority parliaments – 1963, 1965, and 1972 – all involved Liberal governments. In both 1963 and 1965, the Liberal party was close to a majority (four and two seats short, respectively). In both cases, but in 1965 especially, the Liberals were able to govern as a majority. The opposition parties were not keen for an election. The Conservatives were in disarray and the Social Credit were on a losing streak; the NDP were unenthusiastic about both the costs and risks of an election. Both parliaments ended when the Liberal government called an election. In both elections, 1965 and 1968, the Liberals increased their support, achieving a large majority under Trudeau in 1968. The absence of only a few opposition members was enough to ensure government success in the House in these parliaments, and this, as much as third-party support, allowed the government to maintain power. The parliament of 1972 was different. In it the Liberals had only two more seats than the Conservatives, and support of a third party, the NDP in particular, was vital. To maintain power, the Liberals made many policy concessions to the NDP – on welfare programmes and in promoting Canadian ownership of industry. Although the election of 1974 followed a defeat of the government in the House, it was a defeat on an issue (the budget) at a time (spring) chosen by the government, who in effect engineered the NDP into supporting the Conservatives when the government felt its chances were best.[40]

The distinction Franks makes imposes order on events that otherwise appear to have none. In particular, it makes clear that not all minority parliaments and not all minor parties are the same. As suggested earlier in this chapter with respect to Social Credit, third parties whose origins and evolution are identified with charismatic leaders have at most only moderate interest in legislative organization. The contrast with the CCF, and later the NDP, could not be more striking. This was a party committed to comprehensive economic and social policies. Because it subscribed to intra-party democratic methods, its caucus was accountable to party members; yet, notwithstanding the importance of policy and party, it accepted the primacy, in exceptional circumstances, of steadfastly held beliefs, as when J.S. Woodsworth opposed Canada's declaration of war on Germany in 1939, or T.C. Douglas the invocation of the War Measures Act in 1970. The whole purpose of the CCF and the NDP was to secure legislative passage of a program and to demonstrate the validity of that program by winning popular approval at periodic elections. That said, what happened in Parliament was not what happened in the Saskatchewan legislature, the pre-eminent legislative forum for

Canada's CCF/NDP. In the first, the party was never in government, nor until 2011 did it form the official opposition; in the second, it was (after 1944) the mainstream governing party for the rest of the century. In Parliament, between the 1972 and 1974 elections, the NDP led by David Lewis secured social and economic legislative goals through pressure on those who did govern, the Trudeau Liberals.

The aggrieved political force at this time, and indeed for the three decades from the defeat of the Diefenbaker government in 1963 until the election of the Chrétien government in 1993, was the Progressive Conservatives, who formed the official opposition throughout (except for their nine months in power under Joe Clark in 1979). During the Liberal interregnum of minority government between 1972 and 1974, Tory frustration was palpable, as this quotation from a speech of Robert Stanfield conveys: 'One of these days, Mr. Trudeau will find his courage, or, failing that, perhaps Mr. Lewis will find it for him, and then this Parliament will be dissolved ... The time has come to end "this prolonged period of stalemate, of indecision, of cloakroom coalition, a period in our history that could best be described as almost two years of negotiated inertia."'[41] Palpable discontent perhaps but by no means rare, nor always the product of the partisan perfidy of others. Gordon Aiken, a Conservative, recounts how the controversy over Diefenbaker's leadership in the mid-1960s extended into the work of the House committees: 'A rift had developed in the Conservative party over the leadership. By some quirk of fate, four of the five Conservative members on the committee [on procedure], Balcer, Baldwin, Fairweather and myself turned out to be "rebels" ... so [Gordon] Churchill [the PC House leader] had the additional problem of not even trusting his own delegates.'[42] A decade later Franks said that the 'pettiness of the bickering in the House, and the animosity between [Pearson and Diefenbaker], brought parliament into a disrepute from which it has not fully recovered.'[43]

The narratives of the previous two chapters are, perhaps deceptively, easy to summarize: in the first, the emergence of the classic two-party system, which is the accepted arrangement in support of a government–opposition parliamentary system; in the second, its disappearance. National expansion, war, and depression occurred within those historical 'frames,' but with the exception of the introduction of leadership conventions to select national party leaders, underused by the entrenched Liberals after 1919 and overused by the flailing Conservatives after 1927, the outline of the political world, absent radio until the 1930s and television until the late 1950s, remained largely as it had matured half a century earlier. The same might be said about the tempo of the House of Commons:

> When I first joined the staff in 1960 [where the individual speaking became editor of Debates of the House of Commons], members [from British Columbia] were slowly emerging from a time when their attendance in Ottawa was governed by the railway systems ... because it took them three days to travel by train each way, back and forth between Vancouver and Ottawa, each round trip took a week to complete, and sometimes more ... The same, of course, applied in varying degrees to members from the Atlantic [and Prairie] Provinces ... As a result, parliamentary sessions were geared accordingly, usually only one per annum, and honourable members from east and west stayed put in Ottawa for the duration of the session, a generalization borne out by a study of attendance of MPs, by region, in the twenty-sixth Parliament (1963–65).[44]

And of its conduct:

> When I did become a member of the House of Commons staff the first thing that struck me about its proceedings was how tied were the hands of the government ... Its procedures were far, far behind those in the Oireachtas, the Irish Parliament, where I had, so to speak, cut my parliamentary reporting teeth. The government was locked into rigid time constraints in dealing with matters of supply. The government of the day lacked the will to use its most drastic weapon, closure.[45]

One sub-theme of the period under review would be the long march to modernizing the rules and procedures of the Commons. Since modernization is invariably discussed in terms of efficiency and since time is a scarce commodity for government, opposition sees limitations on the use of House time as aimed specifically at itself. For this reason, guillotine – that is, limitation on debate by legislative stages, introduced provisionally in 1966 and first used to end debate on the defence unification bill – was an incendiary issue for the Tories, and especially for Mr Diefenbaker: 'I ... was virtually alone. Many of my colleagues fell for the argument that Parliament must be made more efficient. That is always the Machiavellian argument used when Parliament is about to be emasculated.'[46] Mr Diefenbaker exaggerates about the subject and his influence.[47] Rules and procedures are important, but they *are* a subtheme of this discussion, and of the chamber. Rule changes are, like

Senate reform, a perpetual topic of debate, but as is not the case with Senate reform, rule changes do occur. Still, at the end of the day, no one seems satisfied with the outcome. Disparagement of the members, of the House, and of its work never flags; for the reason that reform of procedure is not the remedy to what troubles the Commons.

From the viewpoint of the opposition's welfare, other developments than rule changes in Parliament have been more influential. Keith Davey, national campaign director of the Liberal party in the 1960s, signalled one important instance of change: 'Pierre Elliott Trudeau became Prime Minister of Canada for a purpose. Like Mike Pearson, like Brian Mulroney, but unlike John Turner, Pierre Trudeau arrived in Ottawa with an agenda.'[48] The purpose, if not the means of realization, that linked these otherwise quite different personalities was the bipolar topic of national unity. The capacity of that subject to attract or repel support is well known. In any case the force of Davey's observation is found not in the common concern these men had but in when they first demonstrated it: for Pearson and Mulroney, it was while they were in legislative opposition; for Trudeau, who went straight to the government benches on entering politics, opposition was as a public intellectual. In its prominence and focus this was a different opposition from any that had gone before. More than that, it was tied to a large, extra-parliamentary 'constituency' in the form of contemporaneous first ministers' conferences, task forces, and Royal Commissions that had national unity as a principal object of study or negotiation. It also needs to be said that candidacy at leadership conventions (at almost regular intervals in the 1960s, 1970s, and 1980s) that chose these men, as well as Stanfield, Clark, and Turner, had an important influence as well.

5 The Mill of Opposition, 1993–2011

The returns of the 1993 election suggested that the mould of Canadian politics had been broken. The former governing Progressive Conservatives led by Kim Campbell, chosen at a delegate convention of Tories a few months earlier to succeed Brian Mulroney, lost 169 seats, thus being reduced to a rump of 2. The NDP, demoted from 34 seats to 9, joined the party of Confederation in falling below the magic number of 12 to qualify for official party status. By contrast, the Liberals under Jean Chrétien won an additional 94 seats, bringing their total to 177, the largest number of seats since 1949 and the second highest ever. Here, presumably, was evidence enough to support the metaphor that the 1993 election was a mould-breaking event. Yet, from the perspective of a study of opposition, the singular feature of the returns was that the principal parties that would be sitting opposite the new Liberal government – the Bloc Québécois with 54 seats (all from Quebec) and the Reform party with 52 (all but one from the four western provinces) – were ingénues in the theatre of Parliament. Deborah Grey, a candidate in an Alberta by-election in 1989, had been the first Reform MP to take a seat in the House, while the Bloc, formed in 1990 under the leadership of Lucien Bouchard by PC and Liberal MPs disaffected by the Mulroney government's machinations to make the Meech Lake Accord more palatable to English-speaking Canada, had won a single by-election victory in 1990, with Gilles Duceppe (later leader) as candidate.

New to Parliament, Reform and the Bloc were new to most Canadian voters as well. Writing a decade after the event, one scholar commented – and it is still true another decade on – that it was 'surprising that relatively few empirical efforts have been devoted to the study of [the] specific causes' of this electoral upheaval.[1] Reform's object, its founder and leader Preston Manning said, was indeed to break the old partisan mould, not just by replacing old-line parties but by getting rid of old-time practices, in particular that bugbear of the Progressives seventy years earlier, party discipline. Representative not responsible government, ultimate accountability to the people not the legislature – here was prospective reform of major proportions. The Bloc went even further: its members wanted to end not traditional political practices – as will be seen later in this chapter, on procedural matters the Bloc was more orthodox than Reform – but to end the country itself by promoting Quebec's withdrawal from the federation. Rooted in distinct regions, each of the new opposition parties was transformative in ambition and pedigree. What they shared was inexperience. Of the more than one hundred members of the two caucuses, fewer than ten had parliamentary experience before entering the House. The implications of such unpreparedness may be imagined, even when traditional Canadian experience is placed alongside that of Great Britain.

> In Britain, an MP on either side of the House will belong to a party which has actively participated in formulating many policies and programmes. His party while in power will have been responsible for administering even those programmes which it did not initiate. Regardless of his party affiliation, he will have a commitment to much of what the government does. In fact, the range of policies about which there is great disagreement between the two sides in Britain is not large, and there is a consensus between both parties in support of the bulk of government activities.[2]

The permanent phenomenon of legislative impermanence, illustrated in Canada by repeatedly high turnover rates of MPs – as much as 40 per cent on occasion – produces amateurism in Parliament and personal uncertainty. (It explains, as well, the disposition of parties to impose, and the readiness of MPs to accept, party discipline.) It also means that new members know as little about what their counterparts on the other side of the chamber do as they know about what is expected of them. David Docherty has labelled the freshman member 'the apprentice.'[3] Every legislator's career, at some point, would fit that description. The distinctive feature about Canadian politics is that the road to legislative office is so 'subject to chance' that MPs feel they have arrived in the Commons 'largely by accident.'[4] To the extent this is true, Reform and Bloc caucuses after 1993 wore a common national political badge – extravagantly so, since neither group had the incentive, commitment, or knowledge to make government work. It is not too much to say that after 1993 the very notion of parliamentary opposition itself became diffuse and uncertain.

Unlike traditional federal parties, Reform had no provincial base. The House of Commons was all it knew about federal politics, and what it saw of the House it disliked. By Reform's populist measure, an MP was an MP was an MP. It rejected manifestations of hierarchy. The initial Reform caucus elected in 1993 eschewed internal party distinctions: there was, for instance, no semblance of a 'shadow cabinet,' with critics assigned to specific areas, but instead 'clusters' of MPs commenting on various issues, which left areas of government inadequately monitored; as well, the 'leader' sat amidst his team in the second, rather than the front, row of the Commons. The resulting policy confusion and lack of prominence encouraged the party to conform to accepted practice in the new Parliament elected in 1997. Because it believed in the principle of electoral democracy inside and outside the legislature – party discipline discouraged in the first instance, consultation with the voters encouraged in the second – Reform presented a challenge to the principle of parliamentary democracy, none more so than in its ignorance of how that system worked. For instance, following the narrow federalist victory in the Quebec referendum of 1995, 'Manning suggested there should be a method of impeaching [Jean] Chrétien in case there is a "screw loose" in his office.'[5] This misinterpretation of how to exact executive accountability in a modern Westminster-style Parliament derived from a reconstituted (eighteenth-century) view that a legislature's duty is to oppose the executive. Here too, in part, was the reason for Reform's commitment to a renovated bicameralism as an antidote, in Manning's words, to 'our current system [which] tends to keep partisans in water-tight compartments, and [which uses] party discipline … to discourage any building of coalitions across partisan lines.'[6]

But a reformed, Triple-E Senate (elected, effective, and equal) had another attraction for Manning's party: it would give the provinces a direct voice in Parliament. One interpretation to be placed on the goal of equality was that Quebec would be treated like any other province, which is to say with no special status and with a consequent downgrading of the Official Languages Act as national policy. Of central importance for a study of parliamentary opposition in Canada is that after 1993, the common bond of government and opposition parties in their quest for national unity, on display in past support for first ministers' accords, vanished. Leaders of the Bloc, when it was the official opposition, might speak in placatory tones about 'playing by the rules' until

'Quebec becomes sovereign.'[7] Their actions, however, belied any false sense of security that promise might engender. Lucien Bouchard, who led the defection on the Meech Lake Accord, took (ultimately unsuccessfully) the lead in the Yes campaign in the Quebec referendum of 1995 (when it was failing in Jacques Parizeau's hands), and the following year abandoned federal politics to assume leadership of the Parti Québécois. The Reform party under Manning appeared scarcely more dependable on the issue of national unity: 'approach[ing] the American ambassador to discuss potential scenarios in the event of a YES vote, a revelation that shocked Ottawa veterans';[8] insisting that a Yes vote meant separation, whatever the magnitude of the vote – and subsequently pitting Reform against the Chrétien government's Clarity Bill; and organizing a nationwide phone-in survey on Canadian unity in which 'for a looney, people across the country could respond to questions about Canada's unity.'[9] From this last innovation it was reported that 'more than 90 per cent of callers wanted national unity settled once and for all, and said it should be solved by ordinary Canadians, not politicians.'

Any idea that stability and continuity of participants in a Westminster-styled parliamentary system might arise in part from government and opposition being locked in a relationship of dynamic tension, with a periodic changing of roles, finds no support in Canadian politics after 1993 (and truthfully, not a great deal before). Arguably, as Jeffrey succinctly states, 'there was no alternative government-in-waiting' in the last decade of the twentieth century.[10] The explanation lay in the destruction of the Progressive Conservative party in the 1993 election and in the long journey back to unite the right, through stages – Reform, United Alternative, Canadian Alliance, and finally, the new Conservative party late in 2003. The intricacies of that evolution are less important to this discussion than the fact that, notwithstanding the important contribution of extra-parliamentary venues such as party conventions, the forum for integrating these activities was the House of Commons. Equally important, however, is that neither Stockwell Day nor Stephen Harper was a member of the House when he became leader of his respective party. Here is the career path blazed by Mackenzie King, retraced by John Turner and Jean Chrétien, and more recently, copied by their Conservative-inclined opponents. The theory of parliamentary opposition that posits a new government with a new leader, possessing parliamentary experience, emerging from across the aisle seems increasingly improbable. The Bloc, Reform, then the shifting alliances that succeeded Reform, have diminished the language associated with, and public understanding of, opposition in Parliament. If words are to be taken literally – for instance, that governments are 'democratically elected,' and that power cannot be taken 'without asking you, the voter' – then in the Conservative lexicon there is no place, as theory has customarily described it, for the official opposition as the alternative government *in* Parliament.[11]

An important moment in that evolution was the decision of the Speaker of the House of Commons (Gilbert Parent) in February 1996 that 'the Bloc Québécois would retain its status as Official Opposition and the leader of that party would be recognized as the Leader of the Opposition until a further review was warranted.'[12] At issue was the point of order of Reform's House leader that the leader (Mr Manning) of his party (with fifty-two seats) should be recognized as leader of the opposition instead of the leader (Mr Bouchard) of the Bloc (with fifty-three seats). By the time the Speaker gave his ruling, Mr Bouchard had resigned his seat and the two parties each had fifty-two seats in the House. Reform argued that its caucus included members from five provinces (versus the Bloc's one) and that Reform had received a larger share of the popular vote than the Bloc. In his decision the Speaker noted that Canadian Speakers possessed neither the 'precise powers to designate the Official Opposition, [n]or to specify the criteria upon which the designation of Official Opposition is to be made.' 'In our system,' he continued, 'the Speaker chooses neither the government nor the government-in-waiting. That prerogative belongs to the Governor General of Canada on the advice of his Privy Council ... The designation of the Official Opposition has never been decided on the floor of the House of Commons.' Nor has 'the question of which party would assume the role of the Official Opposition ... been an issue in our House of Commons until now.' (Compare this assertion of non-intervention to the situation in the British House of Commons, where 'opposition to the government of the day is both legitimate and institutionalized,' with the Speaker having a statutory duty to designate the leader of the largest party not in government as Leader of Her Majesty's Opposition.)[13] Citing precedents from provincial jurisdictions, New Brunswick in particular, Speaker Parent concluded that 'in the case of a tie during the course of a Parliament incumbency should be the determining factor and the *status quo* should therefore be maintained.'[14] He did not cite a contrary example, Saskatchewan, where the Legislative Assembly Act (1960) provides that 'in case of equality of membership of two or more such groups (that is, sitting opposite the government), the allowance and the grant provided for by this section shall be divided equally between the respective leaders of those groups having the largest and equal membership ... It was decided [as well] that the status, privileges and responsibilities in the Assembly traditionally held by the Leader of the Opposition should, in like manner, be shared whenever possible.'[15]

Speaker Parent's ruling is quoted here not to quarrel with its reasoning but to note implications to be drawn from its conclusion, particularly when placed in the following context:

> A substantial component of the Reform party's position [not explicit in the decision itself] had been that the Speaker should take an active role in deciding the official opposition. Much of the commentary advanced by the Reform's spokespersons had questioned the BQ's credibility given that party's separatist position. Thus Reform's strategy consisted of developing the case whereby an opposition party other than the largest one could be recognized as the official opposition.[16]

The next year the same two parties were again tied. This time Preston Manning sought the support of ten non-government MPs to ask the Speaker for a vote to replace the Bloc as official opposition. That scheme failed when 'none of the NDP, Conservative or five independent members of Parliament answered Manning's call: "Each of them chose," he said, "to put their partisan reasons ahead of federalism versus separatism."'[17] The attribution 'partisan' in this remark is not altogether clear, nor is it important. It is the pre-eminence assigned the issue of 'federalism versus separatism' that requires examination, because the compass of the statement is broader than its language suggests. At virtually the same time that Manning was making this distinction, he was clouding its meaning by asserting that 'federal politicians from Quebec such as [then] Conservative Leader Jean Charest or Prime Minister Jean Chrétien ... would be disqualified [in negotiating with separatists] because of their "conflict of interest." Instead, separatists would find themselves "with some hard-nosed lawyer from Toronto or Calgary" who is going to say, "We want money. We want territory. And we want the date nailed down for the revoking of passports."'[18] Another way of making the same point, as Manning did, was to say that 'Quebecers have controlled the national unity deb[ate] for too long and other Canadians want a say.'[19]

Seen as the party of a single province, or as the party of a single issue (although in Parliament on issues other than nationalism – social and moral ones, for instance – the Bloc aligned itself more often than Reform with the Liberals and the NDP), or seen, in Manning's words, as 'mollycoddled separatists,' the Bloc was a political spoiler. Lawrence Martin recounted 'Alberta premier Ralph Klein … expressing wonderment that the leader of the Opposition wasn't expelled from the House of Commons. "I mean, Louis Riel was."'[20] Reform, but not only Reform supporters, resented the Bloc, and especially, from the perspective of this discussion, resented toleration of the Bloc as official opposition. Jean Chrétien's reply that 'Canadians elected a separatist party as the official Opposition and "we're treating them that way,"' proved unconvincing to critics both then and afterward. Indeed, it was events more than a decade later – the failed scheme in 2008 to replace the minority Conservative government under Stephen Harper with a Bloc-supported Liberal–NDP coalition (with Stéphane Dion, the Liberal leader, as putative prime minister) and, subsequent to 2008, government predictions (denied by the other parties) that in the absence of a Conservative majority a similar scheme would be resurrected – that demonstrated the modern Tories' evergreen distrust of opposition parties.

Adapting the title Hugo Young gave his biography of Margaret Thatcher, the Reform and Conservative parties (and intervening similar ideologically inclined formations) thought of other partisans as 'not one of us.'[21] (Conservative campaign literature said the same thing about Michael Ignatieff, in reference to his long residency outside Canada, after he returned to enter federal politics in 2005.) On the subject of federalism, it is clear why the new Tories took that view of the Bloc; and since from their perspective the Liberals and the NDP (and the Mulroney Progressive Conservatives, for that matter) appeased the separatists, it was understandable why they found no community of interest with other members of Parliament either. Such lonely solidarity of the Reform and new Conservative parties has no counterpart in Canadian political history. The sense of difference went further than that, however. It was a tenet of Reform that politics should be unmediated. The central complaint about party discipline was that it made representation, as far as individual constituencies were concerned, unrepresentative. Here was the keystone to the edifice of direct democracy. Similarly, when in 1999 'more than 100 women [from the National Action Committee on the Status of Women] tried to storm his parliamentary office … [Preston Manning] suggested people [were] getting tired of the influence exerted by special interest groups.' He vowed that 'his MPs will not meet as a group with special interest organizations.'[22] The bill of indictment that labelled the Liberals enablers of a 'court party' – which is to say of a new, privileged class whose concerns ran to such matters as national unity, social equality, civil liberties, and post-materialist interests such as the environment – drew its force from the presumption that the other parliamentary parties spoke on behalf of these elites and not of the common man or woman. Both the Canadian Charter of Rights and Freedoms, especially its guarantees for identifiable groups, and the courts, charged by Parliament and the higher law of the constitution with enforcing those rights, fell under the same opprobrium. Special interests led to special pleading, which in turn secured special treatment.

Given that they held these views, it might be expected that after 1993, Conservative politicians (of whatever name) would support the level-playing-field value customarily attributed to Canada's election expense regime. Stephen Harper himself had at one time used the metaphorical adjective favourably, when he criticized the CBC for not being 'on a level playing field' compared to private broadcasters.[23] As explained in chapter 4, the system of subsidies and tax credits introduced in the 1970s was intended, on the one hand, to promote public engagement in the electoral process, and on the other, to reduce party dependency on large corporate or union donations. Further provisions followed in the form of amendments to the Canada Elections Act to restrict third-party (i.e., citizen and lobby) groups from buying political advertising during an election campaign. After much litigation, the Supreme Court, in 2004, decided in *Harper v. Canada (Attorney General)* to uphold sections of the Canada Elections Act that limited the amount a third-party might spend during election campaigns. Critics of these provisions, the most prominent being the National Citizens' Coalition (NCC), whose president between 1998 and 2002 was Stephen Harper, had for some time challenged the spending limits, labelling the offending sections a 'gag law' because they constituted a restraint on freedom of expression. In a 6–3 decision, the judges acknowledged that the law abridged freedom of expression, but they also found the limitation reasonable in the name of 'the over-arching objective … [of] electoral fairness.'[24]

The new Conservatives did not accept, as the old Tories, Liberals, and New Democrats of thirty years before had, that, in the words of the Court, 'equality in political discourse is thus necessary for a meaningful participation in the electoral process.' On that temporal contrast, it is relevant to note that at the time (1983) the amendments the NCC opposed were adopted, 'other groups [than the three political parties] and interested persons had little chance to influence the … amendments … It is not inappropriate to ask whether the three political parties [whose representatives formed what was referred to as the 'ad hoc committee'] in the interests of protecting the election expenses regime, may have circumscribed somewhat the full participation of others in the electoral process.'[25] Freedom, not restraint, in advocating a cause was the object sought. Thus Canada's Conservatives joined Mrs Thatcher's in repudiating political values of the past as they applied to elections, or to debates in the House, or to relations with the public service, for that matter. If for the Iron Lady claims to detachment were a 'chimera,' and objectivity 'a fraud,' a comparable distancing from political custom (a disinclination to use Royal Commissions as instruments of public policy, for instance) when it came to the norms of government (the economy is a different matter) became evident in the ranks of Canadian Tories in the first decade of the new century.[26]

Perhaps it should have been no surprise that Conservatives, with their roots in Reform – the only party without a provincial base to secure representation in the House and, amazingly so, to achieve in short order the status of official opposition – should be wary of what they saw as the cosy arrangements perpetuating the partisan status quo. Here is why Reform set out not only to change electorally the cast of victors but, more permanently, to transform the political caste who set the rules. Having from their perspective made it on their own, they could only be troubled to learn soon after forming a government in 2006 that 'political parties are becoming "empty shells" … relying so heavily on public funds that Canada's party system is headed for a "state system."'[27] To underline the point, between 2000 and 2004 public funding for the Bloc Québécois increased 633 per cent, with the result that 'political supporters of the Bloc … do not need to give money to that party; they are over and above what they had already spent in the previous 10 years of their existence.'[28]

Another Conservative ambition was to end per-vote subsidies to political parties, an innovation of the Chrétien government in 2003 as part of an overhaul of political financing in consequence of the sponsorship scandal. First proposed in 2008, following which it became a precipitating factor in the abortive coalition attempt by opposition parties to unseat the minority Harper government, the proposal was enacted into law following the 2011 general election under the same government that now possessed a legislative majority. Against, it might be said, strong authoritative opinion, from a former Chief Electoral Officer, that under present arrangements Canada maintained an 'incredibly "fair political" system.'[29]

As the party committed to separating Quebec from Canada, the Bloc's extra-parliamentary focus was territorially defined. On non-unity but socially divisive issues, such as gun control, same-sex rights, and access to abortion, it generally stood alongside the Liberal and New Democratic parties in the House. In contrast, the Reform and Conservative parties positioned themselves in support of an improved (less centralized, more responsive) federation but outside, or at least on the margins, of the political and social consensus their contemporaries and, even, Tory predecessors supported. That last comment is a broad generalization: it does not acknowledge Reform's opposition to bilingualism or what it perceived as special treatment for Quebec. It was these positions that made Preston Manning's unity quest poignant yet unrealizable: 'I desperately wanted to invite Quebecers ... to see me as Baldwin representing those in English Canada who wanted to change the federal system fundamentally for the benefit of all Canadians. But what we Reformers from outside Quebec wanted to know was, "Où est LaFontaine?"'[30] The authoritative version of Canadian federalism, handed down by Pierre Trudeau but, as Brooke Jeffrey has argued, eventually so destructive of Liberal unity, had long been buttressed by a consensus of official – governmental, scholarly, and media – opinion that offered no sanctuary for those inclined towards Conservative political thought or practice. The inter-party alliance that for nearly four decades had embraced an array of diverse politicians – Pearson, Trudeau, Chrétien, Stanfield, Clark, Mulroney, as well as Douglas, Lewis, and Broadbent, among others – ended with Reform (and the Bloc). While each (of the pre-1993) parties' leaders held distinctive positions on Quebec and the unity of the federation, all devoted enormous energy, thought, and attention throughout their leadership to 'solving' these questions. Few public figures had the audacity to complain about the answers offered. One who did was Eugene Forsey, who told Tommy Douglas: 'You cannot build a party on a lie [the 'two-nations' theory],' to which warning, he recalled, Douglas 'chuckled'; while another party worthy told Forsey not to worry, 'It was "just words."' A quarter of a century later the gadfly criticized Broadbent for 'the ceremonial kow-tow to the Quebec nationalists at every opportunity.'[31] It was this sense of the Quebec-in-Canada conundrum being a 'swamp' (Lucien Bouchard's word) from which no party seemed able or willing to extricate itself, that Reform brought to Parliament, first in opposition and then (as the Conservative party) in opposition and, finally, in government.[32]

A distinctive feature of Canadian politics (in the federal sphere alone, and leaving the provinces to one side) is the number of third parties in the twentieth century that have achieved electoral success, some great and some less great, in Parliament. One theory offered for this phenomenon, not found in Australia, another parliamentary federation that shares many characteristics with Canada, is that a third party acts as a release valve in a country with strong regional and cultural tensions but with unresponsive electoral and party institutions.[33] The validity or explanatory value of that theory is not the concern of this book. Still, it needs to be acknowledged if only to emphasize that however it applies to Reform, it applies differently than it did to the Progressives, to the CCF/NDP, or to Social Credit. Reform went in one election from no Members of Parliament to two fewer than the official opposition (BQ), to official opposition at the next election. Unlike the Progressives, it fought to be recognized as the official opposition, and unlike the Progressives, it sought not just to lessen party discipline but to realign Canadian political parties and Canadian political debate along a Conservative–Liberal axis. It is necessary to be reminded of this ambition, because from the beginning Reform saw itself, either as opposition in Parliament (where it viewed the Bloc not as a competitor but as the product of a dysfunctional federal system) or as the 'second' federal party, in the role of agent of political transformation.

Liberals and Progressive Conservatives did not think this way; nor did Social Credit, whose esoteric creed offered no practical foundation for a national policy; nor, even, did the CCF/NDP, for whom economic planning was a pre-condition for social programs. Reform and its lineal descendants were different because they were popularly and electorally based movements. In comparatively short order they had organized and reorganized themselves and entered into a succession of leadership contests; during his time as prime minister, Jean Chrétien saw six leaders of the Reform, Alliance, and Progressive Conservative parties come and go. The practice of looking to votes and voters, evident from the time Reform first appeared in federal politics, explains the larger membership base than other parties and also the disposition to look outside Parliament to establish the party's validity. In 2008, the Conservative counter-argument to the proposed Liberal–NDP coalition initiative drew from this 'external to Parliament' sense of legitimacy.

Although, ultimately, the Governor General granted the prime minister's request for a prorogation of Parliament, the argument then and earlier, when a request for dissolution of Parliament seemed possible, cited the electoral record: in the general election only weeks before, the Conservative party had won the largest number of seats (143 versus 77 [Liberal] and 37 [NDP]) and the largest percentage of the vote (37.6 versus 26.2 [Liberal] and 18.2 [NDP]). In addition, the Conservative party had increased its vote in seven of the ten provinces and in all three of the territories, while the Liberal vote had declined in eight provinces and in each territory. Statistical reasoning of this kind received an unsympathetic hearing from those who maintained that governments in a Westminster-styled system depend for their legitimacy upon the support of Parliament and – more to the point for the focus of this book – on the conduct of the party or parties in opposition. Specifically, there was no support from among more than a dozen of the country's 'leading scholars and writers in the fields of constitutional and parliamentary studies,' who in an edited book assessed the controversy.[34] Echoing (but not of) the Reform school, one reviewer of the book dissented from this 'consensus ... among the country's intellectual class,' describing it as 'tunnel vision.'[35]

Following decades of a stable, albeit fluctuating, array of partisan sentiment in the House, the kaleidoscopic changes occurring in opposition after 1993 proved both mesmerizing and distracting. One consequence of the arrival of two new contingents of almost equal size sitting opposite the government was to rigidify House practice by granting a new authority to numbers. As long as there were no financial benefits attached to a party's presence in the House, then speaking and other privileges associated with the conduct of House business could be allocated in light of the issue at hand. Before the introduction of the twelve-member threshold required by the financial provisions of the Parliament of Canada Act, 'the full rights of an opposition party' continued notwithstanding the size of the particular caucus. (In 1992, when the House was debating the Charlottetown Accord, neither Reform nor BQ qualified as an official parliamentary party; thus the speaking privileges of each were restricted.) Before 1963, House procedure was the product of pragmatic and often 'compassionate' rulings and agreements. That was Speaker James Jerome's word for what he described as his 'worst decision.'[36] While the details may be found elsewhere, the following excerpt from Speaker Jerome's memoirs communicates a flavour of House behaviour:

In 1974, when it appeared that the Social Credit Party might fall below [12 seats], the House agreed, as a courtesy to a long-time and beloved veteran, Mr. Real Caouette, to continue to treat him as a Party leader as long as he remained in the House. In fact, after his death, we continued to extend the same courtesy to his successor. But in 1979, with only five Social Credit seats, everyone knew the end had come. That didn't make the transition any less awkward however, certainly not for me. To begin with I had to be the final arbiter of disputes over seating. There were serious arguments about whether the Social Credit Party was entitled to sit as a group, and if so, whether they should occupy any front row seats – which had been looked upon as a badge of party status. I gave them the benefit of the doubt on both counts ... That issue was barely settled when the next one arose, and it was not under my control.[37]

The Social Credit imbroglio deepened, usually, at the Speaker's admission, because he tried to soften succeeding blows 'by extending [further] courteous treatment.'

The significance of this vignette lies in two aspects. First, it conveys the collective sense of the House as a (genderless) inner fraternity in the years when its institutional form grew more visible, that is, from the late 1960s onward. Arguably, it was this clubby atmosphere that Reformers and their successors found objectionable. Second, it poses a sharp contrast to life in the House after the 1993 election; sharper still, because the precedent of Speaker Jerome's compassion for Social Credit in its decline, invoked later to salvage the fortunes of the New Democrats whose caucus numbers went from forty-three in 1988 to nine in 1993, proved unpersuasive to Speaker Parent. Bill Blaikie, the NDP member who raised the matter, concluded (in his 'Reflections' on the events), that this 'passive' ruling placed 'the rights of small political parties ... in the hands of the large political parties,' since, according to the Speaker's reasoning, he was but an instrument of the House.[38]

Until the thirty-fifth Parliament elected in 1993, a simple characterization of the House – with qualification to accommodate the minor party or parties who might be sitting to the Speaker's left – was to view the official opposition as the logical counterpart to the government. In short, they were reverse sides of the same coin. Where one proposed, the other opposed; where one acted, the other cautioned; where one was positive, the other was essentially negative in its deportment. After the election of 1993, a new angle of observation of the House appeared: the homogeneous character of the government's principal opponents, whether of Bloc or Reform persuasion, took its tone from opposition to the constitutional order however that order might be described, be it of parliamentary or federal complexion.

In different circumstances, such a purposeful strategy for systemic change on the part of either the Bloc or Reform and its successors might have been repelled by the Liberal governments of the following decade. Instead, circumstances, such as the 1995 Quebec referendum on separation, and policies of the federal government, such as the irregularly administered sponsorship program (intended to promote the loyalty of Quebeckers) following the near-victory of Yes supporters, inflamed passions on the part of the government's opponents at the same time as they discouraged its supporters. From the perspective of the subject of political opposition generally, as distinct from that of the government's critics across the aisle, the element of long-term significance in these events lay in the contribution made by the media and in critical comments made by the auditor general (Sheila Fraser): officials at Public Works Canada, she provocatively wrote of the sponsorship program, 'broke just about every rule in the book' in the awarding of contracts.[39]

Created in 1878 during the administration of Alexander Mackenzie in the shadow of the Pacific Scandal, which had precipitated the resignation of John A. Macdonald, the auditor general is an officer of Parliament. The subject of officers of Parliament as they relate to the work of parliamentary opposition is discussed in chapter 6, 'Opposition, More or Less.' It is mentioned here because the officers and the media, another key influencer of events and public opinion in the decade that saw Liberals and Conservatives trade places in the House of Commons, are, in manifestly different ways, independent of Parliament. It is their separation from institutionalized political opposition that deserves attention here. For their rise in prominence – in the case of the media because of technological developments that in the main are not political by definition – highlights a simultaneous trend, the decline of parliamentary opposition. Whether it signifies the trend's cause or its effect, the opposition parties proved inadequate in publicizing or even pursuing the sponsorship scandal – for explicable reasons, it should be said, in the case of the Conservatives, who were preoccupied for the first half of the decade with leadership and organizational matters. The opposition parties also were inattentive to the growing public distaste for adversarial politics and for those (political parties in Parliament) who practised them. Arguably, disquiet at the policies and leadership of the Chrétien government was most evident, unprecedentedly so, from the government side of the House, in particular from Paul Martin, who aspired to and, late in 2003, secured the leadership of the Liberal party and with it the position of prime minister. It was Martin who promised a reduction in party discipline and a greater role for parliamentarians in matters such as prerogative appointments hitherto made solely on the advice of the prime minister;[40] and it was Martin who established the Commission of Inquiry into the Sponsorship Program and Advertising Activities under Mr Justice Gomery, an initiative whose consequences continued for another decade to produce anti-Liberal grist for the opposition's mill (and after the Conservatives came to power in 2006, for the government's).

Opposition from within the government's ranks had secured what opposition from across the chamber had not – a new government; and it had achieved this object in the name of openness. Like the officers of Parliament and the media, Martin was speaking to the public, although never with the security of an officer like Fraser, whom Ipsos-Reid reported in 2004 was 'immensely trusted by Canadians because "she has no vested interest and is viewed … as being above politics."'[41] None the less, and in contrast to the theory of parliamentary opposition set down in chapter 1, examples of audiences courted outside of Parliament multiplied. Changes in political party finance laws, which placed a premium on individual, as opposed to corporate, contributions, thus encouraging mass membership strategies, in company with a succession of minority governments in the first decade of the new century, with the attendant possibility always that the government might be defeated in the House and an election follow, introduced what Tom Flanagan has described as a 'garrison party (the Conservative)' and a 'permanent campaign.'[42] To the extent that the other parties failed to follow the Conservatives' lead, they paid an electoral penalty and incurred an inextinguishable financial debt. Modern communication mechanisms worked in the same direction, that is, to bring politics outside, a migration not confined to federal politics. In the far west, British Columbia appointed a Citizens' Assembly on Electoral Reform, and in the far east, New Brunswick created a Commission on Legislative Democracy; both echoed (in 2004) the call heard in Ottawa for greater public involvement in political affairs.[43]

The theory that there is no constituent power external to Parliament in a Westminster-styled system appeared to be just that. As the logic of its parliamentary institutions was ignored, the legitimacy of Canada's constitutional system fell into doubt, a consequence, it might be said, of living simultaneously in two different historical periods. The results of the general election of 2011 deviated from expectations based on the past as much as those of 1993 had. This time the Conservatives received their long-sought majority, while the BQ was reduced to 4 seats, the Liberals to 34 (from 77), thus becoming for the first time in Canadian history a 'third' party, and the NDP, with 103 seats (from 36), more than 50 per cent of these from Quebec, forming the official opposition. Unexpected, the results also were difficult to interpret.

What is significant, particularly in light of Jack Layton's death before the Forty-First Parliament resumed (after a two-week emergency meeting in June to deal with a postal strike), is unanimous agreement on the qualities Mr Layton exemplified as leader. Whether that explanation was accurate is irrelevant to the positive response that Layton elicited and the negative view of other politicians it implied. John Sewell, a former Toronto mayor and the person who brought Layton into electoral politics, spoke of Layton's 'skill ... at helping people find common ground.'[44] Words like compromise, civility, and inclusiveness appeared and reappeared in news reports as descriptions of the man. These are not characteristics the public applies to parliamentary politicians or to politics. One reason the consensual style attracts people is that this is how they perceive agreement is (and should be) reached in their personal and local affairs.[45] Layton was a municipal politician – of a large municipality to be sure (Toronto) – and he was a leading figure in the Federation of Canadian Municipalities. That provenance was unique, for none of his predecessors as leader of the official opposition could claim it. It was important for another reason: its non-partisan complexion promoted a tolerance for the opinions of others and encouraged the search for consensus. Decisions may have numerous reasons, and it is rash in the absence of compelling evidence to read especial significance into a single cause; yet early in the 2011 campaign Layton stated categorically that 'we will live in Toronto,'[46] which is to say that were he to become leader of the official opposition, he would not live at Stornoway, the government-owned property provided for the individual holding that office.[47] In this self-abnegation of a perquisite of office he followed, but for quite different reasons, his predecessors, Lucien Bouchard and (for a time) Preston Manning. Manning eventually moved into the residence on the rationale that not to do so 'showed disrespect for the office [of leader of the official opposition].'[48] Predictably, Stornoway had proven one more flashpoint in the taut Diefenbaker–Stanfield relationship: '[Stanfield] does not want me in the House,' Diefenbaker told Gordon Churchill, 'and [i]t was also obvious that I should get out of the house.'[49] The Chief vacated Stornoway but remained in the Commons until after his successor stepped down as party leader and leader of the official opposition.

PART THREE

Challenges for Parliamentary Opposition

6 Opposition, More or Less

The practice of opposition in the Canadian Parliament has never conformed to the theory of opposition found in political science textbooks. That blanket assertion is perhaps misleading, for as this chapter will argue, the realities of Canadian politics in any case have tempered the sense of precision implicit in the labels government and opposition. The architecture of the House of Commons in Ottawa may mirror that at Westminster, with MPs in both locations aligned in groupings that face each other, but in Canada for over ninety years there have been intermediate shades of colour in the legislative spectrum rather than the dominant two-party system of the model Parliament. There are two explanations for the deviation: the strength of regionalism in Canadian politics, particularly as manifested in the recurring, weak hold the country's governing parties have on western Canadian voters, and the imperative to accommodate Quebec's interests through partisan and governmental structures at Ottawa.

A Westminster-like opposition does not fit easily with the accommodative style of politics demanded of Canadian leaders. By the time of Canada's centennial in 1967, past practice and immediate pressure as a result of the Quiet Revolution in Quebec saw that political style reinterpreted, in European theoretical terms, as a North American example of consociational democracy. Consociational democratic practices are deserving of comment on several grounds, but from the perspective of this discussion that of greatest import is their suppressive effect on opposition. By definition, opposition is not conducive to accommodation. Neither, it should be said, are other features of Canadian politics that this chapter will examine, specifically the use of public inquiries as a mechanism to explore policies conducive to federal–provincial harmony (and therefore included in the discussion of consociational democracy); the proliferation in numbers and expansion in purpose of officers of Parliament; and, finally – although it is not a phenomenon unique to Canada – the transformation of communications in such a manner as to breach the walls of Parliament and to obliterate the distinction traditionally drawn between official or institutional, and non-official or popular, politics.

Consociational Politics

One reason for Canadian exceptionalism in the legislative realm lies with minor or third parties, whose presence, for nearly a century, has required adjustment to a simple binary view of parliamentary politics. Minor parties on a number of occasions have deprived major parties of control of the House of Commons; and furthermore, they have complicated life on the opposition side of the chamber by multiplying the voices critical of government. In short, legislative politics at the national level – the situation in the provinces is the subject of the next chapter – is more complicated than is implied by the exposition found in classic British texts, such as Ivor Jennings's *Parliament*. Of course, the growing strength of regionalism in British politics, acknowledged a quarter-century ago with the devolution of a measure of legislative power to Scotland and Wales, means that the theories of parliamentary government may require adaptation in the country of their origin. None the less, regionalism and federalism are not the same thing, and more to the point, Canadian political parties, with notable exceptions such as the Reform party and the Bloc Québécois, have been in practice (where possible, which was not always the case for the Conservative party in Quebec) federated organizations.

Minor parties make minority government possible, not inevitable; and where a minority government is formed, minor parties do not necessarily enfeeble it: those led by Lester Pearson (1963 to 1968) and Pierre Trudeau (1972 to 1974) are considered unusually productive, the familiar illustration to support the claim being the passage of national medical care legislation. Medicare, as the program was popularly known, had been introduced in Saskatchewan in 1962 by the province's CCF government. The former Saskatchewan premier and generally acknowledged 'father' of medicare was T.C. Douglas, the first leader of the New Democratic party (the renamed national CCF) and by then a member of Parliament. The presence of Douglas was important to the outcome, as was that of Paul Martin Sr, a senior Liberal and long-time articulate advocate of national health care. Finally, the leader of the Progressive Conservative party (and leader of the official opposition), John Diefenbaker, had been instrumental when he was prime minister in modelling Canada's national hospital insurance program after the scheme introduced earlier by the CCF in Saskatchewan. In other words, there was a convergence of support between government and opposition parties for this and comparable social programs, such as the Canada and Quebec pension plans, which belied the negative stereotype of opposition in the parliamentary system. This is not to say there were no strong partisan differences to overcome and interests to meld, but to underline that it was parliamentary debate and action that ultimately propelled rather than obstructed the development of policy.

Nor is it the case, where a government enjoys a majority in the House, that policy convergence across the aisle may not also happen. In fact (as discussed in chapter 4), this was the strategy adopted by party leaders in their attempt to secure caucus support for the mega-constitutional agreements of the 1980s and 1990s. Canada is a double federation – of provinces and cultures – where agreement among the parties in Parliament has been deemed as important to constitutional stability as agreement between federal and provincial jurisdictions. Deemed, that is, by party leaders although not necessarily echoed by their followers.

In fact, the unity of the country and the integrity of political parties are not always compatible. Long-time political observer Tom Van Dusen attributed Joe Clark's defeat at the 1983 PC leadership convention to just such dissonance:

> Joe's problem was that he failed to assess the disillusion in his own party. A lot of Tories were annoyed with Joe because he had failed to rid the country of Pierre Elliott Trudeau. Trudeau was back … and more than a little boring with his endless constitutional preoccupations and his harping on bilingualism. A substantial segment of the voters wanted all that gone.
>
> And Joe was buying it all. Buying patriation of a constitution that had been drawn up in Canada in the first place. Buying a Charter of Rights that guaranteed protection to minority rights in every province but one – the only one where French was not the minority language. There were dimly felt but powerful unseen pressures undercutting Joe's security.[1]

Brian Mulroney, who succeeded Clark as leader, fell victim to the same complaint. Tom Flanagan, chronicler of Reform's transformation into the

Conservative party led by Stephen Harper, noted two causes for his own disenchantment with the Progressive Conservatives at the end of the 1980s. One was 'out-of-control spending,' the other, Mulroney's seeming 'obsess[ion] with meeting ever-escalating constitutional demands from Quebec.'[2] This responsiveness was explained in part by the absence of a Tory party in the province to shield him from direct pressure.

The constitutional labours of prime ministers Trudeau and Mulroney elicited overt support from the opposition parties in Parliament. (In any case, freedom to dissent contracted once members of the Bloc – the prime dissenters – took their seats.) Whether support was wise, or whether there was an alternative in light of the strong separatist and nationalist sentiment evident in Quebec at the time, are matters outside the scope of this discussion. What calls for attention is that on this issue the parties in Parliament (before the arrival of Reform and the Bloc) stood as one. In that context, it needs emphasizing that the proposition that unity requires accommodation is as old as Canada – older, if one looks at the structure and conduct of politics in the province of United Canada. At least, that perspective became the mainline view of Canadian politics after the terms of reference of the Royal Commission on Bilingualism and Biculturalism (which spoke of 'two founding peoples') were released in 1963, and after the same commission reported, in 1967, that its 'guiding principle [was] the recognition of both official languages, in law and in practice, wherever the minority is numerous enough to be viable as a group.'[3] The principal policy to result from the commission's recommendations was the Official Languages Act, 1969, which, despite the divisions it caused in the PC party, received all-party approval.

Donald Creighton (among others) volubly dissented from the interpretation of Canada as a cultural compact of English and French.[4] That conclusion was not necessarily the one to be taken from the commission's research studies, but it could be. The dualism that was so much a feature of politics in the decade before 1867 did not continue into the leadership and work of the Canadian cabinet: there was only one prime minister, although on occasion there might be a French lieutenant, Cartier to Macdonald and Lapointe to King.[5] None the less, alternation (normally) in the great offices of state (usually appointed) by representatives from the official language groups offered ammunition to those who challenged what appeared to be a modern-day policy of official dualism. Of this policy there were competing versions: the 'two nations' depiction that Eugene Forsey tireless sought to refute, and the Trudeau goal of Canada as, at least for federal purposes, a bilingual country.[6] Creighton and Forsey were unhappy with both since in their reading of the Confederation Debates and Canadian history there was no support for either. From the viewpoint of a study of opposition in Parliament, the proposition that the object of the conferences in 1867 was to create a country that was culturally and/or politically divided is difficult to accommodate. For the following reason: in countries where ethnic, religious, or linguistic cleavages are prominent, mechanisms that depoliticize conflict arise. Arend Lijphart's description of politics in the Netherlands in 1967 makes this point: 'potentially divisive issues and disintegrative tendencies are ever present, but they are carefully controlled.'[7] Simply but starkly put for a system like Canada's whose constitutional practices copied those of Westminster: opposition disappears or is drastically demoted from the prominence the Westminster model demands of it.

What has small and densely populated Netherlands to do with Canada? Until the B and B Commission's research studies, very little, but like Belgium and Switzerland (among other countries for commission study), the Netherlands was seen as a culturally segmented yet politically stable state. Implicit in this research was the suggestion that Canada, immense and sparsely populated but in the 1960s experiencing rising tensions between Quebec and the rest of the country, might learn governing principles of value for political stability. As well, there was another suggestion, that consociational practices were not so much foreign to Canadian experience as in need of recognition for what they were. For instance, regarding selections he had made 'to illustrate various aspects of consociationalism in Canada,' Kenneth McRae, the Canadian authority on the subject, acknowledged that 'some of the material cannot be linked explicitly to the concept as it has been developed in recent political literature.'[8] Still, there were examples.

As the principal institution that acknowledges through its composition the diversity of the Canadian federation, the cabinet has been at the centre of political life since Macdonald. The selection of ministers is the sole preserve of the prime minister, a prerogative that accounts as much as any other for the prime minister's dominance of Parliament from the very beginning of the federation. Provincial representation in the cabinet is roughly proportionate to the provinces' populations, and where a province has several ministers, then representation of significant minorities – for instance, Irish Catholics or English-speaking Protestants from Quebec, or French-speaking Catholics from Ontario – has long been considered a convention of the constitution. Is this practice an example of

Canadian consociational democracy? Probably so, although Canada's vast territory and its large immigrant population complicate easy attributions of representation, or comparisons with European countries. More than that, the diversity of regions and their different economic bases adds a further complication: when in 1965 Lester Pearson appointed J.J. Greene, a lawyer who sat for the Ontario seat of Renfrew South, his minister of agriculture – the first non-westerner to hold the agriculture portfolio since Laurier appointed S.A. Fisher, a Quebec farmer, in 1896 – the innovation did not go unremarked (negatively) on the prairies, or by Mr Diefenbaker in the House. Similarly, the fisheries portfolio was traditionally considered the rightful possession of a coastal province, transportation Ontario's, and public works Quebec's. There may have been exceptions to this geographic imperative, but the expectation none the less remained perennially strong, although subject to change: at one time, senior portfolios, such as Finance and External Affairs (as then known), remained closed to French-speaking Quebeckers, an exclusion that disappeared during the time of the Trudeau government.

Does this practice affect opposition? Undoubtedly, the answer is yes, especially when it is viewed in the context of the long history of patronage in Canadian politics. There may or may not have been a French lieutenant when the prime minister was English-speaking, but there have always been regional lieutenants, no matter what language the first minister spoke. In the last half-century, Allan MacEachen, Alvin Hamilton, George Nowlan, and Brian Tobin are four names among many that might be cited. Their control of patronage, influence over local nominations, and prominence in the business of Parliament made them and their respective parties formidable adversaries for opposition to overcome. That they were regional political chiefs only magnified the opposition's problem. No one individual may be considered representative of this ministerial genre, since the personality, history, and political context of each is distinct. Still, the breadth of their activity and its potential implications for the conduct and history of opposition in Canada may be highlighted by summarizing the career of one notable and long-lived representative of their type, James G. Gardiner of Saskatchewan.

Gardiner held, without interruption, first provincial and then federal public office from 1914 until 1958. In those forty-four years he sat as a backbencher, a cabinet minister, premier (twice), leader of the provincial opposition, and then minister of agriculture in Ottawa from 1935 until 1957, and finally in federal opposition for one year, being defeated in 1958. For most of these decades he was the Liberal party's lieutenant on the prairies, as the party's organization in Manitoba and Alberta, compared to its 'machine' reputation in Saskatchewan, where it held office for thirty-five of the province's first forty years,[9] verged on mediocre. The Liberals were weak in those provinces because there – but not in Saskatchewan – the organized farmers had entered electoral politics provincially at the end of the First World War. More than that, Mackenzie King, prime minister for much of the period afterwards, believed that the way to deal with the farmers' threat provincially was the way he was dealing with it in Parliament, through cooperation and cooptation. Gardiner was contrarily minded, in every sense of that term. He had stood with Laurier at the time of Union government; he considered Liberals who crossed the aisle apostates; when the farmers in his own province and those to the east and west set out to compete with the Liberals, he was determined to crush them. In his mind, third parties were constitutionally and politically suspect. First, they undermined 'British responsible and representative government,' an ideal he never tired of celebrating; second, they did not serve the interests of the West. The only way the West would be heard and heeded was if the region held the balance of political power. In his calculation, this was possible if Quebec remained tied to the Liberal party and Ontario split its vote between Liberals and Conservatives. Then with its growing number of Commons seats, as the immigrant population swelled, the West would guarantee victory for the Liberals. Until the 1950s, when Saskatchewan ceased to have the third-largest number of seats in the Commons, the strategy worked. At least as far as Saskatchewan was concerned.

Gardiner's 'relentless Liberalism' put him at odds with his prime ministers and with most of his cabinet colleagues.[10] According to Grant Dexter, journalist and later editor of the *Winnipeg* (before 1931, *Manitoba*) *Free Press*, 'Jimmie [was] desperately unpopular with the cabinet at large for some time. Ralston once remarked to me that Jimmie was the most difficult colleague he had ever known.'[11] Some of this unpopularity arose from his dogged persistence in support of agricultural policies that most of his colleagues did not understand, delivery quotas being one example, and whose significance – for the farmers and for farmer support of the Liberals – they did not appreciate. Much of it, however, originated in his tireless partisanship, which both as a policy and as a practice they did not share. At the same time King was courting such farm leaders as E.C. Drury and T.A. Crerar, Gardiner spared no effort in organizing the Liberals to vanquish the movements they led. When in 1929 the Saskatchewan Liberals met their first electoral defeat, winning

46 per cent of the popular vote and 44 per cent of the legislature's seats, more votes and seats than any other party or grouping (Conservative, Progressive, or Independents) but not a majority, he refused to resign. When his opponents said they would act in unison once the legislature was called into session, Gardiner put them to the test: 'Responsible self-government,' he said, 'calls for a decision by the Legislature itself, not by informal group caucuses held behind "closed doors."'[12] When in the 1957 election the federal Liberals led by Louis St Laurent lost their majority but won more votes than the PCs, although seven fewer seats, Gardiner proffered the same advice, but to no avail. St Laurent listened instead to Lester Pearson and then resigned. Without citing evidence, Gardiner attributed the decision to a discredited source – Manitoba Liberals – via a distrusted route – the Senate.[13] The result, he never tired of complaining afterwards, was that 'for the first time we have a government which came into being when the House was not in session without being able to demonstrate that it had the support of a majority of those elected to the House of Commons.'[14] In 2006, Paul Martin went one better than St Laurent: he refused to lead the Liberals in opposition until a successor was chosen; as a result Bill Graham became leader of the official opposition for ten months.

St Laurent, who had never sat on the opposition benches or on the government backbenches, who had never organized an election, and whose succession to King at the 1948 leadership convention (848 votes to Gardiner's 323 and C.G. Power's 56) was a foregone conclusion, found Gardiner's 'narrow, almost sectarian' partisanship distasteful.[15] In a phrase that gained currency after he died, Gardiner by the 1950s had become 'yesterday's man.' Not only did non-Liberals find his partisanship excessive and threatening, but so too did Liberals. Another phrase not yet current, 'politically incorrect,' described him as well, especially in reference to cultural matters. Gardiner died in 1962, the year Pearson, still federal leader of the opposition, proposed that a Royal Commission on Bilingualism and Biculturalism be appointed. Yet the inclusive ideal was already in circulation: 'About two weeks before the end of the [1957] campaign,' Gardiner wrote a former cabinet colleague, 'a report came over the radio to the effect that it had been stated at one of the Prime Minister's meetings in Quebec that it might not happen in our time but the time would come when everyone holding an important position would have to be bilingual ... They have sown a new form of nationalism which put[s] more emphasice [sic] upon the nationality of the candidate than upon his Liberalism.'[16]

Gardiner's opinions might be, indeed were, dismissed as antediluvian. Yet they were prescient. He, as did John Diefenbaker, accepted the understanding made in Saskatchewan's early days that provided for French Catholic representation on the province's courts. In the same manner he defended the constitutional protection afforded denominational schools, as provided in Section 93 of the Constitution Act, 1867, and in Section 17 of the Saskatchewan Act, 1905. It was on this last issue, and its anti-ethnic rhetoric, that he fought the Ku Klux Klan in the 1929 election, and lost.[17] Still, as early as the 1948 convention, he rejected as without foundation the claim that the Liberal party alternated leaders between English- and French-speaking Canadians. He was a 'majorities man' who accepted the Confederation bargain. Living in the West, he could not be insensitive to minorities, but he rejected symbolic representation, into which category, in his mind, fell official bilingualism because it discouraged participation. The test of an opinion or a policy lay not in claims that it was wise, or desirable, or deserved, but whether voters accepted it. The ballot box was the ultimate democratic test.

In this opinion there is the (politically) unexpected – and no doubt for the individuals themselves, unpalatable – parallel to be drawn between Gardiner and a later Saskatchewan premier, Allan Blakeney. Like Gardiner, Blakeney spent time on the opposition benches – in his case, twice, for a total of six years to Gardiner's five. He too was convinced of the power of parliamentary politics to achieve good, and suspicious of limitations on legislative sovereignty, now in the form of the Canadian Charter of Rights and Freedoms and the power conferred on the judiciary to interpret those rights. There were differences between them – Blakeney the public administrator turned politician with a profound commitment to social democratic principles and programs; Gardiner partisan to the core and with a deep suspicion of bureaucrats. What they shared was the belief in representative and responsible government and the efficacy of free elections to secure that object. Although they never faced each other in the same chamber, they personified a political and partisan, but not cultural, duality that, from the rise of the CCF (under the name Farmer-Labour) at the very time Gardiner dominated Saskatchewan provincial politics, continued for the much of the rest of the century. In this respect the tone and alignment of legislative politics in Regina was more like that found at Westminster than in Ottawa.

The next, and last, Liberal to be premier of Saskatchewan (1964–71) was Ross Thatcher. A former CCF Member of Parliament, who returned to Saskatchewan and crossed the aisle to become the most prominent political opponent of the introduction of medicare in the province, he was viewed by federal Liberals much as Gardiner had been a decade earlier. In the words of Lester Pearson's campaign director, Keith Davey, Thatcher was 'rude, crude' and right-wing.[18] In Ottawa, Pearson's left-leaning Liberals faced the PCs and NDP in opposition, but they shared policy goals, such as medicare, with the NDP and needed its support to realize those goals; in Regina, the CCF, as they were still called, looked upon the Liberals as their adversary. If one were a Liberal, identifying friend and foe depended in large part on where one stood – prairie or Ottawa Valley. In Regina, opposition was the alternative government, just as the theory said it should be; in Ottawa, opposition (or at least some of it) kept the existing government in power.

On the matter of adversaries, it is revealing that Thatcher told Davey: 'Whatever you do, Keith, don't say anything out here that is critical of Dief.' Revealing because while Liberals in Ottawa were solicitous of NDP sympathy, provincial Liberals, for whom the CCF was the party to beat, remained sensitive about the Tories. The reason why was that provincial Liberals were known to vote Tory in federal elections.[19] Tory pre-eminence was a regional phenomenon, not just a Saskatchewan one. In 1958 the PCs won all of the seats in Manitoba and Alberta and all but one in Saskatchewan. In four of the five elections that took place in the decade 1962 to 1972, more than 48 per cent of the seats won by the Progressive Conservatives in the prairie provinces (when measured by the winner's margin of vote) fell into the top quartile of all Tory victories. The exception was the 'Trudeaumania' election of 1968, when only 43 per cent of the prairie victories fell within this quartile. Undeviating loyalty might vary with location and leader; that is not relevant to this discussion. What is relevant is that, except for the first years of the Mulroney era, the prairies were for decades a stronghold of opposition. Their MPs sat opposite the Liberal government in the House of Commons and, except on rare occasions, rejected the policies identified with that government.

The Progressive Conservative hold on the West then, like the Conservative hold today, is scarcely news. Yet the implication of that dominance on the development of opposition in the House of Commons has been inadequately examined. If in political behaviour Gardiner and Thatcher were beyond the pale, defined here as central Canada, when it came to received opinion on subjects such as bilingualism and national unity, Ernest Manning, then Social Credit premier of Alberta, was not a great deal closer, as his remarks to the Confederation of Tomorrow Conference in 1967 testify: 'You cannot say that this particular group has a legal and constitutional right that ... over five million Canadians today who are neither Anglo-Saxon or [sic] French origin ... do not possess.'[20] In 1969, Thatcher, Harry E. Strom (Manning's successor as Alberta premier), and Walter Weir, premier of Manitoba, threatened, but took no action, to challenge the constitutionality of the Official Languages Act. Once again the West was out of step, this time on the new constitutional road, just as, in its eyes, the federal government had long been out of step when it came to caring for the West's interests. It was enough to invoke – as western politicians regularly did – long-nurtured grievances rooted in the subject of natural resources, denominational schools, privileges enjoyed by the CPR, and the protective tariff in order to draw a parallel and see a pattern of regional discrimination. A former prime minister and then leader of the official opposition, John Diefenbaker was more than a regional politician. His rejection of the new flag drew support from all parts of Canada. Still, his parliamentary loyalists, drawn disproportionately from western Canada after 1967, shared his opposition to the new bilingual Canada heralded by Lester Pearson and the B and B Commission, then implemented by Pierre Trudeau. It is important to be clear about the focus of their discontent. They disagreed, first, with the government's elevation of national unity as the central issue confronting Canadians from the 1960s and after; second, with the Liberals' assumption that they were the one party that could be trusted to deal with the issue; and, last, with the belief that Liberal ministers from Quebec held the key to the solution. From the Tories' perspective, in this scenario they were triply handicapped: they came from the wrong part of the country; they were of the wrong party; and they sat on the wrong side of the House. The sense of exclusion that then took root as a result of Liberal condescension proved a hardy perennial: half a century later, quoting Ian Brodie, Stephen Harper's former chief of staff, Lawrence Martin would write that 'Jean Chrétien consistently treated Conservatives as if they were un-Canadian.' That intimation 'stung,' and the 'resentment' it caused 'gave Harper a motivation, a relentless single-minded passion.'[21]

Arguably, the loyalists shared, as well, their leader's suspicion not only of the subject but of its provenance, a Royal Commission. From Diefenbaker's viewpoint, commissions of inquiry were not always the exemplars of reason that academic scholars sometimes assumed. For instance, he never wavered in his belief that the government had appointed the Spence Commission (to inquire into purported security breaches when Diefenbaker was in office) in order principally to embarrass if not destroy the opposition he later led. He and tens of thousands of westerners took offence at the 'two founding peoples' phrase in the B and B Commission's terms of reference, and were equally affronted by Pearson's support for a country-wide nationalism based on bilingualism and biculturalism. In a speech in the House of Commons, which he later described in his *Memoirs* as the one of which he was 'most proud,' Pearson depicted Confederation as a 'settlement between the two founding races of Canada made on the basis of an acceptable and equal partnership.'[22] Like Gardiner earlier and Blakeney later, Diefenbaker championed Parliament because its elected members, both of government and of opposition, embodied the authority that rested in the people. 'One of the problems with amateurs,' Tom Van Dusen, an adviser at different times of Liberal and Tory party leaders, once wrote, 'is they insist on making up the rules as they go along.' Among these 'amateurs' he included neophyte party leaders, such as Robert Stanfield, a former provincial premier; Brian Mulroney, who had held no elected office; and Joe Clark, who had sat in the House for four years before rising to the top of the party. They never learned or, in Mulroney's case, learned painfully through experience 'what the House was all about.'[23] As it transpired, the B and B Commission, the first inquiry on a scale to rival the pre-war Royal Commission on Dominion–Provincial Relations (Rowell–Sirois), whose legal counsel had been Louis St Laurent, signalled a practice that in different forms was to become a recurring feature of politics, with particular ramifications for the conduct of opposition.

Another way of making the point already made – that outside Parliament there is no constituent power – can be found in the words of a solitary Conservative member of nearly a century ago: 'Legislation is only the expression of the will of the people who have no will.'[24] Yet it is the case that the influence of non-elected and extra-parliamentary bodies continues to grow. For Diefenbaker and those who thought as he did, parliamentary politics could not be learned from textbooks, or from those schooled in their study. The core of politics was activity, not theory; the history of the country organic, not the product of some academic design. As he had once ridiculed Joe Clark (when the latter had acted as messenger of young Progressive Conservative opinion critical of the Chief's leadership), so in turn he mocked experiments at soliciting extra-parliamentary opinion by his successor. Early in Stanfield's tenure, a 'policy advisory committee' was created to provide him with 'maximum assistance ... in terms of ... policy speeches.' The first paragraph of a twelve-page 'outline of some topics for study' communicated the ambition of the endeavour: 'There is a need to think through a concept of Canada, to re-interpret the country's character and role in light of present conditions and future opportunities, and to give Canada a new sense of purpose. A national Policy for the second century of Canadian Confederation.' E.D. Fulton, a former minister of justice in the Diefenbaker government, did preliminary organizing work for the committee and in that capacity sought (unsuccessfully) to entice Norman Ward to join. 'There is a real need,' Fulton wrote, 'for some thoughtful and perhaps original work in the elaboration of topics [re: the concept of Canada]. I do hope we will all have a go at this in writing.' Ideas would then be 'pooled'; a 'condensation' produced; and 'a meaningful and important contribution to current political thought' made.[25]

Dates are relevant to this intra-party initiative that reached outside Parliament. It took place before the Liberals selected as leader Pierre Trudeau, the intellectual who would soon triumph over the Tories in constitutional matters, and at approximately the same time as the Pearson government's third-reading defeat on a surtax measure (see chapter 1). Tom Van Dusen records that it was on the advice of Joe Clark and Lowell Murray, at that time unelected aides to Stanfield, that, following the defeat, Stanfield met Pearson (and the governor of the Bank of Canada) and, subsequently, decided not to press the government to resign. From Diefenbaker's perspective, consultation had trumped partisan advantage and long-term interest. That was one man's opinion – not even the one that carried the day; but it was founded on a twofold premise: the leader of the opposition was *the leader*, and the function of opposition was to replace government when the government had failed in its principal task, of controlling the House. Context is important, too. Only a few months earlier, before the leadership convention that selected Stanfield, a 'thinkers' conference held at Montmorency had resolved that Canada was comprised of 'deux nations.' It was a description, although never formally adopted by the PC party, that proved controversial and damaging because it offered the Liberals ammunition, which they used, against the Tories in the increasingly sensitive debate over the constitution.

It may be an exaggeration to say that in a political system committed to the practice of consociational democracy opposition disappears, but it is only an exaggeration. Where the object of national unity achieved through the accommodation of particular interests is paramount, the presumption of a loyal opposition, a constitutional premise for more than two hundred years, loses its certainty. Nor is it a matter of abstract theory. On the contrary, the award of contracts and the distribution of patronage may become subjects for debate and, more to the point, for criticism. But the criticism must be muted, in light of how it might be interpreted. Time and space enter into the matter. Canadian political parties, which normally are federated structures and as such embrace a spectrum of opinion, may be inconsistent in the positions they adopt: at any particular moment a provincial part may disagree with the federal part (the Saskatchewan and federal NDP at the time of negotiations leading to the Constitution Act, 1982), or over time, the federal party may hold contradictory positions (as witness the NDP: in the 1960s, it was 'the first federal party to recognize Quebec's right to self-determination';[26] in the 1990s, the party stood with the Chrétien government on the Clarity Act; and in 2011, Jack Layton campaigned to reopen constitutional discussions with Quebec).

Consociational democratic theory, generally, and its application by academics to Canada, in particular, is coterminous (approximately) with the work of the B and B Commission. Of course, this does not mean that Canadian governments or parliamentary oppositions (of whichever party) were oblivious, although not necessarily sympathetic, to cultural demands before them. The minorities question, of which language, religion, and schools were continuing sub-topics, regularly disrupted provincial, and occasionally federal, politics for decades after Confederation.[27] In the 1890s Laurier led a filibuster against the Bowell government's remedial bill, intended to restore the denominational rights of Roman Catholics in Manitoba, to the point that the Seventh Parliament died, and following the ensuing election the Liberals were in power. In the First World War, the Borden government used closure to pass military conscription over the fractured, Laurier-led Liberal opposition. Military conscription was a matter falling under the jurisdiction of the federal government, but it had predictably divisive effects on national unity and on Quebeckers' trust in the national government. Under Section 93 of the Constitution Act, 1867, education in and for each province is a matter for provincial jurisdiction. By the Pearson years, language and education had, to a degree, become concerns of the federal government: a shift in jurisdiction that helped account for renegade Tory opposition in the West to bilingualism and biculturalism.

In Parliament in Ottawa, the western Tories were the exception, however. Partisanship and the critical function of those whose job it was to hold government to account appeared in decline. If, as the preliminary report of the B and B Commission said, Canada was 'passing through the greatest crisis in its history,' there were few prominent dissenters from the Liberal government's response to it;[28] none the less, the loss of vigour attracted attention (from outside the inner circle), as the following comment in a letter to Richard Bell, former MP, Diefenbaker minister, and national director of the PC party, bore witness:

> To think that no member of the House of Commons sufficiently knows what is the proper position of Opposition, to whom Opposition owes loyalty, and to recognize that Opposition is the sole duly constituted empowered body to be our National Ombudsman and to demand and to obtain account as well as access wherever it need go to obtain satisfaction whether in a case of personal oppression or in matters of more general interest, is certainly beyond me.[29]

For nearly two more decades, the abnegation of the official opposition on the central subject of unity continued, assuring the continuation of Liberal dominance. Joe Clark formed a minority government in May 1979, but had won only two seats in Quebec. His government was defeated in the House seven months later and, in the following election, was reduced to one Quebec seat, while the Liberals won a majority, thereby strengthening Trudeau in his No campaign in the first Quebec referendum on sovereignty, in May 1980. Four years later Brian Mulroney won fifty-eight seats in Quebec, and tried (unsuccessfully) to use that strength to negotiate the province's support for a modified Constitution Act, 1982. In this period there were other issues, to be sure, prominent among these the free trade agreement with the United States (Quebec's Robert Bourassa fought for it and Ontario's David Peterson against), but these did not alter the parliamentary alignment rooted in the central issue of unity. Mulroney's triumph in 1984, the product of an unprecedented melding of Quebec and western interests, did not survive his prime ministership. It was succeeded by two solitudes in opposition: Reform and the Bloc, whose arrival in Ottawa signalled the end of consociational democracy as a governing principle, an outcome, it should be noted, that would have happened earlier had the Yes side in the Quebec referendums of 1980 or 1995 prevailed.

Officers of Parliament

Another parliamentary development, unrelated in its origin to the unity question but because of the Sponsorship Scandal of the Chrétien years to become linked to it, was the proliferation of officers of Parliament.[30] There was background to this development. The Official Languages Act, 1969, created an officer of Parliament, under the title Commissioner of Official Languages, whose essential role is to assure that language equality remains a defining principle of the constitutional architecture of Canada, its Parliament, and its government. The language commissioner was the third officer of Parliament, the first being the auditor general, created in 1878, when Alexander Mackenzie was prime minister, in response to irregular accounting practices of the Macdonald government; and the second being the chief electoral officer (1920), in response to the Union government's manipulation of the franchise in the election of 1917. Privacy and information commissioners appeared in the 1980s (reflecting values associated with the Canadian Charter of Rights and Freedoms), ethics commissioners (for the two chambers) after that, and then with the election of the Conservative government in 2006 and its subsequent Federal Accountability Act, several officers in areas such as lobbying and integrity. Writing before this Act, Paul Thomas remarked upon the absence of study of the federal officers, a lacuna that remains true a decade later despite their growing numbers.[31] By contrast, the proliferation of legislative officers in the provinces has elicited more focused analysis.[32] Significant in this latter exposition – because it almost never arises in discussion of the parliamentary officers – has been the occasional reference to the influence they may have for the conduct of opposition. For instance, 'in 1967, Alberta became the first jurisdiction in North America and the tenth in the world to create an OmbudsOffice.' (As of that year, the province had been governed for more than three decades by one party, Social Credit, in an assembly with what could best be described as vestigial opposition.) With that history in mind, 'a commentator in the *Edmonton Journal* contended that an Ombudsman would "do some of the chores ordinarily reserved for the House Opposition."'[33]

Whether that was a reasonable presumption, and whether later evidence verified it, is unimportant. What is significant is that the influence of officers of Parliament on the work of the opposition parties, as opposed to parliamentarians generally, goes unexplored. Once more, Thomas writes that officers of Parliament are 'independent, accountability agencies created first to assist Parliament in holding ministers and the bureaucracy accountable and, second, to protect various kinds of rights of individual Canadians.'[34] While that description may sound helpful, the interposition of officers of Parliament in the operation of responsible government raises the question whether their activities strengthen or undermine that foundational principle of the constitution. To take a specific example: Does the work of the auditor general assist the Public Accounts Committee of the Commons, or does it supplant that committee? Independence and accountability are contradictory principles, whose realization is further impeded by the triangular set of interrelationships that exist between officers, government, and the legislature. An example of the contradictory pressures at work may be discerned from the following opinion of Anthony Birch, who has written extensively on parliamentary government: the convention of ministerial responsibility, he says, has been used 'to prevent alternative scrutiny procedures from developing, with the result that "far from ensuring that the departments are subservient to Parliament, [it] actually serves to protect the departments from Parliamentary control."'[35] Responsibility versus accountability – here is the nub of a conflict of constitutional proportions, so to speak, and in Canada in the last decade accountability has prevailed – with deleterious consequences for legislative opposition. Consider the response of Suzanne Legault, information commissioner in 2011, to a court ruling on access to cabinet records that found against openness: 'Canadians should be concerned … As it stands, the access-to-information law is the *only* way Canadians can ensure they can hold the government to account and are able to participate in the democratic process in a meaningful way.'[36] Whither the opposition in Parliament?

The creation of officers of Parliament has become 'a tactic in political conflict.'[37] An embarrassment of riches is at hand to support that claim. Two suffice: Tory justice critic Peter MacKay demanding in 2001 that 'the federal privacy watchdog be found in contempt of parliament for appearing to side with Jean Chrétien in a fight over access to the prime minister's agenda books' (resolved, as just noted, unhappily for opposition a decade later); and Gilles Duceppe relentlessly using the auditor general's criticisms of the sponsorship program ('I am appalled by what we have found'[38]) to attack the Liberals (with the unintended consequence of promoting the new Conservative party as the most experienced and trustworthy federalist alternative). Like the 'war on terror,' vigilance (in this case, to prevent 'inappropriate interference from government') must never flag.[39] Yet the results are disappointing for those who seek certainty in matters of trust, while the explanation confounds: 'Our mistrust of government and preoccupation with uncovering waste led to expensive layers of control and oversight that made government no more accountable or transparent but certainly more risk-adverse and inefficient and therefore less worthy of trust: a self-fulfilling prophecy.'[40] If there were any doubt as to the accuracy of that assessment – six years after the sponsorship scandal – 'an *Ottawa Citizen* analysis of question period transcripts show[ed] the Liberals asked about ethics three times as often as they did about the economy.'[41] Caution about the political implications of officers of Parliament is rarely expressed from within the reaches of government. Therefore, when it does arise, in the form of a warning from a former national security adviser to the prime minister, it stands out. Asked to comment on a recommendation, originating with the Air India bombing inquiry, to create a national security 'czar,' Margaret Bloodworth replied that 'because this new czar would be unelected, it would raise questions of ministerial accountability.'[42]

The relationship between ministers and the officers, and between the officers and Parliament – whose agents they are – is fraught with uncertainty. The essential feature that distinguishes the officers has broadened, in the view of some observers, from protection against political influence to separation from Parliament. Controversy in 2010 and 2011 surrounding the integrity commissioner (Christine Ouimet), saw the auditor general 'castigate' her for 'failing to do her job,' and then seven officers send a joint letter to Commons committees in which they diplomatically observed that 'it is timely to examine whether the issues reported by the Auditor General could have been identified [by parliamentarians] sooner.'[43] A reversal of the principal–agent relationship appears to have occurred, one that in the opinion of legal scholar John Whyte has 'constitutional weight.'

With respect to many of the functions of governments we have created every form of parliamentary watchdog office, parliamentary information office and parliamentary policy office. Implicit in this dramatic development is distrust of the good faith of government in implementing legislated policies, and in forthrightness of government in informing legislators what they are doing and what they are achieving, and in helping legislators meet their responsibility for, and their ability to grasp, details about the operations of the government. The growth of independent legislative officers from one perspective might be seen as the refinement of legislative oversight of government but, in reality, it represents a significant shift in how political accountability is achieved in our constitutional system. This system of specialist review represents a new element of separation of powers – one that has acquired constitutional weight, at least in the sense of constitutional practice.[44]

Duff Conacher, of Democracy Watch, concurs: 'We have these watch-dogs over government accountability, but the laws that govern them mean that they cannot be held accountable.'[45] Indeed, the media have fallen into the habit of referring to officers of Parliament as czars, argu-ably unexpected nomenclature for protectors of rights. Recall the find-ing reported by Ipsos-Reid, that Sheila Fraser was 'immensely trusted by Canadians because "she ... [was] viewed by Canadians as being above politics."'[46] Rule by the non-elected expert; election as a positive disqualification for gaining trust. Once again, the implication of this development for elected politicians, especially in opposition, is im-mense. They are without influence because the political contest is no longer perceived as taking place across the aisle but, in Whyte's words, 'between executive government and the more neutral, more specialist and more normatively driven agencies of accountability – the courts, regulatory agencies and the oversight officers and commissions ... Political engagement [focuses on] ... resort to the formal rules and pro-cesses by which government is held in check.' There is a movement away from custom and convention as guides for parliamentary behav-iour and, in their place, the demand to codify rules and penalties, the last of which, Whyte concludes, 'may be a more effective way of check-ing the misuse and abuse of power, but it likely weakens legislators' sense of their responsibility for prudent political judgment and invites less nuanced political engagement from them.'[47]

In this context, a synonym for 'less nuanced' might be *vituperative* as a description of debate in the House. Criticism of the 'tone' of House proceedings, pleas for a return of (lost) civility, claims that the conduct of MPs from both sides of the chamber is reproachable – all of these are so common as not to require comment, except in a sense that goes be-yond political etiquette. Australian scholar Judith Brett argues that 'from the perspective of those experienced with the modern, informal meeting and its consensual means of reaching a decision, parliamen-tary procedure is no longer seen as enabling but as precluding coopera-tive action.'[48] In short, the public does not like the way parliamentarians behave and, contrary to the accepted societal norm of cheering for the underdog, they blame the opposition for what they dislike. While it may take two to argue, the public sees the opposition as the more cul-pable, and for a reason that infuriates parliamentary purists – it is not elected. Elections convey legitimacy, notwithstanding the fact that un-der the Canadian constitution, governments are not 'elected,' only members of Parliament are. For years the media and the public have referred to governments being elected, and for 'terms.' Now governments, particularly the Harper government, have adopted the same stance. In the spring of 2010 a fund-raising letter to members of the Conservative party of Canada offered as a rationale for the plea for money that 'the party [must] fight back against "the hailstorm of negative attacks on our democratically elected government."'[49] As noted earlier in this book, when in 2008 the leaders of the Liberal and New Democratic parties in Parliament entered into discussions with the object of forming a coalition and thereby defeating the Harper government, the Conservatives rallied public opposition to this scheme with the argument that their government, formed following the 2008 election, was about to be supplanted by unelected pretenders. Here and later in criticism (on myriad matters) of those across the aisle, the Harper government behaved like the opposition, although it did not look like one, because it did not suffer from the opposition's democratic deficit of being 'unelected.'[50]

This redefinition of the executive undermines the capacity of opposition to present itself as *the* alternative government – and that, it needs emphasizing once more, is the role the theory of parliamentary opposition assigns those who sit across the aisle from the government. By contrast, in the new depiction MPs are indistinguishable one from the other; only government, as the administration that can get things done, matters. Here is a major reason for the emerging perception of a legislative opposition without influence.

A coda to this discussion concerns the method of appointment of officers of Parliament. In light of their position, it is to be expected that selection would involve more than action on the part of the government alone. That said, contact with the opposition parties over the decades has taken a variety of forms of communication: consultation, concurrence, agreement, or a combination of these. Similarly, the form of involvement of the Senate in appointment of officers of Parliament has varied. A rare survey of practice, relating to the Chief Electoral Officer, the Commissioner of Official Languages, and the Information Commissioner, over the period 1927 to 1990, was prepared by Eugene Forsey.[51] Its principal finding was that no consistent procedure was followed in making appointments. Notwithstanding lack of uniformity in the matter, it was unprecedented, as happened in 2011, to have the members of one opposition party 'walk out of the House of Commons and the Senate ... rather than take part in a vote to appoint [an officer, in this case the Auditor General],' and of the official opposition 'to sta[y] in the House to vote against the resolution.'[52] At issue was the candidate's lack of fluency in French, despite bilingualism being an understood criterion for appointment. Unprecedented, too, was to have the government reprimanded by another officer, the Commissioner of Official Languages, for making the nomination. Most significant for a study of parliamentary opposition – but not unprecedented – was the perspective from which this last act in the controversy was reported – that of the 'watchdog scolding,' another indication of the decline in expectation of legislative oversight.[53]

Media and Communications

The reference to 'negative attacks' in the fund-raising letter quoted above was directed not at the legislative opposition but at the media, whom the letter described as 'the real opposition in the new Parliament.'[54] For most of the first century of Confederation such unilateral antagonism towards the only medium there was – print – was unthinkable and, more to the point, went unvoiced. Government depended upon and at the same time sustained, through advertising and subscriptions, friendly newspapers across the country, to the extent, Norman Ward has shown, of being a founding and for some years supporting partner in the Canadian Press Association. In his study 'The Press and Patronage,' Ward quotes Sir John Willison, long identified with *The Globe*, who described the hermetic worlds of partisan allegiance: 'Very often the correspondents of friendly journals had access to blue books and returns before they were submitted to Parliament.' Edward Blake went so far as to complain to Macdonald that 'in constituencies represented by government supporters blue books "reach no one in Opposition."'[55] On the only occasion he received an invitation to dinner from a Conservative, Willison 'telegraphed to *The Globe* and was assured that acceptance would not be treated as a betrayal of the Opposition.'[56] In a word, patronage of the press reinforced partisanship.

That is until the 1960s, when consolidation, signalled by the closing of many legendary afternoon dailies, made partisan newspaper competition in urban markets impossible. In its place, the spread of television to most parts of the country; the creation of commercial television networks to compete with the public broadcaster (the CBC); the proliferation of local (and 'talk') radio stations; the rise of investigative journalism with a critical perspective focused on government and on institutions of authority generally, influenced by scandals such as Watergate in the

United States and the contribution made by the *New York Times* and the *Washington Post* to their investigation; and later still, the arrival of news networks with their twenty-four-hour news cycles; as well as satellite technology that permitted instantaneous news coverage worldwide, and, of course, the introduction of the Internet and social media. These developments are too well known to require elaboration here except to note their relationship to the subject of legislative opposition, one alluded to as early as 1967 by Robert Stanfield in his maiden speech to the House of Commons: 'Despite the advances and improvements in communications I think the average citizen feels more remote from institutions such as this and from the people who represent him here than formerly.'[57] While it is a thoughtful analysis of the distance separating representative from represented in centennial year, Stanfield's description is hardly an accurate portrayal of politics in the twenty-first century. More indicative – if awkward in presentation – of today's sentiment, is Stockwell Day's celebration of what he described as 'the democratized media of the blogospheres and the twitterspheres': 'I am so glad that that technology has come to the place where everyone can have an opinion and voice it.'[58] Instances to support Day's confidence in the new world of communication are not difficult to find, although few would be as apposite as the action of an opposition MLA in the Alberta legislature, made unhappy by the decision of that province's new premier in 2011 to hold a shorter-than-expected sitting of the legislature before adjourning: 'Rob Anderson [it was reported] ... turned to Twitter to describe the decision as a "disrespect for democracy" and "shameful."'[59]

Rather than reinforce existing partisan allegiances, as once was the case, modern communications and the practices they make possible, such as 'permanent campaigning,' redirect political debate along an axis that emphasizes government versus opposition.[60] Events unique to Canada in the last decade, such as changes to campaign finance laws introduced by the Harper government, occurring at the same time as the formation of, and commitment to, a mass-membership Conservative party, help explain this new alignment, whose consequence, says David Taras, is a 'new political style' that 'limit[s] debate, make[s] compromises with and tolerance for opponents more difficult and delegitimizes politics as a whole.'[61] That said, this transformation in behaviour is not a Canadian phenomenon alone. It is equally true of legislative politics in Great Britain and the United States, where a century ago the media sought to aid the political party of their choice, but half a century ago adopted an *en haute* position from which they judged political parties – particularly the governing party – and now seek 'to represent and empower their audience.'[62] Here is one explanation for why government today is suspicious of the media: they do seek to bring inside, in order to influence decision making, those who were hitherto outsiders, individuals who are more likely critical than supportive of government. In the process, legislative opposition is shunted aside – its façade maintained perhaps but its import in eclipse. Contrary to the McLuhan-like aphorism that 'television is itself part of the opposition,' in this interpretation it has now taken full possession.[63]

If, as critics maintain, Parliament has been superseded by the Charter and the public interest has been displaced by judges who act on behalf of a new, privileged class whose concerns run to such matters as national unity, social justice, civil liberties, and post-materialist interests, such as the environment, then a comparable rise in status may be discerned in the media. In this new order of relations, concerns that a decade ago occupied the attention of reformers, changes to the electoral system being one example, have lost their edge. Rather than altering the electoral system with the intent of changing the representative composition of the House of Commons, attention is now paid to how responsive Parliament and the government are to public, and not just partisan, opinion. A form of direct democratic consultation appears to have arrived via the media, one that offers the public access in the formation of public policy. To the extent this is true, it is important to emphasize its significance for what Lord Campion once described as 'the parliamentary method,' which, he argued, was 'control of government by talk.'[64] There are no vetoes or requirements for supermajorities in Parliament. The function that such provisions perform in legislative systems elsewhere is the job of opposition in Parliament. There can be no sharing of the task because political opposition in systems based on the Westminster model is 'institutionalized.'[65] The media may (admittedly, a big 'may') offer the public some influence over a policy, but it does not secure what responsible government is supposed to secure, which is, accountability of the executive to the legislature. On the contrary, it undermines opposition by promoting independence of the executive from the legislature.

Direct Democracy

The term 'direct democracy' sounds in some respects antique, and for good reason: Canada has been this route before.[66] A century ago the western provinces devised 'mechanisms whereby the electorate could participate more directly in the sponsoring of legislation' – mechanisms that the judiciary, however, found, implicitly and explicitly, 'obnoxious and invalid since [they] detracted from the constitutional position of the lieutenant-governor ... divest[ing] him of his power of granting or withholding royal assent.'[67] The direct democratic cause entered western Canada from the states of the American Midwest. Here as there, it was seen as a means to an end, most prominently social improvement through the promotion of temperance and women's suffrage. Disillusioned with legislative politics, social reform advocates then, as supporters of the environmental movement do today, looked initially to civic groups (such as the Woman's Christian Temperance Union, which was founded in the United States but spread through much of the English-speaking world), religious groups (particularly the Nonconformist denominations and churches), and occupational groups (at that time, principally farmers') to advance their ends. 'The period,' as one scholar has noted, 'generally, was featured by a reaction to the influence of big business, a demand to make government more responsive to the people, and a desire for more government intervention for general welfare.'[68] Direct democracy depended upon the non-mainstream newspapers to promote the ends its proponents sought. The major parties (Liberals and Conservatives), and their newspaper allies, set out to check the populist wave; they were most successful in Saskatchewan, less so in Alberta, and least in Manitoba, with its well-organized urban labour groups and Social Gospel ministries.[69]

At the beginning of this century, as at the beginning of the last one, the traditional fidelity to political structures – which, it should be recalled, were medieval in origin but democratized over time, albeit in details only – is in abeyance. Deference to authority has disappeared, and trust in the unwritten constitution (conventions generally) has been dismissed as a thing of the past. People now as then want equality, clear rules, and penalties. The most obvious consequence of this reversal in attitude is a public life less centred on the House of Commons than it once was. Although extreme in ambition and design, an online petition posted 'on the site of the [Quebec] National Assembly, calling for the resignation of Premier Jean Charest, [and which] within 24 hours of ... being posted ... had gathered more than 50,000 signatures [and] the following day ... word spread like wildfire on Facebook and Twitter,' illustrates the transformation at hand.[70] The swirl of changing ideas and reactions explains why politicians seek to avoid being locked into positions. For the opposition, holding the government to account and advancing alternative policy ideas have become less important than in the past. Individuals once entered Parliament 'to make a difference'; today, they leave for the same reason. In November 2010, the *Globe and Mail* reported that veteran MP Keith Martin was leaving Parliament because he was 'tired of "rabid partisanship."'[71] Arguably, Jack Layton's electoral appeal the following year lay in the public's identifying him as holding the same sentiment: as leader of the official opposition, Layton pledged, he would 'propose' instead of 'oppose.'[72]

In the focus of their activity and in their organization, the initiative and the referendum seem like old-fashioned mechanisms, although in 2011, as a result of a citizen-sponsored initiative, a referendum held in British Columbia overturned the province's harmonized sales tax. More contemporary, however, are what Chantal Hébert calls '"hypothetical parties" whose existence is not even a certainty ... When you have an outsider candidate, a maverick candidate, that's coming in and on a populist platform, the last thing you want to throw at that candidate is insider support for the opposition ... Social media are allowing citizens to connect with each other better than the conventional politicians are connecting with them.' The new communications technology – today's manifestation of direct democracy – is, she says, 'the sleeping giant.'[73]

While initiative and referendum lie at the core of direct democratic mechanisms, their intended use in the last quarter-century has been as much for strategic purposes – for instance, to block constitutional or social change – as to provide legitimacy. An example of the former is Alberta's Constitutional Referendum Act (1992), which requires a direct vote on any prospective change to the Constitution of Canada, and comparable legislation that appeared at the same time in Saskatchewan and British Columbia.[74] As Boyer notes in his study of referendums, most proposals to subject changes in social legislation – abortion and capital punishment would be prominent examples – to a public vote came from opposition in Parliament in the 1970s, and most of those proponents were members of the Progressive Conservative party. Fifty years ago, women in the public gallery of the House might disrupt a sitting in an attempt to publicize their support for liberalizing sections of the Criminal Code dealing with abortion; or farmers angry at low grain prices might (and did) storm the Parliament buildings to vent their wrath. In that period, such demonstrations might be treated as opposition by other means, just as Occupy Wall Street (OWS) encampments in North

American and European cities are in 2011. Except that in Canada, the OWS protest is not concentrated on Parliament Hill, as thirty years ago opponents of Cruise missile testing were. Instead, they are in most large cities. The speed of their formation and the persistence of their public profile are a consequence of the Internet and of social media generally, which in extent and duration are the new and, compared to the past, more disruptive 'other means' of opposition.

7 Opposition in the Federation

Divided jurisdiction is the *sine qua non* of federalism: without it, a political system is unitary in character. While there is a substantial literature on federal government, references to the structure and conduct of opposition within the federal, as opposed to legislative, dimension are rare. Silence is due to the isolation implicit in 'the federal principle,' defined by K.C. Wheare as 'the method of dividing powers so that the general and regional governments are each, within a sphere, co-ordinate and independent.'[1] For instance, and in contrast to Germany, concurrency in administration or jurisdiction is uncommon in Anglo-American federations. In Canada the tendency is to see the jurisdictional spheres as hermetic – 'watertight compartments' is the famous phrase employed by the Judicial Committee of the Privy Council in the *Labour Conventions* opinion – and to treat counter-examples as deviations from the rule.[2] The notable exceptions, of course, are the national political parties, whose most important labour after Confederation, as seen by themselves and their critics, was to unify the country. On the premise that a Liberal or Tory voter in a provincial election would be Liberal or Tory when it came to casting a vote federally, the national parties organized themselves, more or less, on the federal principle too.

At some times and in some places – Saskatchewan under the suzerainty of the 'relentless Liberal' Jimmy Gardiner, perhaps – voter loyalty may have conformed in practice to the theory. Still, decades of seeing Ontario voters return Progressive Conservatives to Queen's Park under leaders like John Robarts and Bill Davis, at the same time as they strongly supported the Liberal party led by Lester Pearson and Pierre Trudeau, suggests the theory's inadequacy as a dependable predictor of behaviour. Furthermore, the theory does not acknowledge the preferences held by political leaders. In his autobiography, journalist Craig Oliver recounts that in the 1980 federal campaign, one of Bill Davis's 'top aides had been assigned to tell us [journalists] privately in what low esteem [Joe] Clark was actually held by the Conservative government of the country's largest province. They would, he indicated, even welcome a return of the Liberals to power.'[3] Inconstancy in federal and provincial elections on the part of voters and leaders has given rise to another theory of opposition in Canada, one of some longevity. Writing in 1955, in the period this book labels the Liberal ascendancy, Frank Underhill offered the following maxim:

> This blanketing of our Canadian federal politics by one national party, with the resulting impossibility of an effective opposition at Ottawa, has had a further effect. By some instinctive, subconscious mental process the Canadian people have apparently decided that, since freedom depends upon a balance of power, they will balance the monopolistic power of the Liberal government at Ottawa by setting up the effective countervailing power, not in Ottawa but in the provincial capitals. Her Majesty's loyal Canadian Opposition now really consists of the Social Credit governments in Alberta and British Columbia, the C.C.F. government in Saskatchewan, the Conservative governments in Ontario and New Brunswick, and the Union Nationale government in Quebec. These are all governments who got elected in their own provinces in order to save their people from the malign influence of Ottawa.[4]

The proposition that, in a political system where the dates of federal and provincial elections are neither synchronized nor, until recently, 'fixed,' voters might divide their partisan loyalties in so rational a fashion is open to debate and is peripheral to the subject of this chapter, which is, the influence that Canada's being a federation has on the conduct of opposition in Parliament. Let it be noted, though, that provincial and federal politicians have traditionally sought to keep electoral contests in the two jurisdictions separate while at the same time ensuring they are of mutual benefit. An early illustration of such a strategy is found in John A. Macdonald's advice to M.C. Cameron, a prominent Conservative member of the Ontario legislature at a time when Edward Blake was premier:

> My idea is this – that in the summer or autumn the Dominion elections should be brought on, and if, as I believe it will, the result of the elections shows that we hold our own at all well in Ontario, and are thereby in posses-

sion of the reins for the next five years, we can bring a tremendous leverage to help you in the Local Legislature in the session of 1872–73. If a new local election takes place before Blake has a fair trial, the verdict of the country will go against you, and that will greatly damage, if not destroy, our chances at the Dominion elections. Depend upon it, the long game is the true one.[5]

The advent of fixed election dates has now complicated such calculations. In 2011, at the time this book was being written, five provinces and the Northwest Territories were scheduled to hold elections between 5 October and 2 November 2015, while a federal election was set for 19 October of the same year. In consequence of this impending tide of public consultation, which would mean two campaigns taking place at the same time, the premier of Saskatchewan requested that the prime minister change the date of the federal election.[6] In the United States, the dates of state and national elections are coterminous, a synchronization that contributes to stronger (than in Canada) identification with the same party at both levels of government. The implication of electoral separation on the organization and conduct of opposition has never been studied in Canada, except by inference in the rich literature on third parties, which have benefited from the convention.

It has long been held that national political parties are the glue that binds the federation: in R. MacGregor Dawson's alliterative phrase, they are 'unifiers of dissident elements in a diverse population.'[7] While this is reassuring as a general principle, the actual practice of political parties in the furtherance of this object is both diffuse and on occasion contradictory. Even the strongest national parties have weak support in some parts of the country, sometimes for long periods. The Progressive Conservatives in Quebec for much of the last century, and the Liberals on the prairies for much of the last half of that century, are cases in point. For the CCF/NDP the problem has been more pervasive over time and territory. Because parties do not like to vacate the field without a show of a fight, one practice that arose was to move partisan forces from strong to vulnerable areas. Flexible voting dates enabled this process, since an electoral blitzkrieg would not be possible were provincial and federal contests held on the same day. Parties act this way because what matters is to win, or appear to try to win, the election. That is so self-evident a purpose as not to require stating, except for its consequence, which is to ignore the opposition. In the final analysis the story of the official opposition is always the same: winning fewer votes than the victor but more votes than any other loser.

There are important exceptions to the generalization that national political parties in Canada are federated structures. Some of these are considered later in this chapter, although for the moment the focus is on the provincial wings, or branches, or parts of national parties. The reason for the attention lies in the fact that at any particular time a constellation of relationships may exist between a national party and its provincial namesakes, thereby revealing a spectrum of behaviour ranging from antagonism to support, which the simple designation of party would disguise. Neither a government composed of a single party nor one composed of a coalition of parties is as uncomplicated as the individual party labels might suggest, principally because the partisan composition of governments, and of potential governments, at one level may not – and probably does not – mirror the other level. The point requires explanation: in Canadian legislative history, coalitions are the exception to the rule of single-party government. That much is quite clear. What is less clear, and also less noted, is the implication this poses for opposition. Coalitions affect opposition, and if the experience of the provinces, where coalition has been more frequent, is any guide, adversely so.

Union government in 1917 was not a textbook coalition, since a substantial part of the Liberal party, including its leader, stayed in opposition. Its primary effect – to encourage the formation of the Progressive (farmers') party – indicates that long-term consequences may follow decisions taken for immediate gain, however justified these last appear at the time. Looking forward, outcomes may be unclear; looking backward, consequences seem to have been predictable. Close to half a century would pass before Conservatives, now with the adjective Progressive, would reappear in western Canada and lead their parties to power, Peter Lougheed in Alberta and Duff Roblin in Manitoba. Farmer governments and Social Credit in the former and farmer governments and coalition in the latter explain the lag, which, in Roblin's description of the Manitoba interlude, took the form of 'self-indulgent lethargy.'[8]

From the perspective of partisan loyalty as well as nomenclature, there is substance to this negative appellation. A non-partisan farmers' movement (the United Farmers of Manitoba), led by John Bracken, came to power in 1922. In 1928, they abandoned electoral politics, and Bracken and his supporters became known as Progressives. Then they fused with the Liberals in 1932; depended upon the support of a handful of Social Credit MLAs after 1936; and, in 1941, formed a non-partisan coalition of Liberal-Progressives, Conservatives, CCF, and Social Credit. The

Roger Graham quotes Frost as saying: 'Hepburn, of course, hates King. The result is that when George [Drew] enters dominion affairs he finds himself thrown in with Hepburn and ... is accused of ganging up.'[23]

Aberhart enters the picture as a colleague-in-arms when the issue is the constitution. For instance, he and his central Canadian counterparts opposed the appointment in 1937 of the Royal Commission on Dominion–Provincial Relations (Rowell–Sirois) for its terms of reference and its later recommendations, both of which they saw as a trespass on provincial terrain. Aberhart and Duplessis shared another, quite different, constitutional objection: the federal government's use (in the case of Alberta) and threatened use (in the case of Quebec) of its power to disallow provincial legislation within one year of its passage (Constitution Act, 1867, s.90). In the first instance, the offending legislation arose when the Aberhart government sought to implement Social Credit policy, particularly as it touched upon monetary matters, a field Ottawa deemed to be its sole jurisdictional prerogative. At almost the same time that Underhill was propounding the thesis of provincial opposition to the federal government, J.R. Mallory wrote his book, *Social Credit and the Federal Power in Canada*.[24] In Mallory's eyes, the exercise of the by then little-used powers of disallowance and reservation amounted to the reassertion of federal power, while at the same time it shifted the weight of legal pressure against the provinces. Disallowance constituted opposition at once extreme and effective, for it negated the legislation that occasioned its use, an outcome denied to legislative opponents. Too much may be made of the power. It has not been used since the late 1930s and, more to the point, was not used at that time to strike down the so-called Padlock Law (to suppress communist propaganda) of the Duplessis government, which civil libertarians believed unconstitutionally restricted freedom of expression and assembly – an opinion the Supreme Court of Canada sustained twenty years later in *Switzman v. Elbling and the Attorney General of Quebec*.[25]

If differences over the constitution became the source of one provincial alliance against the federal government, then differences in 1939 and 1940 over that government's prosecution of the Second World War were the source of another, which in composition and ambition exceeded the first. Aberhart and Hepburn, and George Drew, then Conservative leader of the opposition, thought that the King government was not doing enough to prosecute the war effort, an opinion the Ontario politicians placed in a legislative resolution opposed in the Ontario Legislature by only a handful of Liberal back-benchers. 'Opposition' from Queen's Park gave King a reason to go to the people in a general election (in

March 1940) to determine whether voters shared this view. As it turned out, they did not – King won the largest number of seats he was ever to win and an absolute majority of the popular vote.[26] In Quebec, three months earlier, Duplessis had requested a dissolution of the provincial legislature for similar reasons: that is, to test public support for his suspicion of the federal war effort, especially his presentiment that war would mean, as it had in 1917, military conscription for overseas service. Only, in this instance, the three most prominent ministers from Quebec in the King government (Ernest Lapointe, Arthur Cardin, and C.G. Power) threatened to resign if Duplessis and the Union National were re-elected. They offered themselves, in Black's words, as 'the sole guarantors that there would be no conscription.'[27] Here, with a vengeance, was federal opposition to a provincial government.

The story of opposition in the provinces is as varied as that of provincial influence on opposition in Parliament. In Alberta, legislative opposition is numerically weak and fluid in partisan make-up; sometimes the Liberals are the official opposition, on other occasions it is the NDP. Academic commentary in 1989 phrased the situation this way: 'The present distribution of seats in the legislature, in which the government outnumbers the combined opposition by approximately 3 to 1 represents, by Alberta standards, a relatively strong opposition.'[28] The nadir of its fortunes came in 1984, when a four-man contingent was reduced, through the death of one of their number (Grant Notley, the leader of the official opposition), to three – one NDP MLA and two Independents. The Speaker's ruling on recognition of a successor acknowledged the difficult situation confronting him: he could designate the Independents the official opposition; or the remaining NDP member as such; or designate no one and arrange a sharing of salaries. In the event he opted to recognize the remaining NDP member as leader of the official opposition. The primary reason he gave for this decision is the significant aspect of this vignette of Alberta legislative history:

> What we are concerned with here ... is a special workload and function deriving in part from our Standing Orders. This function is quite apart from leading a group. In other words, here we are not concerned so much with leadership of a group in the House but with additional functions, staffing, and funding which should be available to someone in the opposition.[29]

In the words of the subtitle to chapter 1, 'Somebody Has to Do It.' In short, there must be a leader of the opposition.

Yet it can happen that there is none because there *is* no opposition, as occurred in Prince Edward Island between 1935 and 1939, and in New Brunswick between 1987 and 1991. Opposition-less legislatures must adapt: in PEI, an 'unofficial opposition' selected from the government's own (Liberal) ranks appeared; in New Brunswick, accommodation to necessity rejected the idea of such a 'pretend' opposition and created alternative procedures:

> Conservative and NDP requests for funds to be used at their discretion were turned down. Premier McKenna instead offered the two parties a comprom-ise that included: free office space; use of the legislative Library; permission to take notes of legislative proceedings from the public gallery; representa-tion (one member without voting rights) on the Legislative Administration Committee which oversees the administration of the building, MLA office space, and legislative services; permission to submit written questions to the Public Accounts Committee; and commitment by the Government to submit its bills and estimates to legislative committees where the opposition parties will be able to appear and express their opinions.[30]

It is invariably said of parliamentary procedure that the most pre-cious resource is time. From the government's perspective it is a re-source to be husbanded, and thus the defence of closure; from the opposition's perspective it is an ally to be used against government, and thus resort to closure. From that standpoint, perhaps the most imaginative innovation in New Brunswick was 'the so-called "opposi-tion media-day," whereby the day after a major Government announce-ment such as the Speech from the Throne is set aside, with no legislative sitting, for the opposition parties to deliver their comments at a news conference.'[31] Stewart Hyson, who has written extensively about the 1987 election and its legislative consequences, asks, in so many words, this intriguing question: 'What difference to governing does the ab-sence of an opposition make?' Too often there is an 'assumption,' which he describes as 'debatable,' that New Brunswick before 1987 had 'an effective opposition.' Unfortunately for the present study of opposi-tion, an assessment of the net benefit to a province from having no op-position – Did legislation pass more quickly? Was government more effective? – has not been published. More generally, one wonders, is legislation affected in any qualitative way by the size of a government's majority, as opposed of course to having no majority at all? And from the other side of the aisle, how does the size of the opposition caucus influence the work of members of the legislature seated opposite their government colleagues in the chamber or in committee?

New Brunswick has had a policy of official bilingualism since 1969. Subsequent provincial governments have expanded language rights; for instance, after 1987, the McKenna government sought to increase bilingualism in the province's public service. Frank McKenna was premier throughout much of the time of Canada's mega-constitutional negotiations (Meech Lake and Charlottetown), and his presence nationally and in Fredericton, as a premier highly supportive of efforts at accommodating Quebec's interests in the federation, performs a useful, if paradoxical, service in this discussion of opposition. The first legislative opposition he encountered appeared in 1991 in the form of the Confederation of Regions party–New Brunswick (COR-NB), which won eight seats and became the official opposition. At the next election (1995), COR-NB lost all its seats and collapsed as a populist movement, which is the interpretation usually given this momentary deviation from province's two-party tradition.[32]

COR began life as an interest group, the English-Speaking Association, an organization one scholar has described as 'a party-in-waiting.'[33] One reason for its transformation into a political party was the elimination earlier of the Progressive Conservative party, to which its supporters might have gravitated to express opposition to the McKenna government's bilingualism policies. As already noted in discussion of Progressive Conservative provincial fortunes in the West before 1957 and 1958, the federal party had been treated by default as the barometer of party values. In New Brunswick in these years the same attitude prevailed, only this time it was highly negative. There was a strong distaste for the Mulroney government and the Charlottetown Accord he had nurtured. In the House of Commons, Reform and the Bloc benefited from the demise of the Progressive Conservatives in 1993; in New Brunswick, the defeat of the Accord and then of the Mulroney government exhausted the main motivation behind COR.

In its linguistic composition, New Brunswick is more like the rest of Canada than any other province. More than that, its two traditional provincial parties, the parties of Confederation, aligned themselves after the late 1960s, as did their federal counterparts, with policies to promote unity and accommodation. In the United States the same two parties (Republicans and Democrats) are found in fifty-one jurisdictions. Such duplication is not found in all parts of Canada. In a number of provinces and for long periods of time, 'non-traditional' parties have dominated: Saskatchewan today, British Columbia until recently, Manitoba for decades, Alberta from 1921 to 1971. Opposition in the Canadian federation, even more so than in the Canadian House of Commons, follows diverse and unpredictable paths.

Nowhere more so than in Quebec. Canada is a double federation – of provinces and of founding cultures, English and French. If, as this chapter maintains, there is an oppositional dimension in the relationship of provinces to the federal government, as well as across the aisle in Parliament, then how much more textured is the relationship between Quebec and the federal government, where the ties that comprise the skein are multiplied? More is at issue here than governments, or legislatures, or political parties. Before the Quiet Revolution (and on some issues some of the time still), the Roman Catholic Church was the institution of influence par excellence. In the hierarchical society that was then Quebec, the Church dictated not everything but a great deal, from education policy to the conduct of Catholic trade unions to personal morality. The Church as a force of opposition was a prominent factor in Quebec political life, to a degree not seen elsewhere in Canada – but only to a degree. Many CCF-ers in Saskatchewan had no difficulty understanding the point about ecclesiastical opposition when it was directed at them as apostles of 'godless' socialism. Nor was the concept lost on adherents of sect, cult, and church in Alberta.[34] Half a century later, moral issues – which for some of their proponents assume the tone of crusades, for or against abortion or same-sex marriage being current examples – still roil politics, but they are no longer the property of hegemonic institutions. Labour, too, has moved out from under the direction of the Church, although this does not make organized labour any less of a non-legislative political force in Quebec today than in the past. Nor is Quebec unique in this respect. In 2010, Carole James, the NDP leader in British Columbia, was forced out of her position because 'she could tell that labour, the spine that ran down the back of the party, was not ready to fight to the end.'[35]

All of which is to say that Quebec is not unique – except where it is, which is to say in its political, institutional, and constitutional relationships with Ottawa. At one time, until the arrival of the Bloc, one of the dicta of Canadian politics was that Quebec sat on the governing side of the Commons. In other words, Quebec would rarely sit in opposition, an orientation that set it apart from western Canada, which through most of the Liberal regnum did sit in opposition. For a chapter devoted to examining opposition in the federation, the contrasting locations are important. A variation on the enunciated dictum was that the national party that embraced Quebec's members made retaining the support of the voters who sent them to Parliament a central concern of their government. Until the Quiet Revolution and, later, the federal government's official languages policy, this response to the presence of (French-speaking) Quebec MPs in government was no different from the response to other provinces' MPs, except for the fact that the universe in question was so large: there were more Quebec MPs in the governing caucus than those of any other province, and they remained there for so long. The convention of alternating individuals as leaders of the Liberal party, according to competency in one or the other of the country's (later) official languages, was viewed as one such overture, although it was the case that St Laurent and Trudeau, each of whom had one English-speaking parent, spoke flawless English.

Liberal party dominance and Pierre Trudeau's aversion to any suggestion of special status for Quebec in the Canadian federation set in motion currents that the parties in Parliament, and in Quebec, found difficulty navigating. From the moment he first appeared in national politics, Trudeau became a subject for attack, and often as not from Quebec Liberals. As early as 1967, Jean Lesage, then leader of the Quebec Liberal party, considered in many parts of Canada the father of the Quiet Revolution, and once a junior minister in the St Laurent government, charged Trudeau, who had denounced the two-nations theory, with being out of touch with the aspirations of the Quebec people. From the federal position, Lesage's attack amounted to an endorsement of the constitutional position of the province's Union Nationale premier, Daniel Johnson. Using an argument that was to be heard many times over the next forty years, Lesage pleaded that 'French-Canadians must stop fighting among ourselves.'[36] Phrased more theatrically, Johnson's Union Nationale successor as premier, Jean-Jacques Bertrand, argued that Quebec's political parties should join in '"a sacred union" to defend the province's interests.'[37]

The language is dramatic, the sentiment expressed less so. In their relationship with Ottawa, most political parties in most provinces share a common stand. When expressed in economic terms, which is what provincial interests usually become when provincial governments negotiate with the federal government, the partisan affiliation of the provincial politicians at the table is far less important than might be thought. Except in Quebec, where behind any policy matter stands, always, the nationalist question. In contrast to all other provinces, divisions in Quebec between government and opposition over relations with the federal government pervade every discussion. Starkly put, there is a double axis – nationalism distorts federalism. Parallelism between parties of the same name in the different spheres long ago disappeared. As a consequence, 'Quebeckers have lost any understanding of what a federation is and how federal parties work ... Indeed, for 20 years, the Bloc kept repeating that in federal politics, it's better to be in the opposition, since all governments (according to the Bloc) fail Quebec.'[38]

Within the province, the same resolute verdict might be rendered of both government and opposition. And for the same reason: the promotion and the defence of the separatist cause are never enough. The Parti Québécois is repeatedly fractured by internal divisions over how hard or soft its leadership is on the issue of sovereignty. Pauline Marois in 2011 and 2012, Lucien Bouchard a decade or so earlier, and even René Lévesque before that (as PQ leader and much earlier as a Liberal backbencher who supported the Fulton–Favreau constitutional amending formula of the early 1960s), experienced the sting of rebuke.[39] The federalist alternative (the Liberal party) is scarcely in a better position, since it attracts the same criticism from the same sources even while, at the same time, it carries the opprobrium that accompanies association with the Liberal Party of Canada, and more particularly leaders such as Trudeau and Chrétien. In the other provinces, attitudes about the constitution and especially Quebec's place in it may momentarily rise to the surface – consider, for instance, Newfoundland's Clyde Wells at the time of Meech Lake, or Lougheed, a decade earlier, who opposed the Victoria Charter's amending formula (accepted by eight provinces), which gave Ontario and Quebec each a veto over constitutional change – but they are neither anchored nor systemic. In that context, the Underhill version of Canadian opposition originating with the provinces (published on the eve of the Quiet Revolution), and the more recent Ibbitson version, are both wide of the mark; for both treat all opposition as the same, a generalization that can never be applied to Quebec for the reasons just cited.

Part of the answer for lack of discrimination lies in looking at executives rather than legislatures as the source of opposition: 'Her Majesty's Loyal Canadian Opposition,' says Underhill, 'really consists of ... governments.' For a long time – in the context of the present discussion, sixty-seven years – legislatures have lived under the lengthening shadow of their executives. It is for this reason that the twentieth-century anxiety about the decline of legislatures assumes added alarm when the part of it that sits opposite the government is the subject for analysis. Parliamentary federations compound the problem because they multiply the number of governments, a proliferation that is a source of worry to those concerned about issues of accountability and representation. Critics of executive federalism have arraigned this development on just these grounds, though seldom so epigrammatically as in the comment by former Liberal cabinet minister Roy MacLaren: 'In a real sense, the House was never the cockpit of the constitutional debate ... the centre was always elsewhere.'[40] Perhaps there is no alternative in light of the fact that Anglo-American federations offer little in the way of non-executive structures to promote cooperation or harmonization.

To cite the weakness of provincial legislatures, as opposed to executives, is to acknowledge the incongruity of parliamentary and federal institutions. Canada was the first country to marry the two arrangements, although in the terms of the Constitution Act, 1867, there is a strong disposition towards central as opposed to provincial jurisdiction. This is why Wheare called Canada 'quasi-federal in law.'[41] The signal feature of federalism to note is that it is – and was adopted for that reason – a technique, a mechanism, a device to meet a need, which, in every country where it has been employed, is the same: to promote unity or, conversely, to recognize diversity. Federalism and its component parts, such as executive federalism in Canada today, are pieces of that machinery. One piece long considered defective as an instrument of federalism is the Senate of Canada, one part of the country's tripartite Parliament, and the only part, it should be recalled, purposely designed by the Fathers of Confederation to serve the new federation. Federalism, if not the structure of the Canadian Senate, reflects the influence of the United States.

The Canadian House of Commons, its structure, procedures, and conventions, reflects more than the influence of Great Britain – it is the lower house of the British Parliament transposed to Canada and necessarily adapted to the conditions of British North America. A critical part of the Westminster model that crossed the Atlantic Ocean was the concept of opposition.[42] Opposition is integral to parliamentary government, and when it does not exist, as was the case in New Brunswick for a time, compensatory arrangements are required. Federalism is not an integral part of parliamentary government, as Senate reformers never tire of noting. Federalism and parliamentary institutions do not fit well. This is one of the main reasons for Canada's long history of third or protest parties; it is also one reason why relationships between partisans, even of the same party, at the two levels of jurisdiction are so often fraught with controversy. Because Liberals and Conservatives have historically been economical in respect to ideology, party unity is less likely to snap in times of tension. Such is not the case with a movement bound by ideology, as in the NDP. In 1993, when the NDP government of Ontario, led by Bob Rae, embarked on severe deficit-cutting measures, the federal party's finance critic, Steven Langdon, denounced it for diverging 'from the priorities and vision of the New Democratic Party.' Langdon was fired from his position by the national party leader, Audrey McLaughlin, because in making his attack, she said, 'he defied the wishes of the NDP caucus.'[43]

On rare occasions, provincial governments may even enable opposition to be carried to the doors of Parliament. In 1999, the government of Saskatchewan, then led by Roy Romanow, 'paid for ... farmers' tickets to Ottawa' so that they might protest what they saw as inadequate financial support for western agriculture from the federal Liberal government led by Jean Chrétien.[44] Three weeks later, following a provincial general election that saw the NDP reduced to a minority (and win fewer votes than the opposition Saskatchewan party), the NDP approached 'the Liberals, who held the balance of power with three seats, to form a workable majority.'[45] In the event, all three crossed the floor. A participant in these negotiations, and a key figure as well in the subsequent, aborted federal coalition strategy in 2008, was Brian Topp, the premier's deputy chief of staff.[46] In 1999, the Liberals had won 20 per cent of the provincial vote; in contests over the next decade, they still took more than 10 per cent, but by 2011 support had fallen to only 1 per cent. Arguably, coalition did not save – but rather destroyed – the Liberal party; nor did it help in the long term the NDP, who in 2011 lost their majority and were reduced to nine members in a chamber of fifty-eight. The three-way contests that had kept them in power evaporated with the disappearance of the Liberals and benefited the Saskatchewan party, which this time won 64 per cent of the votes. Thus, the most successful provincial wing of Canada's NDP was reduced to a corporal's guard just weeks before the NDP swept Quebec in the federal election. The effects of these disparate results for the party's future remain unclear at the beginning of 2012. The ever-shifting ambitions and disappointments of governments, opposition, and political parties (federal and provincial) are captured in the contrasting outcomes of these events separated by less than a decade. With apologies to Kipling: 'Who knows political opposition in Canada who only parliamentary opposition knows?'

8 Whither Parliamentary Opposition?

'Perhaps the British view of opposition retains its fascination,' writes Neville Johnson, 'because it is unusual in its clarity of definition.' Its 'failings,' he says, are an 'over-simplification of the issues,' 'exaggeration of adversarial relationships,' and 'a certain kind of brutal disregard for those parties which are not players in the big league. And after all there can only be two in any big league.'[1] Elizabeth May, leader of Canada's Green party, can speak to the subject of disregard. On a decision of a consortium of broadcasting executives, she was excluded from the televised leaders' debates in the 2011 campaign. The consortium had made the same decision during the 2008 campaign and then reversed itself after public criticism. In 2011, it held firm. Coupled with the regime that has regulated election expenditures for some decades and whose rationale from the outset was invariably articulated as 'levelling the playing field,' exclusion from the central event of the national campaign appears restrictive (May called it 'capricious' and 'arbitrary'). In a political system that has demonstrated a continuing regard for the needs of parties once they enter the legislature, there would seem to be substance in her case.[2] Except that at the time, the Greens lacked a seat in the House and were, as a result, in the unenviable position of being outside Parliament looking in.

From the perspective of a study of opposition, the issue is less whether the leader of a political party participates in a televised debate than it is the logic that leads to the decision to exclude. Of course, there are practical considerations that limit the number of participants in a debate; of course, not every leader of every movement who says she wants to take part can realistically be accommodated. Still, there was a discernible echo to the consortium's decision in 2011: not only of the one they had made (then reversed) in 2008, but also of the Liberal–PC–NDP troika's control of House affairs for decades before the collapse of the Mulroney government and the arrival of the Reform party and the Bloc Québécois. After the election results were in, Preston Manning surveyed the scene:

> Lest we forget … Westerners especially know what it is like to be 'out' of the federal power block … In the past, both of the major federal parties, the Liberals and the old Progressive Conservatives, bent over backward to accommodate Quebec's demands. In doing so, they increasingly alienated major segments of the electorate in the rest of the country. In the end, their Quebec supporters turned against them.[3]

The new political order Manning saw from the right bank of the Ottawa River was unusual in two respects: it embraced the West, and it excluded Quebec, and in both instances to an unprecedented degree. At the same time it was old, or at least traditional, in the sense that it was territorially defined. Certainly, there was no suggestion of an alternative world online. Perhaps this grounded orientation was to be expected from a leader who was identified with Senate reform; who promoted a movement with the slogan 'the West Wants In'; and who, as leader of the Reform party, had been unstinting in criticism of federal policies and politicians that coddled another region, Quebec. Still, his summary constituted an incomplete acknowledgment of what the election had wrought in legislative terms. For the first time in seven years, there was a majority government, and for the first time the Conservative Party of Canada enjoyed dominance. As important as that outcome might be in the long term, the immediate damage lay across the aisle in the cataclysmic results visited upon the Liberals and the BQ and in the unpredicted sweep of Quebec voters by the NDP. If, as theory maintains, one task of opposition in a parliamentary system such as Canada's is to present itself as the alternative executive, that was a duty no one seated opposite the government after the 2011 election was in a position to perform.

There was another feature to Manning's interpretation of politics in Canada post-2011: party was no longer the central idiom of his analysis. Rather he envisioned 'bridges [to Quebec, for instance] … built … by private-sector decision makers and provincial leaders on the grounds of economic and interprovincial relations.' The concern of parties, he maintained, should be with their long-term survival, measured less in electoral success than in healthy 'democratic infrastructure,' an obligation he placed upon the extra-legislative party to meet if the legislative elite neglected its duty. Absent in this analysis was reference to movement-like linkages, such as united proponents of the environment, civil liberties, or minority concerns and that pervaded the social media and attracted the attention of young Canadians. For that matter, there was no reference to mechanisms to ensure governmental accountability and responsiveness, values that had animated the Reform party's narrative in its early incarnation.[4] At that time, when the new party's object was to reform Parliament, election had constituted the sole criticism of representation; now Reform's successor, the Conservative Party of Canada, controlled Parliament.

There are several observations to be made about Manning's line of thinking, which essentially champions the democratization of politics. First, it is the prevailing view of a legion of reformers that there is too much power at the centre, which in the context of this discussion means Parliament and the parties in it, on both sides. Second, and fortuitously, modern attitudes come to the aid of advocacy by promoting the popular over legislative opinion: democracy is centrifugal in its reach, Parliament centripetal. There is no shortage of descriptive adjectives that make the point: open and closed, inclusive and exclusive, accommodating and non-accommodating. Except there is ambiguity with the last pair: Are they in the right order? Which is the more accommodating: the people or Parliament? Manning's summation of the 'new order' neatly, although unintentionally, epitomizes the central problem of Canadian politics today: the continuing erosion of parliamentary opposition. Arguably, there are other contenders for this unhappy distinction: the suffocating power of prime ministerial government is an obvious candidate. All the same, this chapter will argue that the perils of the opposition eclipse that and other sombre assessments.

The place to begin is with the mandate. In political terms this means that a legislator has the authority to make decisions because he or she has been authorized to do so by the action of the electorate. While the concept is not unknown in Canadian politics, its use is rare. The 'free trade election' in 1988 – with the Mulroney government for the agreement and the opposition parties against – is the exception that proves the rule, however often that example is cited to illustrate the concept. None the less, the mandate had a heyday during the period of the Progressives, when farmers' suspicion of backroom politics and the politicians of old parties who were part of them was most active.

The question on which that debate turned was the following: Was the MP a representative or a delegate? If the answer was the latter, then the constituents controlled the MP. The spoiler in this relationship was party discipline because of the distortion it might impose on the agent's carrying out the wishes of the principal. Two points need to be noted: first, the subject of the role of the MP is well-tilled ground (beginning, customarily, with Edmund Burke's 'Speech to the Electors of Bristol,' from 1774) and requires no elaboration here; and second, except for the farmers and their long-nurtured reserve of prairie anger at the federal government, the banks, the railways, and the elevator companies, references to delegate and mandate in matters of representation are few in the traditional texts on Canadian government, or elsewhere.[5] The reason for the silence is that if, as this and other studies of parliamentary government argue, there is no constituent power outside of Parliament, there is no controlling agent either. Central to refuting the mandate argument is the fact that the source of executive power provided for in the Constitution Act, 1867, rests not in representation, and thus the people, as found in the Constitution of the United States, but rather in the Sovereign (s.9).

In the political arena in Canada there has been no need to refute the theory of the mandate since no politician has advanced it in a concerted way, although, according to Conrad Black, Maurice Duplessis was fond of saying, after the Union Nationale had come to power in 1936, that 'the public has given me a mandate to judge the *ancien régime*.'[6] One exception to that generalization would be a party like the CCF in Saskatchewan, which, as a government, used provincial elections after 1944 as referendums on their policies and promises, most particularly those associated with the introduction of publicly supported hospital and medical care.[7] This suggests that the concept of the mandate has greater applicability to parties that are ideologically committed. In Great Britain after 1945, the subject arose more usually in contexts where Labour rather than Conservative party policy was being discussed.

Whether viewed as revival or original, the mandate has appeared in Canadian politics in recent years in elaborate form, with ramifications that touch numerous aspects of the constitution and its conventions, among the most affected being parliamentary opposition, itself a major component of the unwritten constitution. The source of the change, which might be attributed to the Conservative Party of Canada and the government formed by it under the leadership of Stephen Harper – but whose gestation this study maintains is older than that – is less easy to isolate than illustrations of its influence in present-day politics. Two publicized examples make the point. The first was the passage in 2012 of Bill C-18, the Marketing Freedom for Grain Farmers Act, which removed the monopoly enjoyed by the Canadian Wheat Board (CWB) over foreign marketing of western grain. The CWB was a creation of the Bennett government (Conservative) following the collapse of the cooperative pool organizations during the 1930s; the monopoly was a wartime measure pressed upon the reluctant King government (Liberal). Opposition to the CWB was part of a more general opposition to the grain-handling 'system,' which included freight rates and transportation infrastructure.[8] Long a divisive but simmering issue, the CWB assumed electoral significance when the Conservative party focused attention on its statutory monopoly. The Harper government promised 'marketing freedom,' and when C-18 was passed, it declared: 'We have delivered.'[9] To critics who said the government had to amend the act establishing the board before it could end the monopoly, the responsible minister's reply echoed the rationale of a mandate: 'The general election last spring [May 2011] served as the only vote ... needed since the vast majority of CWB ridings voted for Conservative MPs.'[10]

C-18 was the first piece of legislation enacted by the Harper majority government, and it was, said one reporter, 'pushed through Parliament with lightning speed, using every procedural trick in the book, including time allocation, closure and extended sessions of the ... committee on house and committee procedures.'[11] Opposition parties could not keep up. If at one time, the parliamentary method was 'to control government by talk,' Canadian opposition parties might be disposed to turn that maxim around and say that it has become control of talk by government.[12] Yet it would be a mistake to think that Parliament's problem today is the consequence of this or any other government alone. The fact is, no one seems interested in, or listens to, legislative debate anymore.

Very different in terms of its provenance was the long-gun registry, another statute from the Liberal years that the Conservative government was committed to abolishing. According to Ed Komarnicki, a Saskatchewan Conservative MP, the registry was 'a touchstone issue' in a double-geographic sense, 'symbolizing where the former Liberal government lost touch with Western Canadians and ordinary Canadians, and were passing something that pandered to a narrow view of Canadians in the East.'[13] When the Conservatives celebrated repeal of the registry with a cocktail party to which pro-gun lobbyists were invited, criticism followed. Bob Rae, interim leader of the Liberal party, called the event 'inappropriate.' 'All of us,' he said, 'should be sensitive to the feelings of Canadians across the country.'[14]

'Our point, exactly,' Conservatives might respond. The registry was not a political but 'an ivory tower' response to the Montreal Polytechnique massacre in 1989. (The phrase is Gary Breitkreiz's, another Saskatchewan Conservative MP and vocal critic of the registry.) Neither then nor more than two decades later could the opposition in Parliament (all but two of whom opposed repeal of the registry) bring their views to bear on the legislation at hand. Perhaps there was no alternative but to see the difference in legislative opinion as a product of regional divisions of opinion in Canada. Except that there was. There are two ways of viewing Parliament: as an institution that initiates, and as one that transmits. In the first incarnation, policy originates usually within the executive and the public service, and is debated, amended (where deemed necessary), and passed through the two chambers. During that process, intensity of feeling for or against a bill is moderated and support for it is generated through the methodical procedures of the respective chambers. While doubtless there will be disagreement expressed over the wisdom of specific policies, it is this initiating orientation of Parliament that explains the early (when compared, for instance, to the United States) passage of legislation that, among other matters, abolished capital punishment and permitted same-sex marriage. A second way of looking at Parliament is as a transmitting institution, one that communicates, through representation, constituency or, more generally, public opinion. The role assigned opposition varies significantly according to whether Parliament is viewed as a body that transmits or initiates. Generally, it may be stated that in the former, opposition contracts, and in the latter, it expands.

To return to the CWB and its monopoly over wheat and barley sales: from the Conservative government's perspective, the issue was not one for Parliament to decide but for the wheat farmers, and then not all of them but rather those who supported the government, as demonstrated in a general election. Although Parliament is the premier aural location of the nation's politics, legislative and political debate had no contribution to make to the outcome of the decision. As regards the gun registry, it was viewed as a policy that had been introduced to assuage aroused opinion that was geographically concentrated, then passed and maintained through imposition of party discipline. Its repeal had been pledged by the Conservatives, and by Reform before them, and when the Conservatives won a majority of seats in 2011, they saw themselves as possessing a mandate (sometimes the language spoke of 'legitimacy') to carry through on their promise. ·

The contradictory positions on where legitimacy lay in the Canadian political system were foreshadowed in controversy surrounding a Speaker's ruling in 1996 (see chapter 5). At issue was whether, after Lucien Bouchard left the House and Reform and the Bloc had equal numbers of seats, Reform should replace the BQ as the official opposition. The Liberal party accused Reform party members of contempt of Parliament for publicly lobbying the Speaker, Gilbert Parent, by means of a letter-writing campaign, to select them. Reformers circulated a leaflet in the largely francophone eastern Ontario riding of the Liberal whip (Don Boudria), saying that he '"backs separatists" because [he] isn't supporting Reform's bid to replace the Bloc as the official opposition.' Boudria called it 'harassment.' Stephen Harper, then an MP, retaliated, accusing Boudria of 'trying to quash both the rights of Reform MPs and Canadians to even express an opinion on the issue. If the government or the [S]peaker get too involved in that they could create a very serious crisis of confidence in Parliament and the country at large.' In the event, the Speaker sustained the Bloc. In retrospect, Harper's prediction on the eve of the debate that 'it could well lead to the most divisive Parliamentary debate that this country has ever seen' proved prophetic.[15]

The aborted Liberal–NDP coalition in 2008, with support from the Bloc and only two months after a general election that saw the Conservatives continue in power as a minority government, reprised in stark terms the dual claims to legitimacy – Parliament or the people – that the 1996 fight over who would form the official opposition had presaged. As one radio advertisement opposing the scheme phrased it: '[Dion] thinks he can take power without asking you, the voter. This is Canada. Power must be earned, not taken.'[16] How is one to reconcile protestations of loyalty to the Crown, which the Harper government has been at pains to make and which under constitutional principles established as long ago as 1688 means the Crown-in-Parliament, with such exhortations to Conservative supporters? A variation on the theme of legitimacy-from-the-people proved electorally effective in the election of 2011, when the Conservatives campaigned for a majority on the rationale that in its absence 'the three main opposition parties [Liberal, NDP, and BQ] will move "the next day" to form a coalition government to replace him.' A second-place party seeking a mandate to govern, the Tories pronounced as 'illegitimate.' A coda to this theme, one that leads back to the discussion of the mandate above – in this instance, to do the reverse of what Conservatives said their opponents would do – attributed to their opponents the following policy positions: '"anti-military"policies, "soft on crime," make it too easy to collect employment insurance premiums, and would raise taxes.'[17]

If governments are not made and unmade in the House of Commons – if, in other words, the House is not an electoral college as well as a deliberative assembly – what does this mean for the status of Parliament? More particularly, what does it mean for the official opposition, which derives its status from Parliament? One consequence of the transfer of government's legitimacy to the electorate outside Parliament, as opposed to perceiving that it is derived from the chamber, is a determination by government to appear inflexible in Parliament. Interference with the people's will in its transmission into statute law may not be permitted. Executive or prime ministerial dominance of politics is a familiar journalistic and academic lament, only now the critique is sharper. Because of controls in the form of use of closure and time limits on debate, as well as access to committees, the claim is made that Parliament is being suffocated. A reversal, this time of traditional roles, appears to be under way: government adopting an oppositional tone to those across the aisle, the opposition parties adopting the rhetoric of the mandate and complaining, for instance, that 'Harper did not raise the [Old Age Security changes] in the last election and ... he lacks a mandate to change the system.'[18] It is too early to ask but not unreasonable to wonder, perhaps, whether the public will accept, if not now then in the course of time, legislation that the opposition has had so little part in passing.

Following the election of 2011, in which the Liberal party was relegated by the voters to third place, that is, not government, not official opposition, but plain opposition, commentary ensued usually along the lines that the Liberals were a centre party and that there was no centre anymore. Some interpreters saw the disappearing Liberals as a parallel manifestation to the disappearing middle class. Conservatives in power and socialists as official opposition lent some credence to this analysis, although the concentration of the NDP in Quebec, where it had hardly before elected an MP, suggested the lingering influence of territory and deep dissatisfaction with the status quo therein. More than territory accounted for the results: the Conservatives had displaced the Liberals from many metropolitan seats whose populations were markedly ethnically heterogeneous. Still, territory was a pre-eminent factor for the parties in opposition, either as in the case of the NDP, which now drew two-thirds of their members from Quebec, or in the case of the Liberals, who had for decades dominated the national unity issue but no longer were capable of doing so. The Conservatives had secured their long-sought majority, yet they too had a territorial problem in the sense that they were viewed, from the vantage point of Quebec, as being antipathetic to the province. Several explanations might be offered for that conclusion; the Tories' promotion of monarchical symbols was one. Most critical, however, was the perception that the Conservatives did not share the belief, long ascribed to by Progressive Conservatives, NDPers, and Liberals, in the fundamental importance of national unity and in the cooperative, non-partisan promotion of that object.

That perception was accurate, as Reg Whitaker, author of *The Government Party: Organizing and Financing the Liberal Party of Canada, 1930–58* (1977), acknowledged in an obituary-like analysis titled 'Is the Government Party Over?':

> The new Conservative party under Stephen Harper is not another Mulroney-type brokerage party; instead it incorporates the conservative ideological drive of Harper's old party into a more flexible vote-seeking organization. While there are some brokerage elements in this approach, it resembles the Mike Harris Ontario party ... The sharp divisiveness that marked the Harris years was part of a wedge-politics strategy ... Current Conservative success in party financing from a broad base of small donors is a sign of their capacity to keep their base persistently energized.[19]

The importance of this interpretation lies in what it signifies for parliamentary opposition. On the one hand, there is the ideology. Canadians and their politicians are not used to it. There is no shortage of examples, although the one that follows, from Lawrence Martin's *Harperland: The Politics of Control*, makes the point in two respects. During the Liberal leadership campaign in 2006, Harper accused 'all the [Liberal] candidates' of being anti-Israeli. Bob Rae rejected the charge, calling it divisive, and went on to say that 'we cannot carry on politics in this country like this.'[20] Peter Newman concurs with that sentiment: in ideological communities, he says, 'adversaries are enemies,' and 'we cannot afford to be an ideological community.'[21] Of the Alliance party, one of the parents of the present Conservative Party of Canada, Joe Clark earlier made the same observation: 'It [was] an alliance of people who don't like other people.'[22] Ideological discourse – some would call it argument – uses exclusionary categories: at home, for instance, tough (or soft) on crime; abroad, behind (or against) Israel (or some other power). Foreign policy, which except in rare instances, such as Suez, was at one time non- or multi-partisan in advocacy, has become morally charged and often militarily clothed. On the other (non-ideological) hand, there is the commitment to permanent campaigning – a form of trench warfare, if the metaphor is to the Great War, or to an arms race that never ceases, if the reference is to the Cold War. Whichever allusion obtains, the focus is usually electoral and the tone bellicose. Battle analogies are not misleading. The continuities of Canadian politics have been lost and, with them, the assumption that Parliament is the centre of political attention.

In the interest of balance, it needs to be stated that the divisiveness of which Bob Rae complains originates not solely in the behaviour of one political party. As a case in point, some members of the Liberal party seem unable, in Andrew Coyne's words, 'to acknowledge the legitimacy of the Conservative government. They are not merely a government whose policies some find disagreeable ... They are, quite literally, anti-Canadian.' At issue, according to this analysis, is the putative 'need for Quebec as a counterbalance.'[23] If there is truth in this analysis, then it is only a partial one. The Liberal party's problem is that, since the days of Mackenzie King, it has been constructed and operated wholly for the purposes of government; the raison d'être of the Conservative party (and its antecedents) has been to oppose. In that last assignment, the Conservative party was not often successful, when measured by the frequency with which it displaced the Liberals, but that was its parliamentary lot, none the less.

Such was not the destiny of the CCF or NDP. They occupied a position unknown to the theory of parliamentary government: they were confined to permanent opposition. The alternative government role that theory assigns the official opposition was denied them. That of course was the fate of Social Credit too, but Social Credit was a party without great expectations in federal politics. Earlier still, the Progressive party had spurned the silver medal of official opposition when it was on offer, and then disappeared within a decade. The socialists were another matter. They sought power federally and they secured power provincially, but that was as far as it went. The results of the 2011 election, which made the NDP the official opposition, presented the possibility for the first time that it could cross the aisle to sit as government. The probability of that happening remains a subject for speculation. The history of the parliamentary party has yet to be written; when it is, doubtless the relationship between the parliamentary party and the provincial parties will be an important component of the story. The tension between the Saskatchewan and parliamentary parties has been mentioned elsewhere in this study. The source of the strain arose from the contrast between the provincial NDP, which followed a path of conviction politics, and the parliamentary party, which despite periodic jousting with the (usually governing) Liberals was at its heart a supporter of consensus politics.

The principal issue that required consensus was the preservation of national unity; to that end, Lewis and Broadbent, in company with Stanfield, Clark, and Mulroney, joined the Trudeau Liberals in seeking to accommodate forces for change while maintaining constitutional and territorial integrity. Of course, there were strong policy differences over how to achieve those conflicting objectives. The Meech Lake and Charlottetown Accords elicited condemnation from Trudeau because of the special treatment they provided Quebec; the failure to secure provincial and popular support for the respective accords attracted comparable criticism from others, for example, David Peterson, premier of Ontario (1985–90). Preston Manning, when leader of the Reform party, and Stephen Harper consistently did not align themselves with their fellow party leaders in the unity enterprise. As a result, the dissolution of the long parliamentary consensus ensued. However that decision might be judged from the perspective of consociational politics, it set the leaders of the Reform and Conservative parties apart from their peers on an issue that had been viewed for nearly half a century as of paramount importance. Thus, when the Conservatives formed a government in 2008, they brought not an alternative government – as the theory of opposition would have it – so much as an alternative form of national politics.

Reformers and the Harper Conservatives saw Quebec as a vested interest of the Liberals during that party's hegemony, one around which other parties coalesced. In retrospect, it might be more accurate to describe preoccupation with national unity as a vested idea, one that was central to the party's sense of itself and to the province's continuation as part of Canada. While the new parties of the right held other policy ambitions – such as, for instance, freedom from state control – opposition to what they perceived as concessions to Quebec was a prominent part of their platform. In itself, that is not an unpatriotic stance, although it brings with it practical complications for a country that is constitutionally bilingual and whose civic practices acknowledge that fact. The difficulty with the Conservatives' position on concessions to Quebec is that concession making is the essence of parliamentary government in a country as diverse as Canada. That is why there are comparatively few divisions in Parliament – the details of bills are worked out in committee. Here is Parliament in its role as mediator. Divisiveness and incivility in debate in the House ultimately ensure agreement on the foundation of society. If the opposition does not control what happens in Parliament, because it usually has smaller numbers than the government, how then does it prevail? The answer is, as Macdonald recognized from the outset, 'in the long run.' Perspective is an essential parliamentary virtue: 'Apart from seeking to demoralize the government and lower it in the public estimation, the Opposition performs no other vital parliamentary function.'[24] That is because opposition is played out almost totally within the parliamentary dimension.

People do not elect an opposition any more than they elect a government, although when it comes to forming the latter, that common parliamentary provenance is in danger of disappearing in the eyes of the voters. From where they stand, there is a government – which they see themselves as having chosen – made up of ministers, the most dominant of whom is the prime minister, and there is a legislature. Members of that last body may come from different parties, but, irrespective of affiliation, the majority of them think their most important job is to serve their constituents. A counter-argument may be made that the time and attention demanded of constituency service undermines a member's legislative function. In any case, prime ministerial dominance, reinforced by threat of the party whip, paradoxically renders the parliamentary party to the right of the Speaker apolitical for legislative purposes. In this vacuum, parliamentary opposition, which needs the oxygen provided by government activity to survive, grows weaker as time for debate is rigorously allocated or cut off altogether. In consequence, opportunities for Parliament to resolve the conflicting interests of national life shrink. Although the subject was the Harper government's non-negotiable stance on the always contentious issues of Canadian federalism, the succinct criticism it elicited from the premier of Quebec, Jean Charest, had wider import: 'In a democracy, you can't just say, I won, you lost, I'm going to do what I want.'[25]

Roy Romanow, premier, leader of the opposition, and member of the Saskatchewan legislature for a combined total of thirty-four years, says that 'people no longer pay attention.' The Assembly in that province is a 'mere shell to what it was.'[26] The last quotation originated from an interview; but almost the exact same words were used by a Conservative MP in a different context: '[The House] has become an empty shell of a legislature and such a weak legislature.'[27] Which came first, one wonders: lack of attention or lack of attraction? Only scandals attract attention now, and even then, people 'have no confidence in Parliament to get to the bottom of [them] ... The institutions we trust to hold government to account in this country are so weak – well, do we trust them anymore? ... People have so lost confidence in these other institutions that a public inquiry becomes almost their fallback response.'[28] Or at least, an officer of Parliament, who is viewed as being independent; so independent, indeed, that in the case of Elections Canada, for example, it 'does not comment on its investigations and refuses to confirm or deny any element of its probes in a bid to stay out of the political process.'[29] Admirable in the abstract, independence is politically enervating, which in this context is its whole point. Opposition is judged to be without influence because it is partisan and, therefore, partial. When Robert Walsh, the eminent Law Clerk and Parliamentary Counsel, retired in 2011, he articulated a more optimistic view: 'The beauty of the parliamentary system is that everything devolves to a political decision. Ultimately, it's all politics.'[30] Recourse to independent officers, to statutory codes of conduct, to rigidity in procedure argues for a less benign verdict, at least as to the condition of parliamentary opposition at the present time.

How does Parliament make up for what it has lost? Or is this the wrong question? In politics, the retrospective view is always that the past is not only another country but also a better one: more civil, more rational, less personal, less partisan. This is a selective interpretation: 'John Diefenbaker tormenting Lester Pearson every step of the way, that was no walk in the park.' Here is an assessment with which a participant observer, a former Speaker of the House, Peter Milliken, concurs and amplifies: 'Exactly, and the yelling in the House at the time was quite vigorous, as I recall.'[31] Yet studies of cross-party attitudes and personal recollections testify to alternative behaviour, too. When it took too much time to return every weekend to constituencies outside of the St Lawrence heartland, MPs of different parties mixed socially and established long-term personal relationships.[32] Politicians who establish in public and academic minds reputations as partisan warhorses may belie that characterization: Mitch Hepburn, for instance, sent to Leslie Frost just before his maiden speech 'a nice little note: "Good luck on your first big try"'; and Ross Thatcher, Liberal premier but once a CCF

MP, crossed the floor to the opposition side of the Saskatchewan chamber to tell Roy Romanow that he was 'a young legislator with promise' and that he should not repeat Thatcher's mistakes, as in kicking the legislature's doors for the benefit of the media during the tumultuous medicare debate: 'I never lived down the reputation I earned as a tough guy from this incident.'[33] Jet travel, constituency demands, high turnover once in the House, and rudimentary political involvement before nomination combine now to discourage association across the aisle or even within caucus. The sixty-five former MPs surveyed in the Samara study, *The Accidental Citizen?* (2011), 'were not raised on politics' and 'considered themselves outsiders [to Parliament],' but, say the survey's authors, possessed 'strong community connections and experiences.'[34] Surprisingly, because it is so rarely noted, one of the bonds throughout much of the last century in Parliament was military. A large percentage of members on both sides of the House were war veterans or had children who had enlisted. Many of the latter, including Jimmy Gardiner's eldest son in 1942, died in combat. For a long time, a military background was a positive feature in a candidate's résumé, as when Ellen Fairclough pressed George Drew, the PC leader in 1951, to support Gordon Churchill's nomination in Winnipeg, because he had 'a distinguished record in two world wars.'[35]

There have been more leaders of the official opposition than there have been prime ministers. On balance, prime ministers last a long time in office in Canada. Leaders of the official opposition tire of waiting for their turn, or their supporters lose confidence in their ability to lead them across the floor. Since 1993, there have been three prime ministers (Chrétien, Martin, and Harper). In the same period, there have been eleven leaders of the official opposition (Bouchard, Duceppe, Gauthier, Manning, Day, Harper, Hill, Graham, Dion, Ignatieff, and Layton). In addition, there have been five interim or acting leaders of the official opposition. The conclusion to be drawn from this disparity, and from earlier comparable numbers, is unclear and also uninformative. Many of these individuals had been on the political scene, although not in a leadership position or even in Parliament, for some time. Mr Harper is one example, Mr Manning another. The periodization of parliamentary politics according to who is leader, especially on the opposition side of the chamber, conveys a misleading sense of impermanence. Counterexamples would be Joe Clark, who was in Robert Stanfield's office when Stanfield was leader of the official opposition, and leader of the young PCs before that; or Brian Mulroney proffering advice on the subject of language and national unity to John Diefenbaker through a PC stalwart in Quebec nineteen years before securing a seat in the House.[36] It is as if there was a political dimension behind and out of sight of the public one.

In the Progressive Conservative party, the long reach of John Diefenbaker could be seen right up to Joe Clark's opposition to the merger of Reform and the PC party. There is a long, and sometimes damaging, echo in Canadian party politics, proof of this being the fate of John Turner, who when in opposition dissented from the Liberal party orthodoxy of Trudeau and Pearson. Turner's 'curse,' says his biographer, 'was to be forever forging compromises over complex issues in an ideologically divided caucus.'[37] The party on whom the past hung least heavy was the NDP:

> With none of the old guard in the House of Commons there was no continuity between the founding fathers and the handful of troublesome offspring ... The product of this almost classic confrontation of generations was a widening rift between executive and caucus, and a growing determination on the part of the caucus to emphasize those aspects of its behaviour that clearly were not the CCF norm.[38]

The NDP benefited immensely from the policies that led to the institutionalization of the parliamentary parties – policies that began to appear in the first decade after its birth. In time, the provincial wings of the party came to exert less influence over their Ottawa men and women than had been the case in the old CCF. True, by the end of the twentieth century the NDP had a past, but it was one largely defined by its four-decade-old federal provenance, especially in the form of support for the package of national unity policies initiated, sequentially, by the leaders of the then two major parties. It was that past, symbolized by the Clarity Act, subjecting a future Quebec referendum on separation to federal oversight, that Jack Layton promised in the 2011 general election to reopen and review.

PART FOUR

Conclusion

9 The Problem of Parliamentary Opposition Today

The outcome of the general election in 2011 – the new Conservative Party of Canada forming a majority government, the NDP for the first time the official opposition, and the Liberal party reduced to mere opposition status – complicates any generalization to be made about opposition in Canadian politics. In a matter of only a few months the backdrop of personalities and parties totally altered. That transformation cannot be ignored, but at the same time it cannot be treated as the logical outcome of a chain of events. Were that true, then somebody might have predicted an election outcome that approximated the final result. Nobody did, or at least not until a few days before the actual vote. All of which is to say that the events of 2011 and 2012, which saw the Liberals and the NDP change their positions opposite the government and both, for separate reasons, spend the next ten months under interim leaders, destroyed the customary sense of continuity in Canadian politics. None the less, although its causes might be different, the disorganization and weakness of the opposition after the 2011 election was not a new phenomenon.

The condition of opposition is the test of the health of Parliament – Lord Campion labels it *'prima facie* evidence.'[1] For that reason, there can scarcely be a more important topic for discussion in Canadian politics; except that politics associated with the great institutions of government are for many people today an activity of the past. Voters have become agnostics about Parliament. Because the kind of power that changes lives no longer is seen to rest in the hands of legislators, the public have small expectations of politicians and what they may do. There is some foundation for that low esteem:

In the Martin minority and the first Harper minority more than half of the opposition day motions were actually adopted by the House, usually against the wishes of the government ... It is perhaps satisfying to the sponsors and to the opposition parties to have their supply motions adopted by the House of Commons but what is the average citizen to think when he reads that Parliament has voted to do something and then nothing is done?[2]

That piece of evidence might be disputed since it refers to periods of minority government. It is open to question, however, whether the public makes a clear distinction between majority and minority situations when it comes to passing judgment on government. In any case, the sense of impotence attributed to politicians originates in more sources than that. The force of ideas and the range of interests are now subject less to political organization and control than they are to the channelling influence of (among other factors) the global economy, information technology, and social media. Legislative politics in general and opposition in particular are treated as bordering on the superfluous.

These comments relate to opposition in Canadian, and not British or any other Westminster-styled system. In fact, in the twenty-first century, the Westminster model is of deceptive application to Canada, as the subject of opposition illustrates. A relevant example is the shadow cabinet, which in Britain 'since the 1950s has in fact turned into a full-scale "shadow government,"' with a 'whole set of sophisticated rules and conventions designed to sharpen [its] organizational profile.'[3] This has not happened in Canada, where cabinet is a federalized body with ministers chosen for reasons of territorial representation as well as administrative competence; and where, historically, turnover of Commons members is high and thus continuity from the opposition to the government side of the chamber is unpredictable. In this country, there are opposition 'critics,' who may or may not, when the occasion arises, make the transition across the aisle. In any case, the keystone concept of opposition as the alternative government is at best a theory that lacks support in literal practice. While the capability of the leader and the standing of the party in the House are central factors in evaluating the stature of any specific opposition and thus make generalizations suspect; still, comments by James Gillies, an unsuccessful PC leadership candidate in 1976, on that party's then 'shadow cabinet' continue to carry authority, notwithstanding the influence that public affairs coverage of Parliament Hill offers today's opposition:

He termed the concept of the 'shadow cabinet' almost a joke, saying that in the period prior to the 1974 election, when the Conservatives thought themselves to be close to governing the country, there was literally no organization of members to act as an executive wing of the government and no continuing record of the party's basic position on issues ... The only ingredient holding the party together in the House is a shared dislike of the Liberals.[4]

Placing to one side, if that is possible, the partisan scheming that goes with opposition – Doug Richardson, John Turner's one-time principal secretary, coined the maxim that 'the problems of the leader of the official opposition begin and end in caucus'[5] – few leaders of the opposition, Diefenbaker excepted, appear to have either enjoyed the position or used it to partisan advantage. More common appears to be Roy MacLaren's view that 'few things are more boring than Opposition.'[6] By contrast, Graham Fraser says of Quebec politics that Lévesque 'was not comfortable in opposition [but used the opportunity] to think about issues that had been put aside during the intensity of day-to-day government.'[7] The difference between Quebec City and Ottawa may be explained by the fact that the PQ – like the Quebec Liberals after 1960 – was more programmatic in its approach to politics and government than the Progressive Conservatives ever were. It needs recalling that the fully formed shadow cabinet at Westminster developed after the first Labour government to command a majority in Parliament, under Clement Attlee, was defeated and returned to opposition in 1951.

The dullness of opposition for federal Liberals stemmed in part from unfamiliarity with the position: between 1920 and the end of the century, they were in power three-quarters of the time. These were the years of the Liberal ascendancy and, except for the governments of John Diefenbaker and Brian Mulroney (and the minority Liberal government of 1972 to 1974), periods of weak and divided opposition. When coupled with co-optation of the opposition parties by Liberal or PC governments on national unity strategies, the result was nothing less than a façade of opposition, until the Bloc and Reform made their appearance in 1993. After the CPC under Stephen Harper formed a government in 2004, the stature of the opposition did not improve. The Liberals appeared to be so eager to return to power that they forgot (or refused) to play the role the election results demanded of them; at least, that was one interpretation of the coalition imbroglio. Once more, there were parliamentary critics without influence. For decades, Canadians had watched oppositions of different partisan hue flail and bluster. The result, perhaps to be expected after such long inculcation, was a stereotyped impression of those politicians facing the government, one that ended up acquiring substance in the public's mind. Certainly, there was no longer the immense respect for opposition that had been evident in Canada and other Western democracies in the years immediately following the Second World War.

The loss of opposition power was felt before it was confirmed. Here is one explanation for the rise of officers of Parliament. The relationship between ministers and officers, and between officers and Parliament – whose agents they are – is fraught with uncertainty. In the view of some observers, the essential feature that distinguishes the officers has broadened – from protection against political influence to separation from Parliament. It needs to said, of course, that this is not solely a Canadian phenomenon; Bruce Ackerman of Yale Law School has written about what he calls 'constrained parliamentarianism' to describe the post-war practice, in Westminster-style legislatures and elsewhere, of 'insulating sensitive functions from political control.'[8]

Take as an example the position of chief electoral officer (CEO), which according to the Elections Canada website 'was created in 1920 by the Dominion Elections Act. The CEO is appointed by a resolution of the House of Commons. He or she reports directly to the Parliament and is thus completely independent of the government of the day and all political parties.'[9] Yet in the controversy occasioned by fraudulent phone messages (robo-calls) aimed at disrupting the vote in multiple constituencies during the 2011 election, the CEO found his independence less complete than that description implied. At one point, the House voted 283 to 0 to pass a motion to give the CEO additional investigative powers; at another, the CEO 'strongly hinted that he would like to be called before a parliamentary committee so he [could] offer more detail about the allegations received'; but then the parliamentary secretary to the prime minister allowed only that 'the Conservatives [were] *willing to let* elections boss Marc Mayrand appear before a Commons committee and brief MPs on the matter.'[10] In this combination of elements, there was a degree of isolation (Ackerman would say 'constraint') in the CEO's position, with the result that independence may (as here) function as a wall between politicians and their agents, and, in time, between politicians and the people. Inevitably, calls were voiced for an 'extra-parliamentary investigation,' analogous to the Gomery Inquiry a decade earlier, into charges related to the sponsorship program during the Chrétien and Martin governments. The reason for such a predictable response, Andrew Coyne believes, was 'the public's loss of confidence in elected institutions.'[11]

A conclusion is supposed to summarize, provide a denouement to a story. Yet when the topic is legislative opposition in Canada, the better analogy is the episodic serial, which has neither a clear line of development nor an end to its plot. Rephrased, the focus that a parliamentary opposition ought to provide is missing. In its place, technology, in the form of the Internet for example, disperses interests and opinions across a spectrum rather than concentrating them on politicians across the aisle. The democratic accessibility of modern technology distracts from the conduct traditionally associated with party leaders as they orchestrate debates in the House of Commons. As recent as two decades ago, a Canadian observer could say with some assurance of accuracy, as Alexandra Kelso does of the British House of Commons, that 'the structured institutional context ensures that elite actors in both the governing party and the main opposition party [that is, Conservative and Labour] will share similar outlooks with regards [sic] to creating an efficient House of Commons.'[12] The institutional reforms to the Commons, discussed in chapter 4, bear out that claim; and it was because of this reciprocal outlook that a sense of what might be called political elasticity existed, with parties in the House moving from government to opposition and back, as electoral and political fortunes decreed. The assertion of a mandate, in company with an electoral calculus to determine legitimacy, have replaced adjustment with confinement to one or the other side of the aisle. To the detriment, one might say, of government and opposition seeing themselves as parts of a shared community.

It is the dissolution of the sense of an institutionalized community that threatens opposition, which depends upon the parliamentary environment to thrive. Only in this forum can opposition fulfil the dual role of auditor assigned to it: as listener and as holder to account. Parliamentary government functions by way of consensus; in Canada in the last four decades of the last century, national unity too depended – in the eyes of the Liberal, PC, and NDP leaders in Parliament – upon parliamentary consensus. That assumption unravelled after 1993, when the Reform party appeared in Parliament. Reform was opposed to what has been described, in another context, as 'the anaemia of consensus,' which resulted in a 'blurring' of the politics of national unity as well as fuzziness in other policy areas. In place of consensus, it aligned itself instead with 'the spirit of majority voting.'[13] Under the

Canadian electoral system, majority in practice often means plurality, that is, more votes than anyone else. It was this kind of arithmetic that informed the rationale for Reform's opposing the Bloc as official opposition in 1996, and for the CPC's response to the Liberal–NDP aborted coalition in 2008.

The dichotomy between inside and outside Parliament arises in ways distinct from the question – which this book considers paramount and will discuss in the concluding paragraphs below – of where constituent power lies. For instance, Bernard Manin has developed the concept of audience democracy, which addresses both the decline of legislative institutions and the proliferation of alternative publics:

> Manin [says one scholar] points to the ceding of power from the political party to opinion polls, consultants, non-partisan mass media, and political leaders. Audience democracy is seen as involving insecure elites lacking a significant and stable core of support, autonomous voters, and television-mediated leaders. The elites chosen tend to be 'media experts' rather than 'political activists.' In this view, parties are seen merely as election machines ... and their policy role is minimal, while individual members are simply parts of this machine.[14]

Writing of Canada in particular, John Ibbitson has divided its politics into two parts, characterized, on the one hand, by 'insiders who have the capacity and energy to fight and remain engaged in the system, and [on the other] outsiders who simply walk away out of frustration and disappointment.'[15] To what extent do these bifurcations coincide, and thus reinforce one another?

While this is a question of peripheral relevance to opposition in Canada, it does allude once more to a factor central to its present condition – fragmentation. Especially is this relevant, when coupled to contradictory claims as to the source of political legitimacy – and, in a Westminster-style system where the political is so often deemed constitutional, constitutional legitimacy. Is that source the people, or is it Parliament? The theory and practice of opposition depend upon the wholeness of the House of Commons: government belongs to Parliament, and not to the people. This is the logic that explains the doctrine of ministerial responsibility, as well as the difficulties experienced when attempts have been made to broaden enforcement of that responsibility. The thesis that there is a constituent power external to Parliament offers no role for opposition. Yet opposition speaks for the people as faithfully as government does. In the words of (then plain) Ivor Jennings: 'The one permits the other to govern because the second permits the first to oppose.'[16] If Parliament has no role, what does being an MP mean? If Parliament possesses no corporate personality, what does privilege signify? How to explain Louis Riel's expulsion – twice?

One symbol of the evanescence of the non-government component of Parliament is the failure to provide, for the third time (as of the first session of the Forty-First Parliament, February 2012), for the right of reply to the speech from the throne. Customarily, there is an obligation to have a confidence vote early in a session. While a vote on the budget, for example, might be considered an alternative, the proceedings of the chamber are not meant to operate in this way. The foundation of Canada's constitution, as of Britain's, is the Queen-in-Parliament. The government's program, which is to say Her Majesty's Canadian government's program, normally comes first. Not to proceed in this sequence is disrespectful of the Crown – a surprising lapse by a government that otherwise conscientiously promotes the symbolism of monarchy. Is this a transformation of the parliamentary system in Canada, or only inadvertence? There is no requirement that Canada's parliamentary procedure follow the British. Perhaps deviation with regard to the right to reply is only a step towards distinctive Canadian practice; if so, it is unacknowledged.

In any case, of what significance is this deviation? Little significance, it might be said, because the Crown in Canada is treated not as the embodiment of the constitution but rather as a non-partisan umpire, an elevated officer of Parliament, to resolve partisan differences when they threaten to get out of hand. This is a role that the present sovereign in Great Britain never plays, because British politicians have been scrupulous in shielding the Queen from such involvement. Here is another difference in constitutional practice on either side of the Atlantic. It is one that deserves attention in this discussion, for, as noted in chapter 1, a healthy opposition depends upon the neutrality of the monarch – and vice versa. The Constitution of the United States provides for a separation of institutions and, except for checks in the form of, for example, the presidential veto and congressional override of the veto, a separation of powers. In a constitutional monarchy such as Canada's, there are no vetoes or supermajorities. Instead, there is loyal opposition.

Lack of understanding of parliamentary opposition, whether it occurs in government, among MPs, or with the public, presents a serious challenge for the achievement of responsible and responsive government in Canada. The source of that problem is more than one government, of whatever political party, and more than government alone. As a first step, resolution of the predicament depends upon clarifying the source of constituent power – is it, in short, where all theories of parliamentary government say it is, the Crown-in-Parliament? If it is elsewhere, that must be unequivocally stated and agreed to. Otherwise, Canada is faced with a constitution embracing irreconcilable principles as they affect the House of Commons: members owing fidelity to their respective constituents, or to their sovereign – it cannot be both.

Notes

Abbreviations in the Notes

AC	Appeal Court (Judicial Committee of the Privy Council)
APSR	*American Political Science Review*
CAR	*Canadian Annual Review of Public Affairs*
CBR	*Canadian Bar Review*
CHR	*Canadian Historical Review*
CJEPS	*Canadian Journal of Economics and Political Science*
CJPS	*Canadian Journal of Political Science*
CNF	*Canadian News Facts*
CPA	*Canadian Public Administration*
CPR	*Canadian Parliamentary Review*
DAC	Diefenbaker Archives Canada
DHOC	*Debates of the House of Commons*
DLAUC	*Debates of the Legislative Assembly of United Canada*
DP	Diefenbaker Papers
GP	Gardiner Papers
HT	*Hill Times*
JCS	*Journal of Canadian Studies*
JPPL	*Journal of Parliamentary and Political Law*
LRC	*Literary Review of Canada*
NP	George Nowlan Papers
NWP	Norman Ward Papers
PSQ	*Political Science Quarterly*
SAB	Saskatchewan Archives Board
SCR	Supreme Court Reports
SLL	Saskatchewan Legislative Library

Preface

1   Jean Blondel, 'Political Opposition in the Contemporary World,' *Government and Opposition* 32, no. 4 (1997): 462–86 at 463.
2   *DHOC*, 20 March 1922, 214.
3   The single previous major study of opposition in Canada is by Thomas A. Hockin, *The Loyal Opposition in Canada: An Introduction to Its Ideal Roles and Their Practical Implementation for Representative and Responsible Government*. Written as a PhD dissertation in 1966, it was never published. From the perspective of the present work, the date of the Hockin thesis is significant because the study appeared before the institutionalization of political parties, a development of determinative influence, it will be argued, for the function of opposition in Canada's Parliament in the last half century.

Chapter One

1   Don Rowat, 'Our Referendums Are Not Direct Democracy,' *CPR* 21, no. 3 (1998): 25–7.
2   Katherine May, 'Parliamentary Privilege Used as "Sword" Against Citizens, Political Experts Warn,' *Ottawa Citizen*, 24 April 2008, A1.
3   Daniel Leblanc and Campbell Clark, 'Harper Threatens Election for Ottawa to "Function,"' *Globe and Mail*, 15 August 2008, 1, 4.
4   John Wilson, 'In Defence of Parliamentary Opposition,' *CPR* 11, no. 2 (1988): 26–31.
5   Anthony Trollope, *Phineas Finn*, vol. II (London: Geoffrey Cumberlege: Oxford University Press, 1949), 163.
6   R.M. Punnett, *Front-Bench Opposition: The Role of the Leader of the Opposition, the Shadow Cabinet, and Shadow Government in British Politics* (New York: St Martin's Press, 1973), 4.
7   Archibald S. Foord, *His Majesty's Opposition, 1714–1830* (Oxford: Clarendon Press, 1964), 37.
8   W. Ivor Jennings, *Parliament* (Cambridge: Cambridge University Press, 1939), 159.
9   Lord Campion, 'Parliament and Democracy,' in Lord Campion et al., *Parliament: A Survey* (London: George Allen and Unwin, 1952), 9–36 at 29.
10   Punnett, *Front-Bench Opposition*, 79.
11   DAC, DP, 334.1, 08811, file: Material for Questions in the House of Commons, January–May 1957, Sevigny to Diefenbaker, 21 January 1957.
12   Preston Manning, 'How To Remake the National Agenda,' *National Post*, 13 February 2003, A18.

13 Preston Manning, 'Parliament, Not Judges, Must Make the Laws of the Land,' *Globe and Mail*, 16 June 1998, A23.

14 John Ibbitson, 'Commons Fully Backs Deployment,' *Globe and Mail*, 22 March 2011, A17.

15 Ralph Heintzman, 'The Educational Contract,' *JCS* 14, no. 2 (1979): 1–2/142–5 at 2.

16 DAC, DP, MG01/1X/B/129, file: Clark, Joe, 1964–65, Van Dusen to Clark, 20 March 1964.

17 Ibid., Clark to Diefenbaker, 7 April 1964.

18 SAB, NWP, A526/184(2), file: Correspondence, 1972–76, Ward to Stanfield, 4 November 1974.

19 'Stop Knifing Clark, Usually Mild Stanfield Advises Dief,' *Globe and Mail*, 23 September 1977, 10.

20 Bob Rae, *From Protest to Power: Personal Reflections on a Life in Politics* (Toronto: Viking Penguin, 1996), 78.

21 DAC, DP, 334, file: Ellen Fairclough, March 1957, Speech to United Rubberworkers, 'The Role of the Opposition in Government,' 08763-08770 at 08768 and 08769.

22 Walter Gray, 'Stanfield in First House Vote Joins Liberals to Defeat Motion,' *Toronto Daily Star*, 18 November 1967, 7.

23 'Stanfield Acquiescence Explained,' *CNF*, 16–30 June 1970, 480.

24 Gordon Aiken, *The Backbencher: The Trials and Tribulations of a Member of Parliament* (Toronto: McClelland and Stewart, 1974), 139; Paul Litt, *Elusive Destiny: The Political Vocation of John Napier Turner* (Vancouver: UBC Press, 2011), 80.

25 'Interview: George McIlraith,' *CPR* 7, no. 4 (1984): 21–5 at 24.

26 Roger Graham, *Arthur Meighen*, vol. III, *No Surrender* (Toronto: Clarke, Irwin and Co., 1965), 94.

27 Norman Ward, ed., *A Party Politician: The Memoirs of Chubby Power* (Toronto: Macmillan of Canada, 1966), 72.

28 John Kendle, *John Bracken: A Biography* (Toronto: University of Toronto Press, 1979), 229.

29 Geoffrey Stevens, *Stanfield* (Toronto: McClelland and Stewart, 1973), 198.

30 The Canadian Collection, 'Show Time: The Decline of the Canadian Parliament,' video (Magic Lantern Communication, 1993).

31 John English, *The Worldly Years: The Life of Lester Pearson*, vol. II: *1949–1972* (Toronto: Alfred A. Knopf Canada, 1992), 215.

32 See, for example, C.E.S. Franks, 'The "Problem" of Debate and Question Period,' in *The Canadian House of Commons: Essays in Honour of Norman Ward*, ed. John C. Courtney (Calgary: University of Calgary Press, 1985), 1–19.

33 R. MacGregor Dawson, *The Government of Canada*, 5th edition, revised by Norman Ward (Toronto: University of Toronto Press, 1970).

34 SAB, NWP, A526/679, Correspondence 1979–83(1), Ward to Shirley Spafford, n.d.

35 See 'Toward a More Responsible Two-Party System,' *APSR* 44, no. 3, Pt 2, Supplement (September 1950): 1–14 at 1–2; and Austin Ranney, 'Toward a More Responsible Two-Party System: A Commentary,' *APSR* 45, no. 2 (June 1951); 488–99 at 495 and 498. A. Lawrence Lowell, *Essays on Government* (Boston: Houghton Mifflin, 1897), [itals. in original].

36 'Clark Would Free Committees,' *CNF*, 1–15 April 1979, 2116; Josh Wingrove, 'Lone-Wolf Province Getting Back in Fold,' *Globe and Mail*, 5 October 2011, A9.

37 Preston Manning, *Think Big: Adventures in Life and Democracy* (Toronto: McClelland and Stewart, 2002), 207.

38 Cecil Carr, 'Parliament and Pipeline,' *CBR* 35, no. 9 (November 1956): 1100–6 at 1101 (quoting Lord Campion).

39 Wilson, 'In Defence of Parliamentary Opposition,' 26.

40 DAC, DP, A526/692, Speech Delivered to Empire Club, Toronto, 21 March 1957, 'The Role of the Opposition in Parliament.'

41 Eugene Forsey, 'Never Have So Many Been In So Long,' *Canadian Commentator* 1, no. 5 (May 1957): 1–2.

42 SAB, NWP, A526/692, file: Stanley Knowles, 'The Role of the Opposition in Parliament,' 10.

43 Carolyn Thomson, '"This Place": The Culture of Queen's Park,' in *Inside the Pink Palace: Ontario Legislature Internship Essays*, ed. Graham White (Ontario Legislature Internship Programme / Canadian Political Science Association, Toronto: University of Toronto Press, 1987), 1–20 at 15.

44 Steven R, Weisman, ed. and intro., *Daniel Patrick Moynihan: A Portrait in Letters of an American Visionary* (New York: Public Affairs, 2010), 412.

45 Peter Van Onselen, 'Major Party Senators and Electoral Professionalism in Australia,' PhD diss., University of Western Australia, 2006.

46 Senator J.S. Grafstein, 'The Mystery of the National Liberal Caucus,' Fourth Allan J. MacEachen Lecture in Politics, St Francis Xavier University, 24 September 2001, compiled by James Bickerton, *Reflections on Canadian Politics*, vol. II (Antigonish: St Francis University Press, 2008), 15–33 at 30.

47 John R. Williams, *The Conservative Party in Canada: 1920–1949* (Durham: Duke University Press, 1956), 80, cited in John C. Courtney, *Do Conventions Matter? Choosing National Party Leaders in Canada* (Montreal and Kingston: McGill–Queen's University Press, 1995), 11.

Chapter Two

1 J.E. Hodgetts, *Pioneer Public Service: An Administrative History of the United Canadas, 1841–1867* (Toronto: University of Toronto Press, 1955).

2 Nicholas A. MacDonald and James W.J. Bowden, 'No Discretion: On Prorogation and the Governor General,' *CPR* 34, no. 1 (2011): 7–16.

3 M.J.C. Vile, *Constitutionalism and the Separation of Powers* (Oxford: Clarendon Press, 1967), 216.

4 DLAUC, 23 June 1849, V111.1.1849, 155.

5 Rosa W. Langstone, 'Robert Baldwin's Proposals to the Legislative Assembly of Canada, on September, 1841,' Appendix J, *Responsible Government in Canada* (Toronto: J.M. Dent and Sons, 1931), 221.

6 Assembly (Lower Canada), *Journals*, 1809, Appendix and *Lower Canada Statutes*, 51 Geo. III, c.4, cited in Gary O'Brien, 'Pre-Confederation Parliamentary Procedure: The Evolution of Legislative Practice in the Lower Houses of Central Canada, 1792–1866' (unpub. PhD diss., Carleton University, 1988), 142.

7 Canada, *Statutes*, 7 Vict., c.3.

8 Ibid., 240.

9 G.M. Trevelyan, ed., *The Works of Lord Macaulay* (London 1871), vol. VI, 127–30, quoted in Archibald S. Foord, *His Majesty's Opposition, 1714–1830* (Oxford: Clarendon Press, 1962), 8–9.

10 *Edinburgh Review* (July 1807), X, no. XX, 413, quoted in Vile, *Constitutionalism*, 216.

11 John Beverley Robinson, *Canada and the Canada Bill* (Toronto: S.R. Publishers, Johnson Reprint Corp., 1967), 191, cited in O'Brien, *Pre-Confederation Parliamentary Procedure*, 87.

12 DLAUC, October 8, 1853, X1-11-1852-3, 932.

13 John D. Whyte, 'Constitutional Change and Constitutional Durability,' *JPPL* 5 (2011): 419–36.

14 O'Brien, *Pre-Confederation Parliamentary Procedure*, 290–1.

15 Rudyard Griffiths, ed., *Dialogue on Democracy* (The Lafontaine-Baldwin Lectures, 2000–5, Toronto: Penguin Canada, 2006), xxix.

16 Gordon T. Stewart, *The Origins of Canadian Politics: A Comparative Approach* (Vancouver: UBC Press, 1986), 56.

17 James McCaig, *Studies in Citizenship* (Toronto: The Educational Book Co., 1941), 156.

18 *Halifax Morning Journal*, 23 December 1859, in *Pre-Confederation*, vol. II, ed. P.B. Waite (Scarborough: Prentice-Hall of Canada, 1965), 191.

19 David E. Smith, 'Party Government, Representation, and National Integration in Canada,' in *Party Government and Regional Representation in Canada,* ed. Peter Aucoin (Toronto: University of Toronto Press in Cooperation with the Royal Commission on the Economic Union and Development Prospects for Canada, 1985), 1–68.

20 Norman Ward, 'The Formative Years of the House of Commons, 1867–1901,' *CJEPS* 18, no. 4 (November 1952): 431–51.

21 Sir Richard Cartwright, *Reminiscences* (Toronto: William Briggs, 1912), 125.
22 Oscar D. Skelton, *The Life and Letters of Sir Wilfrid Laurier* (Toronto: Oxford University Press, 1921), 222–3.
23 Cartwright, *Reminiscences*, 128.
24 Donald Creighton, *John A. Macdonald: The Young Politician* (Toronto: Macmillan of Canada, 1952), 289.
25 Cartwright, *Reminiscences*, 121.
26 R.C.B. Risk, 'Blake and Liberty,' in *Canadian Constitutionalism, 1791–1991*, ed. Janet Ajzenstat (Ottawa: Canadian Study of Parliament Group, 1991), 195–211 at 196.
27 Skelton, *The Life and Letters of Sir Wilfrid Laurier*, 160.
28 W. Buckingham and G.W. Ross, *The Hon. Alexander Mackenzie*, 5th ed. (Toronto: 1892), 221, quoted in Norman Ward, *The Public Purse: A Study in Canadian Democracy* (Toronto: University of Toronto Press, 1962), 48–9.
29 Cartwright, *Reminiscences*, 120.
30 Dean E. McHenry, 'Formal Recognition of the Leader of the Opposition in Parliaments of the British Commonwealth,' *PSQ* 69, no. 3 (Sept. 1954): 438–52.
31 Ward, *The Public Purse*, 49.
32 Sir Joseph Pope, *Correspondence of Sir John A. Macdonald: Selections from the Correspondence of the Rt. Hon. Sir John A. Macdonald* (Toronto: Oxford University Press, 1921), 243.
33 DLAUC, 4 December 1854, XII.IV.1854–5, 1579.
34 Skelton, *The Life and Letters of Sir Wilfrid Laurier*, 220.
35 David E. Smith, 'A Constitution in Some Respects Novel,' in *Federalism and the Constitution of Canada* (Toronto: University of Toronto Press, 2010), 40–61.
36 Donald Creighton, *Canada's First Century* (Toronto: Macmillan of Canada, 1970), 80–2.
37 Robert Craig Brown, *Robert Laird Borden: A Biography*, vol. I, *1854–1914* (Toronto: Macmillan of Canada, 1975), 100–1.
38 'Bilingualism Resolution Approved,' CNF, 1 June–15 June 1973, 1026.
39 Creighton, *Canada's First Century*, 144.
40 Ramsay Cook, *Provincial Autonomy, Minority Rights, and the Compact Theory, 1867–1921* (Royal Commission on Bilingualism and Biculturalism, Study 4, Ottawa: Information Canada, 1969).
41 Sir Ivor Jennings, *The Queen's Government* (London: Penguin, 1954), 88.
42 Eugene Forsey, *Freedom and Order: Collected Essays* (Carleton Library No. 73, Toronto: McClelland and Stewart, 1974).
43 David Edward Smith, 'Emergency Government in Canada,' *CHR* 50, no. 4 (December 1969): 429–48.
44 Robert Craig Brown, *Robert Laird Borden: A Biography*, vol. II, *1914–1937* (Toronto: Macmillan of Canada, 1980), 181.

45 Ibid., 182.
46 Ibid.

Chapter Three

1 Margaret MacMillan, *Paris, 1919: Six Months That Changed the World* (New York: Random House, 2003), xxv.
2 W.L. Morton, *The Progressive Party in Canada* (Toronto: University of Toronto Press, 1950), 96.
3 Roger Graham, *Arthur Meighen: A Biography*, vol. I, *The Door of Opportunity* (Toronto: Clarke, Irwin and Co., 1960), 242–3.
4 *DHOC*, 2 June 1919, 3014–15, cited in ibid., 239–40.
5 J.E. Rea, *T.A. Crerar: A Political Life* (Montreal and Kingston: McGill–Queen's University Press, 1998), 87.
6 Ernest Charles Drury, *Farmer Premier: Memoirs of the Honourable E.C. Drury* (Toronto: McClelland and Stewart, 1966), 141.
7 Ibid., 87.
8 DAC, MG01/1X/B/129, file: Clark, Joe, 1964–5, Diefenbaker to Clark (Draft), 9 February 1965. [It is unclear whether this letter was sent.]
9 John C. Courtney, 'Recognition of Canadian Political Parties in Parliament and in Law,' *CJPS* 11, no. 1 (March 1978): 33–60 at 34.
10 The ten volumes, with publication dates in parentheses, were published by the University of Toronto Press: W.L. Morton, *The Progressive Party in Canada* (1950), D.C. Masters, *The Winnipeg General Strike* (1950), Jean Burnet, *Next-Year Country* (1951), C.B. Macpherson, *Democracy in Alberta* (1953), J.R. Mallory, *Social Credit and the Federal Power in Canada* (1954), W.E. Mann, *Sect, Cult, and Church in Alberta* (1955), V.C. Fowke, *The National Policy and the Wheat Economy* (1957), Lewis G. Thomas, *The Liberal Party in Alberta* (1959), S.D. Clark, *Movements of Social Protest in Canada, 1640–1840* (1959), and J.A. Irving, *The Social Credit Movement* (1959).
11 Rea, *T.A. Crerar*, 87.
12 *DHOC*, 20 March 1922, 214, cited in Kenneth McNaught, *A Prophet in Politics: A Biography of J.S. Woodsworth* (Toronto: University of Toronto Press, 2001), 167.
13 McNaught, *A Prophet in Politics*, 210.
14 John C. Courtney, *The Selection of National Party Leaders in Canada* (Toronto: Macmillan of Canada, 1973), 67 [itals. in original].
15 R. MacGregor Dawson, *William Lyon Mackenzie King: A Political Biography, 1874–1923* (Toronto: University of Toronto Press, 1958), 329.
16 SAB, NWP, A526/183 file: Correspondence 1971 (2), Fred Gibson to Norman Ward, 8 September 1971.

17 *DHOC* (1919, Special Session), 551–3, cited in Graham, *Arthur Meighen: The Door of Opportunity*, 257.

18 Murray Beck, *Pendulum of Power: Canada's Federal Elections* (Scarborough: Prentice Hall, 1968), 151.

19 Roger Graham, *Arthur Meighen: A Biography*, vol. II, *And Fortune Fled* (Toronto: Clarke, Irwin and Co., 1963), 10.

20 C.J. Doherty to Sir Robert Borden, 16 April 1920, Borden Papers, quoted in Dawson, *William Lyon Mackenzie King*, 337.

21 Eugene Forsey, *Freedom and Order: Collected Essays* (Carleton Library No. 73, Toronto: McClelland and Stewart, 1974); 'Introductory Note' on the Essay: 'Mr. King and Parliamentary Government,' *CJEPS* 17, no. 4 (November 1951): 451–67.

22 Eugene A. Forsey, *The Royal Power of Dissolution in the British Common-wealth* (Toronto: Oxford University Press, 1943).

23 DAC, DP, 4640–1, 'Never Have So Many Been In So Long,' *Canadian Commentator* 1, no. 5 (May 1957): 1–2.

24 Tom Flanagan, 'Only Voters Have the Right to Decide on the Coalition,' *Globe and Mail*, 9 January 2009, A13.

25 W.L. Mackenzie King, *The Message of the Carillon and Other Addresses* (Toronto: Macmillan of Canada, 1928), 97.

26 Ibid., 151.

27 Beck, *Pendulum of Power*, 165.

28 Norman Ward and David Smith, *Jimmy Gardiner: Relentless Liberal* (Toronto: University of Toronto Press, 1990), 46.

29 Graham, *Arthur Meighen*, II:187.

30 Dawson, *William Lyon Mackenzie King*, 316.

31 Courtney, *The Selection of National Party Leaders in Canada*, 73.

32 *Toronto Mail and Empire*, 6 October 1927, in ibid., 76.

33 Ibid., 79–80.

34 Bennett Papers, vol. 950, McRae to Bennett, 23 December 1929, cited in Larry A. Glassford, *Reaction and Reform: The Politics of the Conservative Party under R.B. Bennett, 1927–1938* (Toronto: University of Toronto Press, 1992), 51–2.

35 Glassford, *Reaction and Reform*, 207.

36 Norman Ward, ed., *A Party Politician: The Memoirs of Chubby Power* (Toronto: Macmillan of Canada, 1966), 270; also 261.

37 Quoted in Stanley Knowles, 'The Role of the Opposition in Parliament,' Address to the Empire Club of Canada, Toronto, 21 March 1957, Press Release, Cooperative Commonwealth Federation in DAC, DP, A526/692, 'Stanley Knowles,' 11pp at 7.

38 *DHOC*, 30 May 1938, 3339.

39 John R. Williams, *The Conservative Party of Canada: 1920–1949* (Durham: Duke University Press, 1956); and J.L. Granatstein, *The Politics of Opposition: The Conservative Party of Canada, 1939–1945* (Toronto: University of Toronto Press, 1967).

40 Reginald Whitaker, *The Government Party: Organizing and Financing the Liberal Party of Canada, 1930–1958* (Toronto: University of Toronto Press, 1977).

41 Glassford, *Reaction and Reform*, 229.

42 'Backstage at Ottawa,' *Maclean's* 53 (1 May 1940): 51, quoted in Beck, *Pendulum of Power*, 240.

43 Granatstein, *The Politics of Opposition*, 43.

44 Ibid., 55–6 (Manion Papers, Vol. 65, speech to caucus, 13 May 1940) (typed copy).

45 John G. Diefenbaker, *One Canada: Memoirs of the Rt. Hon. John G. Diefenbaker*, vol. I, *The Crusading Years, 1895–1956* (Toronto: Macmillan of Canada, 1975), 249; Denis Smith, *Rogue Tory* (Toronto: MacFarlane Walter and Ross, 1995), 558.

46 Arthur Meighen, 'The CBC: A Party Instrument,' in *Unrevised and Unrepented: Debating Speeches and Others* (Toronto: Clarke, Irwin and Co., 1949), 419–34 at 423.

47 David Kynaston, *Austerity Britain, 1945–1951* (London: Bloomsbury, 2007), 212.

48 Ward, *A Party Politician*, 72.

49 Williams, *The Conservative Party in Canada*, 207–9.

50 See Courtney, *The Selection of National Party Leaders in Canada*, 213.

51 Williams, *The Conservative Party in Canada*, 211.

52 Ibid., 213.

53 DAC, DP, MG01/IX/A/596/334, file: 'The House of Commons – The Opposition, 1964,' 'Government in Canada: The Role of the Opposition,' for publication in magazine 'The Educational ABCs of Canadian Industry.' Letter from editor to JGD, 30 December 1963, 012195-012213 at 012204-5.

54 SAB, NWP, A526 175(1), file: Correspondence 1964, Norman Ward to Helen O'Reilly, 17 April 1964.

55 Dale C. Thomson, *Louis St Laurent: Canadian* (Toronto: Macmillan of Canada, 1967), 343.

56 Editorial, 'Is Parliament Free?' *Star-Phoenix*, 17 June 1951.

57 SLL, Stanley Knowles, 'I Believe in Parliament,' lecture Huron College, 19 November 1964, 4.

58 William Kilbourn, *Pipeline: Transcanada and the Great Debate, A History of Business and Politics* (Toronto: Clarke, Irwin and Co., 1970), 136.

59 NP, George Nowlan to Miriam Nowlan, 12 June 1955, Vaughan Memorial Library Archives, Acadia University, cited in Margaret Conrad, *George Nowlan: Maritime Conservative in National Politics* (Toronto: University of Toronto Press, 1986), 166.

Chapter Four

1 DAC, Diefenbaker Papers, Diefenbaker to Elmer Diefenbaker, 11 April 1957 and 24 May 1963, vol. 3, 1608–9 and 2933–4, quoted in Denis Smith, *Rogue Tory* (Toronto: MacFarlane Walter and Ross, 1995), 228 and 511.

2 Robert Bothwell and William Kilbourn, *C.D. Howe: A Biography* (Toronto: McClelland and Stewart, 1979), 312; 'Howe Acting as PM, Fills 11 Other Roles,' *Globe and Mail*, 24 July 1951, 1.

3 Eugene A. Forsey, *A Life on the Fringe: The Memoirs of Eugene Forsey* (Toronto: Oxford University Press, 1990), 139.

4 C.E.S. Franks, *The Parliament of Canada* (Toronto: University of Toronto Press, 1987), 99.

5 Smith, *Rogue Tory*, 217.

6 Lord Hewart, *The New Despotism* (London: E. Benn, 1929); J.A. Corry, *Democratic Government and Politics* (Toronto: University of Toronto Press, 1946); Ivor Jennings, *Cabinet Government*, 3rd ed. (Cambridge: Cambridge University Press, 1959). See *DHOC*, 22 March 1954, 3206 and 3232–3.

7 *DHOC*, 14 October 1957, 5, quoted in Robert M. Belliveau, *Mr. Diefenbaker, Parliamentary Democracy, and the Canadian Bill of Rights*, unpublished MA thesis, University of Saskatchewan, May 1992, 79.

8 Gordon Gibson, 'Democratic Reform Should Be This Election's Central Issue,' *Globe and Mail*, 13 April 2011, A17. See, too, New Brunswick, Commission on Legislative Democracy, *Final Report and Recommendations*, 31 December 2004, http://www.electionsnb.ca/pdf/cld/CLDFinalReport-e.pdf. The first of its three recommendations for 'enhancing the role of MLAs and the Legislature are: 'give the legislature more independence and authority,' 'give private MLAs more independence and authority,' and 'reduce party discipline and the adversarial culture of the legislature.'

9 Further discussion of these and other changes in the procedure of the House is found in the following articles: Donald Page, 'Streamlining the Procedures of the Canadian House of Commons, 1963–1966,' *CJEPS* 33, no. 1 (February 1967): 27–49; John C. Courtney, 'Recognition of Canadian Political Parties in Parliament and Law,' *CJPS* 11, no. 1 (March 1978): 33–60; Paul G. Thomas, 'The Role of House Leaders in the Canadian House of Commons,' *CJPS* 15, no. 1 (March 1982): 125–44; and Élise Hurtubise-Loranger, 'Official Languages and Parliament,' Library of Parliament, Law and Government Division, revised 23 July 2008, PRB 06-28E.

10 Gerald Schmitz, 'Opposition in a Parliamentary System,' Library of Parliament, Political and Social Affairs Division, December 1988, http://dsp-psd.pwgsc.gc.ca/Collection-R/LoPBdP/BP/bp47-e.htm.

11 Linda Geller-Schwartz, 'Minority Government Reconsidered,' *JCS* 14, no. 2, (1979): 67–79 at 76.

12 James R. Robertson, 'Political Parties and Parliamentary Recognition,' Library of Parliament, Law and Government Division, rev. August 1996, http://dsp-psd.pwgsc.gc.ca/Collection-R/LoPBdP/bp243-e.htm.

13 Gordon Aiken, *The Backbencher: The Trials and Tribulations of a Member of Parliament* (Toronto: McClelland and Stewart, 1974).

14 Dean E. McHenry, 'Formal Recognition of the Leader of the Opposition in Parliaments of the British Commonwealth,' *PSQ* 68, no. 3 (September 1954): 438–52 at 443.

15 John Ward, 'In Memory's Eye: Recollections of Canadian Parliamentarians,' http://www.vindicator.ca/In_Memorys_Eye/2_Prime_Ministers.html.

16 SAB, NWP, file: A526 (5) Dawson/Ward, House of Commons, 1962–7, Lamoureux to Ward, 27 September 1967. The request is found in NWP, file:A526/116, Ward to Lamoureux, 21 September 1967; the acknowledgment is ibid., 2 October 1967.

17 Gerald Michael Halabura, *Diefenbaker and Electoral Distribution: Principle and Pragmatism*, unpublished MA thesis, University of Saskatchewan, 1992, 35; see, too, Norman Ward, 'A Century of Constituencies,' *CPA* 10, no. 1 (1967): 105–22.

18 F. Leslie Seidle, 'The Election Expenses Act: The House of Commons and the Parties,' in *The Canadian House of Commons: Essays in Honour of Norman Ward*, ed. John C. Courtney (Calgary: University of Calgary Press, 1985), 113–34 at 116.

19 Seidle, 'The Election Expenses Act,' 117; *DHOC*, 12 July 1973, 5553–4.

20 DAC, DP, reel M–5561, Report No. 12, *The Social Credit Movement*, 15 October 1955, 21515–671 at 21656 and 21659.

21 Aiken, *The Backbencher*, 120.

22 Edwin R. Black, 'Opposition Research: Some Theories and Practice,' *CPA* 15, no. 1 (March 1972): 24–41 at 29.

23 Dianne Pothier, 'Parties and Free Votes in the Canadian House of Commons: The Case of Capital Punishment,' *JCS* 14, no. 2 (Summer 1979): 80–96.

24 Luc Juillet and Ken Rasmussen, *Defending a Contested Ideal: Merit and the PSC of Canada, 1908–2008* (Ottawa: University of Ottawa Press, 2008), ch. 4.

25 'Opposition Defends Auditor-General,' *CNF*, 1–15 April 1970, 427.

26 J.W. Pickersgill, *The Road Back: By a Liberal in Opposition* (Toronto: University of Toronto Press, 1986), 32. Confirmation that 'Pearson became the most astute politician to practise the art of the possible' is found in the reminiscences of John Ward, a former editor of Debates in the House of Commons: 'In

Memory's Eye: Reflections on Canadian Parliamentarians,' http://www
.vindicator.ca/In_Memorys_Eye/2_Prime_Ministers.html.

27 Margaret Conrad, *George Nowlan: Maritime Conservative in National Politics*
(Toronto: University of Toronto Press, 1986), 276–7.

28 Eugene Forsey, 'Canada: Two Nations or One?' *CJEPS* 28, no. 4 (November
1962): 485–501; see, too, Forsey, *A Life on the Fringe* (Toronto: Oxford University Press, 1990), 205–7.

29 Aiken, *The Backbencher*, 126; see also Smith, *Rogue Tory*, 563–4.

30 Desmond Morton, 'A Note on Party Switchers,' *CPR* 29, no. 2 (2006): 4–8.

31 Peter H. Russell, *Constitutional Odyssey: Can Canadians Become a Sovereign
People?* 3rd ed. (Toronto: University of Toronto Press, 2004), 138–9.

32 Chantal Hébert, *French Kiss: Stephen Harper's Blind Date with Quebec*
(Toronto: Alfred Knopf Canada, 2007), 109.

33 Ibid., 221.

34 Judy Steed, *Ed Broadbent: The Pursuit of Power* (Markham: Viking, 1988),
246 and 247; see also Franks, *The Parliament of Canada*, 109.

35 Allan Blakeney, *An Honourable Calling: Political Memoirs* (Toronto: University of Toronto Press, 2008), 137.

36 Franks, *The Parliament of Canada*, 150–1.

37 Brooke Jeffrey, 'The Meech Morass, 1987–1988' in *Divided Loyalties: The Liberal Party of Canada, 1984–2008* (Toronto: University of Toronto Press, 2010),
89–120.

38 Ibid., 15; David E. Smith, *Federalism and the Constitution of Canada* (Toronto:
University of Toronto Press, 2010), 57–8.

39 Hébert, *French Kiss*, 173.

40 Franks, *The Parliament of Canada*, 49.

41 'United PCs Emerge from Convention,' *CNF*, 16–31 March 1974, 1177.

42 Aiken, *The Backbencher*, 78.

43 For exploration of the 'problem,' see C.E.S. Franks, 'The "Problem" of
Debate and Question Period,' in *The Canadian House of Commons: Essays
in Honour of Norman Ward*, ed. John C. Courtney (Calgary: University of
Calgary Press, 1985), 1–19.

44 John Ward, 'In Memory's Eye: Reflections on Canadian Parliamentarians:
Honourable Members – Part 1,' http://www.vindicator.ca/In_Memorys_
Eye/3_Honourable_Members_1.html, accessed 26 October 2010; SAB,
Norman Ward Papers, A526/561 (6), Dawson/Ward, House of Commons,
1962–7, 13-page typescript (n.d.) titled 'Divisions.'

45 John Ward, 'In Memory's Eye: Reflections on Canadian Parliamentarians:
Prime Ministers –Part 1,' http://www.vindicator.ca/In_Memorys_Eye/2_
Prime_Ministers.html, accessed 26 October 2010.

46 'Guillotine Rule Invoked,' *CNF*, 7–20 April 1967, 57, and 'Parliamentary Rule Changes Proposed,' 1–15 October 1974, 1271.

47 See the contribution to debate on procedure of Gordon Churchill, *DHOC*, 25 May 1965, 1643–6; for a history of time allocation, see Yves Yvon J. Pelletier, 'Time Allocation in the House of Commons,' *CPR* 23, no. 4 (2000): 20–8.

48 Senator Keith Davey, *The Rainmaker: A Passion for Politics* (Toronto: Stoddart, 1986), 191.

Chapter Five

1 Éric Bélanger, 'The Rise of Third Parties in the 1993 Canadian Federal Election: Pinard Revisited,' *CJPS* 37, no. 3 (September 2004): 581–94 at 581.

2 C.E.S. Franks, *The Parliament of Canada* (Toronto: University of Toronto Press, 1987), 46.

3 David Docherty, 'Representation, Amateurism, and Turnover,' in *Mr Smith Goes to Ottawa: Life in the House of Commons* (Vancouver: UBC Press, 1997), 31–59.

4 Samara, 'The Accidental Citizen?,' 4, http://www.samaracanada.com/ mp_exit_interviews.

5 Hugh Winsor and Tu Thanh Ha, 'Manning Set to Have PM Removed,' *Globe and Mail*, 14 December 1995, A4.

6 Preston Manning, 'Democracy in the 21st Century: New Imperatives, Old Restraints,' in *Who Decides? Government in the New Millennium*, ed. Richard M. Bird (Toronto: C.D. Howe Institute, 2004), 33.

7 *CNF*, 'Gautier Elected Bloc Leader,' 16–29 February 1996, 5269; 'Bouchard Sounds Battle Call,' 16–30 November 1994, 5030; 'Bouchard Braves English Canada,' 16–30 September 1993, 4810.

8 Brooke Jeffrey, *Divided Loyalties: The Liberal Party of Canada, 1984–2008* (Toronto: University of Toronto Press, 2010), 277.

9 *CNF*, 'Reform Polls Unity Views,' 1–15 October 1994, 5006.

10 Jeffrey, *Divided Loyalties*, 291.

11 Tim Naumetz, 'Conservatives "Lay Track" to Attack Media, Real Opposition Party in Parliament,' *HT* 13 June 2011, 1 and 6; 'Tories Begin Battle Against Coalition,' http://www.cbc.ca/news/canada/story/2008/ 12/02/harper-coalition.html, cited in Tom Flanagan, 'Political Communication and the "Permanent Campaign,"' in *How Canadians Communicate IV: Media and Politics*, eds. David Taras and Christopher Waddell (Edmonton: Athabaska University Press, 2012).

12 House of Commons, Canada, *Selected Decisions of Speaker Gilbert Parent, 1994–2001* (2008), 'The House and Its Members, Official Opposition: Designation: Tie in Opposition, February 27, 1996, Debates, 16–20,' 84–93 at 93.

13 'The Opposition,' *Parliament and Reform* (Politics Briefing, No. 3, London: Constitutional Reform Centre, 1988), 3.

14 For more on the New Brunswick precedent, see Stewart Hyson, 'Determining the Official Opposition in New Brunswick and the House of Commons,' *CPR* 19, no. 3 (1996): 2–6.

15 Gordon Barnhart, 'Tie in Opposition,' *The Table* 46 (1978): 18–22 at 19.

16 Hyson, 'Determining the Official Opposition,' 5.

17 *CNF*, 'Reform Plan Scuttled,' 1–15 April 1997, 5473.

18 *CNF*, 'Manning Uses Quebec Podium,' 1–15 April 1997, 5490.

19 *CNF*, 'Manning Attacked Over Ads,' 16–31 April 1997, 5498.

20 Lawrence Martin, *The Antagonist: Lucien Bouchard and the Politics of Delusion* (Toronto; Viking, 1997), 261.

21 Hugo Young, *One of Us: A Biography of Margaret Thatcher* (London: Macmillan, 1991).

22 *CNF*, 'Reform Makes New Waves,' 1–15 June 1999, 4948; 'NAC Lobbies MPs,' 16–30 June 1996, 5332.

23 Tom Korski, 'Years Ago, I Tried to Trace the Genesis of Conservative Loathing for the CBC,' *HT*, 16 May 2011, 10.

24 *Harper v. Canada (Attorney General)*, [2004] 1 SCR 827.

25 F. Leslie Seidle, 'The Election Expenses Act: The House of Commons and the Parties,' in *The Canadian House of Commons: Essays in Honour of Norman Ward*, ed. John C. Courtney (Calgary: University of Calgary Press, 85), 113–34 at 126.

26 Young, *One of Us*, 413.

27 Kate Malloy, 'Public Funding Too High, Political Parties Becoming "Empty Shells,"' *HT*, 2 October 2006, http://www.thehilltimes.ca/page/view/.2006.october.2.funding. The article reports testimony of Leslie Seidle of the Institute for Research and Public Policy before the Legal and Constitutional Affairs Committee of the Senate of Canada.

28 Ibid.

29 Jean-Pierre Kingsley, 'Political Parties Could Be Forced to Return to Big Money Corporate Funding If Per-Vote Subsidies Scrapped,' *HT*, 11 April 2011, 1, 16–17. Tom Flanagan described the 2008 proposal as 'probably the single worst mistake … in [Stephen Harper's] career as a party leader.' *Harper's Team: Behind the Scenes in the Conservative Rise to Power*, 2nd ed.

(Montreal-Kingston: McGill–Queen's University Press, 2009), 321. After the 2011 election and from the perspective of the opposition parties, Flanagan offered a more sanguine assessment: 'Ending the allowances is in the long-term self-interest of these parties (or at least of their supporters), because it will drive them to co-operate in order to compete with the Conservative juggernaut.' 'Some Day, They'll Thank Mr Harper,' *Globe and Mail*, 31 May 2011, A13.

30 Preston Manning, *Think Big: Adventures in Life and Democracy* (Toronto: McClelland and Stewart, 2002), 201.

31 Eugene Forsey, *A Life on the Fringe: The Memoirs of Eugene Forsey* (Toronto: Oxford University Press, 1990), 205 and 206.

32 *CNF*, 'Bouchard Sounds Battle Call,' 16–30 November 1994, 5030.

33 Seymour Martin Lipset, 'Democracy in Alberta,' in *Voting in Canada*, ed. John C. Courtney (Scarborough: Prentice-Hall of Canada, 1967), 182–5. Originally from *The Canadian Forum*, 34 (November and December 1954).

34 Peter H. Russell and Lorne Sossin, eds., 'Introduction,' in *Parliamentary Democracy in Crisis* (Toronto: University of Toronto Press, 2009), xiv.

35 Andrew Potter, 'Unbalanced Thoughts,' *LRC*, July–August 2009, 3–4.

36 James Jerome, *Mr Speaker: James Jerome* (Toronto: McClelland and Stewart, 1985), 86.

37 Ibid., 87.

38 Bill Blaikie, 'The Status of Small Parties in the House of Commons,' *CPR* 17, no. 3 (Autumn 1994), 29–32; 'Speaker's Ruling (Gilbert Parent), The Designation of Party Status,' 16 June 1994, *CPR* 17, no. 3 (Autumn 1994): 33–5; Blaikie, 'Reflections on the Speaker's Ruling,' *CPR* 17, no. 3 (Autumn 1994): 36.

39 CBC News Online, 'Federal Sponsorship Scandal,' 26 October 2006, http://www.cbc.ca/slash/news/background/groupaction.

40 Privy Council Office, *Ethics, Responsibility, Accountability: An Action Plan for Democratic Reform* (Ottawa: Privy Council Office, February 2004). Not all observers agreed with his analysis. See Jeffrey, *Divided Loyalties*, 656n33.

41 Steven Chase, 'Straight-Talking Fraser Strikes Fear on the Hill,' *Globe and Mail*, 12 February 2004, 4.

42 Tom Flanagan, 'Something Blue: Conservative Organization in an Era of Permanent Campaign,' *Inroads* 28 (Winter–Spring 2011): 90–9. The phrase is reminiscent of Joe Clark's reference in 1964 to a 'perpetual campaign.' See chapter 1, note 17.

43 See F. Leslie Seidle, 'Citizens Speaking for Themselves: New Avenues for Public Involvement,' in *Political Leadership and Representation in Canada:*

Essays in Honour of John C. Courtney, eds. Hans J. Michelmann, Donald C. Story, and Jeffery S. Steeves (Toronto: University of Toronto Press, 2007), 81–109.

44 Michael Valpy, 'NDP Leader Brought Inspiration and a Message of Hope to a Cynical Age,' *Globe and Mail*, 23 August 2011, S8.

45 Judith Brett, 'Parliament, Meetings, and Civil Society' (paper presented as a lecture in the Department of the Senate Occasional Lecture Series at Parliament House, Canberra, Australia, 27 July 2001), http://www.aph.gov .au/SENATE/pubs/pops/pop38/c08.pdf.

46 *Globe and Mail*, 5 March 2011, A13.

47 Built in 1914, then purchased in 1950 by a trust composed of wealthy businessmen for the purpose of housing the leader of the opposition, the property was subsequently bought by the Government of Canada in 1970. Maureen McTeer, *Residences: Homes of Canada's Leaders* (Scarborough: Prentice-Hall Canada, 1982), 84–6.

48 'Manning Accepts Stornoway,' *CNF*, 16–30 June 1997, 5515.

49 Denis Smith, *Rogue Tory* (Toronto: MacFarlane Walter and Ross, 1995), 560.

Chapter Six

1 Tom Van Dusen, *Inside the Tent: Forty-Five Years on Parliament Hill* (Burnstown: General Store Publishing House, 1998), 108.

2 Tom Flanagan, *Harper's Team: Behind the Scenes in the Conservative Rise to Power*, 2nd ed. (Montreal and Kingston: McGill–Queen's University Press, 2009), 13.

3 Kenneth McRae, 'Consociationalism and the Canadian Political System,' in *Consociational Democracy: Political Accommodation in Segmented Societies*, ed. Kenneth McRae (Carleton Library, No. 79, Toronto: McClelland and Stewart, 1974), 238–61 at 254 (quoting from Report, Bk 1, 86).

4 Donald Creighton, *Canada's First Century, 1867–1967* (Toronto: Macmillan of Canada, 1970), 11–12.

5 Frederick W. Gibson, ed., *Cabinet Formation and Bicultural Relations: Seven Case Studies* (Studies of the Royal Commission on Bilingualism and Biculturalism, No. 6, Ottawa: Queen's Printer, 1970).

6 Eugene Forsey, 'Canada: Two Nations or One?,' in *Freedom and Order: Collected Essays* (Carleton Library, No. 73, Toronto: McClelland and Stewart, 1974), 247–69.

7 Arend Lijphart, 'The Netherlands: The Rules of the Game,' in McRae, ed., *Consociational Democracy*, 136–49.

8 Kenneth McRae, 'Applications and Illustrations: Canada,' in McRae, ed., *Consociational Democracy*, 236.

9 Escott M. Reid, 'The Liberal Party Machine in Saskatchewan before 1929,' *CJEPS* 2 (1936): 27–40.
10 See Norman Ward and David Smith, *Jimmy Gardiner: Relentless Liberal* (Toronto: University of Toronto Press, 1990).
11 Frederick W. Gibson and Barbara Robertson, ed. and intro., *Ottawa at War: The Grant Dexter Memoranda, 1939–1945,* vol. VI (Winnipeg: Manitoba Record Society, 1994), 111.
12 *CAR* (1928–9): 469–70.
13 John A. Munro and Alex I. Inglis, *Mike: The Memoirs of the Right Honourable Lester B. Pearson,* 3 vols. (Toronto: University of Toronto Press, 1975), 20–1; GP, Gardiner to Hon. David A. Croll, 15 June 1957, 66589; Gardiner to Paul Martin, 12 December 1958, 66775–6; Gardiner to Howard Winkler, 9 December 1958, 67498.
14 SAB, GP, 'Report from Parliament Hill,' CKCK (Regina), 9 November 1957.
15 J.W. Pickersgill, *My Years with Louis St Laurent: A Political Memoir* (Toronto: University of Toronto Press, 1975), 66.
16 SAB, GP, Gardiner to Ken Mayhew, 9 July 1957, 66737–8.
17 Patrick Kyba, 'The Saskatchewan General Election of 1929,' unpublished MA thesis, University of Saskatchewan, 1964.
18 Senator Keith Davey, *The Rainmaker: A Passion for Politics* (Toronto: Stoddart, 1986), 62 and 63.
19 John C. Courtney and David E. Smith, 'Voting in a Provincial General Election and a Federal By-Election: A Constituency Study of Saskatoon City,' *CJEPS* 32, no. 3 (August 1966): 338–53.
20 Ontario, Confederation for Tomorrow Conference, *Proceedings,* Toronto, 27–30 November 1967, 11 and 4.
21 Lawrence Martin, *Harperland: The Politics of Control* (Toronto: Viking Canada, 2010), 4.
22 Munro and Inglis, *Mike,* 239 and 67–9.
23 Van Dusen, *Inside the Tent,* 62.
24 *DHOC,* 18 August 1920, 547 (John H. Burnham).
25 SAB, NWP, A526/117, file: 'Correspondence, 1968,' Minutes of the Meeting of the Leader's Policy Advisory Committee, 26 February 1968; 'Summary of Discussions and Conclusions of the Advisory Committee on the Setting Up of a Policy Research Organization' (author, E.D. Fulton); D.W. Slater and T.H.B. Symons, 'An Outline of Some Topics for Study by the Policy Advisory Committee,' n.d.; E.D. Fulton to Norman Ward, 28 February 1968.
26 Chantal Hébert, *French Kiss: Stephen Harper's Blind Date with Quebec* (Toronto: A.A. Knopf, 2007), 110–11.

27 Ramsay Cook, *Provincial Autonomy, Minority Rights, and the Compact Theory, 1867–1921* (Royal Commission on Bilingualism and Biculturalism, Study No. 4, Ottawa: Queen's Printer, 1965).

28 Canada, Royal Commission on Bilingualism and Biculturalism, *A Preliminary Report* (Ottawa: Queen's Printer, 1965), 13.

29 DAC, DP, file; MG01/IX/B/41, Pauline L'Orange to Richard Bell, 29 May 1967.

30 Positions that qualify for inclusion under the designation 'officer of Parliament' are occasionally in dispute, although those discussed in these paragraphs are agreed to wear that title. Other offices, of various nomenclature, approximate but do not fulfil all the requirements. See Stewart Hyson, 'A Primer on Federal Specialty OmbudsOffices,' *CPR* 34, no. 2 (Summer 2011), 34–42. One controversial position is the parliamentary budget officer, created in 2006 in consequence of the Federal Accountability Act. Brooke Jeffrey, 'The Parliamentary Budget Officer Two Years Later: A Progress Report,' *CPR* 33, no. 4 (Winter 2010): 37–45. See also David Pond, 'The Role of Parliamentary Officers: A Case Study of Two Officers,' *CPR* 33, no. 4 (Winter 2010): 19–26.

31 Paul Thomas, 'The Past, Present, and Future of Officers of Parliament,' *CPA* 46, no. 3 (2003): 287–314; see, as well, Megan Furi, 'Officers of Parliament: A Study in Government Adaptation,' MA thesis, University of Saskatchewan, 2002.

32 Stewart Hyson, ed., *Provincial and Territorial Ombudsman Offices in Canada* (Institute of Public Administration of Canada, Toronto: University of Toronto Press, 2009).

33 *Edmonton Journal*, 19 June 1963, 1, quoted in Lorna Stefanick, 'Alberta's Ombudsman: Following Responsibility in an Era of Outsourcing,' in ibid., 27–52 at 28.

34 Thomas, 'The Past, Present, and Future,' 288.

35 Birch (1964, 140), quoted in Alexandra Kelso, *Parliamentary Reform at Westminster* (Manchester: Manchester University Press, 2009), 21.

36 Mike de Souza and Amy Minsky, 'Ruling Could Lead to Increased Secrecy,' *LP*, 14 May 2011, A10 (italics added).

37 G. Drewry, 'Reform of the Legislative Process: Some Neglected Questions,' *Parliamentary Affairs* 25, no. 4 (1972): 286–99 at 298–9, quoted in Alexandra Kelso, *Parliamentary Reform at Westminster* (Manchester: Manchester University Press, 2009), 42.

38 Campbell Clark and Daniel Leblanc, 'Fraser Puts Heat on PM,' *Globe and Mail*, 11 February 2004, A1.

39 Daniel Leblanc, 'Retiring Fraser Urges Vigilance over Watchdog's Independence,' *Globe and Mail*, 26 May 2011, A10.

40 Alex Himelfarb, 'We Seem to Have Forgotten the Fact That If We Want
    Government Services (and We Do), We Need to Pay for Them,' *Globe and
    Mail*, 15 October 2011, F4.

41 Glen McGregor, 'Ethics Popular Topic in Ottawa,' *LP*, 4 January 2011, B7.

42 Greg McArthur, 'Harper's Ex-Adviser Urges Caution on National Security
    Czar,' *Globe and Mail*, 17 August 2010, http://www.theglobeandmail.com/
    news/politics/harpers-ex-adviser-urges-caution-on-nation.

43 Jennifer Ditchburn, 'Better Scrutiny of Watchdogs Recommended,' *Globe
    and Mail*, 4 March 2011, A6.

44 John D. Whyte, 'Constitutional Change and Constitutional Durability,'
    JPPL 5 (2011): 419–36; see also Jeffrey Graham Bell, 'Agents of Parliament:
    A New Branch of Government?' *CPR* 29, no. 1 (2006): 13–21. For a contrary
    view, see Gloria Galloway, 'Watchdogs – or Lapdogs?' *Globe and Mail*, 28
    December 2010, A4.

45 Jan Nitoslawski, 'One-Man Ethics in Government Crusader Conacher to
    Leave Gig in Ottawa,' *HT*, 7 March 2011, 4.

46 'Straight-Talking Fraser Strikes Fear on the Hill,' *Globe and Mail*, 12 Febru-
    ary 2004, 4.

47 Whyte, 'Constitutional Change and Constitutional Durability,' 429.
    For an example, involving the Chief Electoral Officer, see Steven Chase,
    'Conservative Senators Avoid Charges in Plea Deal,' *Globe and Mail*,
    11 November 2011, A4.

48 Judith Brett, 'Parliament, Meetings and Civil Society' (paper presented as
    a lecture in the Department of the Senate Occasional Lecture Series at Par-
    liament House, Canberra, Australia, 27 July 2001), 12, http://www.aph
    .gov.au/binaries/senate/pubs/pops/pop38/brett.pdf.

49 Tim Naumetz, 'Conservatives "Lay Track" to Attack Media, Real Opposi-
    tion Party in New Parliament,' *HT*, 13 June 2011, 1 and 6 at 6.

50 Martin, *Harperland*, 27.

51 NA, EFP, 60/16, file: Parliamentary Appointments 1981, 1990, 'Officers of
    Parliament.'

52 Gloria Galloway and Jane Taber, 'Watchdog Scolds Tories for Unilingual
    Appointments,' *Globe and Mail*, 4 November 2011, A6.

53 See, for example, Steven Chase, 'Privacy Watchdog Sounds Alarm on
    E-Snooping Legislation,' *Globe and Mail*, 28 October 2011, A6.

54 Ibid.

55 Sir John Willison, *Reminiscences: Political and Personal* (Toronto: McClelland
    and Stewart, 1919), 121, and Blake to Macdonald, 17 and 22 February
    1883, Macdonald Papers, vol. 188, 166, both quoted in Norman Ward,
    'The Press and Patronage: An Exploratory Operation,' in *The Political*

Process in Canada: Essays in Honour of R. MacGregor Dawson, ed. J.H. Aitchison (Toronto: University of Toronto Press, 1963), 3–16 at 11.

56 Willison, *Reminiscences*, 123.

57 *DHOC*, 20 November 1967, 4460.

58 Naumetz, 'Conservatives "Lay Track,"' 1.

59 Dawn Walton, 'Legislature to Sit for 2 Days, Then Break,' *Globe and Mail*, 21 October 2011, A11.

60 Tom Flanagan, 'Political Communication and the "Permanent Campaign,"' in *How Canadians Communicate IV: Media and Politics*, ed. David Taras and Christopher Waddell (Edmonton: Athabasca University Press, 2012), 129–48.

61 David Taras, 'The Past and Future of Political Communication in Canada: An Introduction,' in ibid., 1–25 at 4.

62 Taras and Waddell, 'The 2011 Federal Election and the Transformation of Canadian Politics,' in ibid., 71–107.

63 SAB, NWP, A526, file: Correspondence, 1974–6, Ward to Otto Lang, 27 September 1976.

64 Lord Campion, 'Parliament and Democracy,' in Campion et al., eds., *Parliament: A Survey* (London: George Allen and Unwin, 1952), 9–36 at 17. See also C.E.S. Franks, *The Parliament of Canada* (Toronto: University of Toronto Press, 1987), 15: 'Words and discussion are the core of effective parliamentary government.'

65 Ludger Helms, 'Five Ways of Institutionalizing Political Opposition,' *Government and Opposition* 39, no. 1 (Winter 2004): 22–54.

66 Patrick Boyer, *Direct Democracy in Canada: The History and Future of Referendums* (Toronto: Dundurn Press, 1992).

67 W.H. McConnell, *Commentary on the British North America Act* (Toronto: Macmillan of Canada, 1977), 248. See, in particular, the judicial opinion arising from Manitoba's legislation: *Reference re* Initiative and Referendum Act [1919], A.C. 935.

68 Lionel Orlikow, 'The Reform Movement in Manitoba, 1910–1915,' in *Historical Essays on the Prairie Provinces*, ed. Donald Swainson (Carleton Library No. 53, Toronto: McClelland and Stewart, 1970), 215–29 at 215.

69 David E. Smith, *Prairie Liberalism: The Liberal Party in Saskatchewan, 1905–1971* (Toronto: University of Toronto Press, 1975); Jared J. Wesley, *Code Politics: Campaigns and Cultures on the Canadian Prairies* (Vancouver: UBC Press, 2011).

70 Lysiane Gagnon, 'An Online Petition with a Popular Twist,' *Globe and Mail*, 22 November 2010, A17.

71 Jane Taber, 'Tired of "Rabid Partisanship," Liberal MP Quits,' *Globe and Mail*, 11 November 2010, A9.

72 John Allemang, 'Layton Stakes His Biggest Bet as Jack of Hearts,' *Globe and Mail*, 28 May 2011, F6.

73 Chantal Hébert, 'Citizens Angry, Engaged, and Ahead of Conventional Parties,' *HT*, 1 November 2010, 1 and 5.

74 Boyer, *Direct Democracy in Canada*, 193–202; see also David E. Smith, *The People's House of Commons: Theories of Democracy in Contention* (Toronto: University of Toronto Press, 2007), 60 and 158n24.

Chapter Seven

1 K.C. Wheare, *Federal Government* (London: Oxford University Press, 1946), 11.

2 *Attorney General for Canada v. Attorney General for Ontario and Others*, [1937] AC 355.

3 Craig Oliver, *Oliver's Twist* (Toronto: Penguin, 2011), 102.

4 F.H. Underhill, 'Canadian Liberal Democracy in 1955,' in Frank H. Underhill, *In Search of Canadian Liberalism* (Toronto: Macmillan Company of Canada, 1961), 227–42 at 237.

5 John A. Macdonald to M.C. Cameron, 3 January 1872, in *Sir Joseph Pope, Correspondence of Sir John A. Macdonald: Selections from the Correspondence of the Rt. Hon. Sir John Alexander Macdonald* (Toronto: Oxford University Press, [n.d.]), 159–61.

6 'Province Asks Feds to Move Election,' *LP*, 16 December 2011, B10. Manitoba followed suit: Canadian Press, 'Two Votes Too Many in 2015,' *LP*, 18 May 2012, C10.

7 R. MacGregor Dawson, *The Government of Canada* (5th ed., rev. Norman Ward, Toronto: University of Toronto Press, 1970), 413.

8 Review (by Heath Macquarrie) of *Speaking for Myself: Politics and Other Pursuits*, in *CPR* 23, no. 2 (Summer 2000), 37.

9 Gregory P. Marchildon, 'Provincial Coalition Governments in Canada: An Interpretive Survey,' in *Continuity and Change in Canadian Politics: Essays in Honour of David E. Smith*, ed. Hans J. Michelmann and Cris de Clercy (Toronto: University of Toronto Press, 2006), 170–94 at 181 (emphasis added).

10 Ibid., 182.

11 Gary Mason, 'Lucky Liberals, NDP Could Be Neck and Neck If Election Held Now: Poll,' *Globe and Mail*, 20 November 2010, A5.

12 Margaret Conrad, *George Nowlan: Maritime Conservative in National Politics* (Toronto: University of Toronto Press, 1986), 143.

13 Peter Oliver, *G. Howard Ferguson: Ontario Tory* (Toronto: University of Toronto Press, 1977), 121.

14 Margaret Prang, *N.W. Rowell: Ontario Nationalist* (Toronto: University of Toronto Press, 1975), 154–5.

15 Robert Bothwell and William Kilbourn, *C.D. Howe: A Biography* (Toronto: McClelland and Stewart, 1979), 305.

16 Norman Ward, 'Hon. James Gardiner and the Liberal Party of Alberta,' *CHR*, 56, no. 3 (1975): 303–22.

17 *DHOC*, 22 March 1954, 3207 (citing *Edmonton Bulletin*, 16 November 1950).

18 John Ibbitson, 'Qualms That Could Keep Harper Up at Night,' *Globe and Mail*, 16 May 2011, A4.

19 Ian Bailey, 'Layton Says He'll Be "Driving Hard" to Strengthen Pensions,' *Globe and Mail*, 12 May 2011, A4.

20 Doreen Barrie and Roger Gibbins, 'Parliamentary Careers in the Canadian Federal State,' *CJPS*, 22, no. 1 (March 1989), 137–45.

21 Ibid., 144.

22 Conrad Black, *Duplessis* (Toronto: McClelland and Stewart, 1979), 182.

23 Trent University Archives, Frost Papers, letterbook 8, Frost to C.H. Hale, 10 February 1942, cited in Roger Graham, *Old Man Ontario: Leslie M. Frost* (Toronto: University of Toronto Press, 1990), 64.

24 J.R. Mallory, *Social Credit and the Federal Power in Canada* (Toronto: University of Toronto Press, 1954).

25 [1957] SCR 285.

26 John T. Saywell, *'Just Call Me Mitch': The Life of Mitchell F. Hepburn* (Toronto: University of Toronto Press, 1991), chapters 18 and 19, 428–70.

27 Black, *Duplessis*, 207.

28 Keith Archer, Faron Ellis, and Peter Nestoruk, 'Legislators and Their World,' *CPR* 12, no. 2 (Summer 1989), 19–23.

29 Gerald Amerongen, 'Speaker's Ruling: Recognition of the Leader of the Opposition, November 16, 1984,' *CPR* 7, no. 4 (1984), 29. Of related interest, see Gerald Amerongen, 'Speaker's Ruling: Statement Concerning Status of the Leader of the Official Opposition, March 11, 1983,' *CPR* 6, no. 2 (1983), 44–5.

30 Stewart Hyson, 'A One-Party Legislature: Where's "Her Majesty's Loyal Opposition": In the Loyalist Province?' *CPR* 11, no. 2 (1988), 22–5 at 24; see also Hyson, 'Determining the Official Opposition in New Brunswick and the House of Commons,' *CPR* 19, no. 3 (1996), 2–6; Christopher Dunn, 'Executive Dominance in Provincial Legislatures,' *CPR* 13, no. 1 (1990), 11–18; and Loredana Catali Sonier, 'New Brunswick's Experiment with a "House of No Nays,"' *The Parliamentarian* 85, no. 3 (2004): 64–7.

31 Hyson, 'A One-Party Legislature.'
32 Geoffrey Martin, 'The Rise and Fall of the New Brunswick CoR Party, 1988–1995,' *CPR* 18, no. 3 (1995), 19–22.
33 Ibid.
34 W.E. Mann, *Sect, Cult, and Church in Alberta* (Toronto: University of Toronto Press, 1955).
35 Gary Mason, 'Inside the Downfall of Carole James,' *Globe and Mail*, 7 December 2010, A5.
36 'Lesage Attacks Trudeau,' *CNF*, 11–31 September 1967.
37 'Quebec Alters Opening Ceremony,' *CNF*, 16–28 February 1970, 407–8.
38 Lysiane Gagnon, 'Quebeckers' Mental Bloc,' *Globe and Mail*, 16 May 2011, A11.
39 Graham Fraser, *PQ: René Lévesque and the Parti Québécois in Power* (Toronto: Macmillan of Canada, 1984), 36–8.
40 Roy MacLaren, *The Fundamental Things Apply* (Montreal and Kingston: McGill–Queen's University Press, 2011), 124.
41 K.C. Wheare, *Federal Government* (3rd ed., London: Oxford University Press, 1953), 21.
42 David E. Smith, 'The Westminster Model in Ottawa: A Study in the Absence of Influence,' *British Journal of Political Science* 15, nos. 1 and 2 (2002): 54–64.
43 *CNF*, 'Rae's Policies Divide Federal NDP,' 16–30 April 1993, 4741.
44 *CNF*, 'Farmers Stage Ottawa Protest,' 1–31 August 1999, 5919.
45 Eric Cline, *Making a Difference: Reflections from Political Life* (Saskatoon: Thistledown Press, 2008), 109.
46 Brian Topp, *How We Almost Gave the Tories the Boot (The Inside Story behind the Coalition): A Memoir* (Toronto: Lorimer, 2010).

Chapter Eight

1 Neville Johnson, 'Opposition in the British Political System,' *Government and Opposition* 32, no. 4 (Autumn 1997): 487–510 at 510.
2 Steve Ladurantaye, 'No Reprieve for Elizabeth May,' *Globe and Mail*, 1 April 2011, A5.
3 Preston Manning, 'New Order Mustn't Threaten Unity, Vision,' *Globe and Mail*, 20 May 2011, A15.
4 Ibid.
5 R. MacGregor Dawson, *The Government of Canada* (5th ed., rev. Norman Ward, Toronto: University of Toronto Press, 1970); Norman Ward, *The Canadian House of Commons: Representation* (2nd ed., Toronto: University of

Toronto Press, 1963); 'Relation of a Member of Parliament to His Constituents: 1.A "Representative or Delegate?,"' *Manitoba Free Press*, 2 August 1919, in R. MacGregor Dawson, *Constitutional Issues in Canada, 1900–1931* (London: Oxford University Press, 1933), 187–8.

6 Conrad Black, *Duplessis* (Toronto: McClelland and Stewart, 1977), 164.

7 David E. Smith, 'Path Dependency and Saskatchewan Politics,' in *The Heavy Hand of History: Interpreting Saskatchewan's Past*, ed. Gregory P. Marchildon (Regina: Canadian Plains Research Center, 2005), 31–50.

8 Grace Skogstad, 'The Liberal Party, Insensitivity, and Western Canadian Agriculture: Does the Account Still Stand Up?' in *Continuity and Change in Canadian Politics: Essays in honour of David E. Smith*, ed. Hans J. Michelmann and Cristine de Clercy (Toronto: University of Toronto Press, 2006), 225–44.

9 Bruce Johnstone, 'Ritz Declares Victory in Battle over CWB,' *LP*, 17 December 2011, B1.

10 Mia Robson, 'Bill to Kill CWB Monopoly Clears Senate,' *LP*, 16 December 2011, D1.

11 Bruce Johnstone, 'Farmers Denied the Right to Decide,' *LP*, 17 December 2011, B1.

12 Lord Campion, 'Parliament and Democracy,' in *Parliament: A Survey*, ed. Campion et al. (London: George Allen and Unwin Ltd., 1952), 9–36 at 17.

13 Kevin Weedmark, 'Long Gun Registry Is History: Komarnicki Feels Relief as Gun Bill Passes,' 20 February 2012, http://www.world-spectator.com/news_story.php?id=51.

14 'Quebec Outrage as Tories Celebrate Long-Gun Registry Vote with Cocktail Party,' 15 February 2012, http://news.nationalpost.com/2012/02/15/long-gun-registry-abolished.

15 Terrance Wills, 'Tough Debate Looms in House over Official Opposition,' *The Gazette* (Montreal), 24 February 1996, A9.

16 Tim Naumetz, 'Conservatives "Lay Track" to Attack Media, Real Opposition Party in New Parliament,' *HT*, 13 June 2011, 1 and 6 at 6; 'Tories Begin Battle against Coalition,' http://www.cbc.ca/canada/story/2008/12/02/harper-coalition.html.

17 Mark Kennedy, 'Harper Sets Sights on Party Subsidies, Warns of Coalition,' *LP*, 13 January 2011, A7; Kennedy, 'Harper Claims Opposition Plans to Form Coalition,' *LP*, 9 October 2010, A12; Randy Boswell, 'Ignatieff Comments on Minority,' *LP*, 20 April 2011, B7.

18 Mark Kennedy, 'PM Says OAS Changes "Being Considered,"' *LP*, 4 February 2012, A5.

19 Reg Whitaker, 'Is the Government Party Over?' *Globe and Mail*, 16 May 2011, A11.

20 Lawrence Martin, *Harperland: The Politics of Control* (Toronto: Viking Canada, 2010), 82.

21 Peter Newman, *When the Gods Changed: The Death of Liberal Canada* (Toronto: Random House, 2011), 223.

22 Ibid., 113–14.

23 Andrew Coyne, 'Justin Buys into Myth of Quebec Progressivism,' *LP*, 18 February 2012, A11.

24 Henry Fairlie, *The Life in Politics* (London: Methuen, 1968), 197.

25 Chantal Hébert, 'Conservative Monarchist Rebranding of Country Seen as an Ill-Advised Return to Canada's Colonial Past,' *HT*, 20 February 2012, 22.

26 Interview, 12 October 2011.

27 Kelly Blidook, 'Symbol vs Substance: Theatre, Political Career Paths, and Parliamentary Behaviour in Canada,' Canadian Study of Parliament Group (2011), 27; http://www.studyparliament.ca/English/pdf/ KBlidookFinal-e.pdf.

28 Andrew Coyne, 'Robocon Is a Scandal with No Clear Pattern,' *LP*, 1 March 2012, A6.

29 Daniel Leblanc, 'Probe Relying on Ex-Mounties,' *Globe and Mail*, 1 March 2012, A4.

30 Kathryn May, 'Walsh Was on Guard for Tradition,' *LP*, 11 February 2012, D9.

31 'Q and A: A Conversation with the Speaker,' *Policy Options* 31, no. 8 (September 2010): 12–16 at 12.

32 See David Hoffman and Norman Ward, *Bilingualism and Biculturalism in the Canadian House of Commons*, Documents of the Royal Commission on Bilingualism and Biculturalism (Ottawa: Queen's Printer, 1970).

33 Roger Graham, *Old Man Ontario: Leslie M. Frost* (Toronto: University of Toronto Press, 1990), 56; interview (Roy Romanow), 12 October 2011.

34 Samara is 'a charitable organization that aims to study citizen engagement with democracy in Canada': Laura Ryckewaert, 'Parliament's Future MPs Need More Help, Guidance, Direction,' *HT*, 2 May 2011, 18. Its publications (all from 2011) include *The Accidental Citizen?*; *'It's My Party': Parliamentary Dysfunction Reconsidered*; and *Welcome to Parliament: A Job with No Description*.

35 Ellen Fairclough, *Saturday's Child: Memoirs of Canada's First Female Cabinet Minister* (Toronto: University of Toronto Press, 1995), 84.

36 DAC, DP, MG 01/1X/A/694.1/391.1 (file: Political Parties–Progressive Conservative Party–Leader of the Progressive Conservative Party, 1964), Richard B. Holden to Diefenbaker, 6 February 1964.

37 Paul Litt, *Elusive Destiny: The Political Vocation of John Napier Turner* (Vancouver: UBC Press, 2011), 350.
38 Walter D. Young, *The Anatomy of a Party: The National CCF, 1932–1961* (Toronto: University of Toronto Press, 1969), 235–6.

Chapter 9

1 Lord Campion, 'Parliament and Democracy,' in *Parliament: A Survey*, ed. Campion et al. (London: George Allen and Unwin, 1952), 9–36 at 31.
2 Gary Levy, 'Who Killed Parliamentary Government?,' paper prepared for the Johnson–Shoyama Graduate School of Public Policy Lecture Series, University of Saskatchewan and University of Regina, 11 January 2011, 6. See also Paul Benoit and Gary Levy, 'Viability of Our Political Institutions Being Questioned,' *HT*, 25 April 2011, 15.
3 Ludger Helms, 'Five Ways of Institutionalizing Political Opposition,' *Government and Opposition* 39, no. 1 (Winter 2004): 22–54 at 27.
4 *CNF*, 1–15 September 1975, 1443 (from Speech to Kiwanis Club, Toronto).
5 Interview, 15 October 2011.
6 Roy MacLaren, *The Fundamental Things Apply: A Memoir* (Montreal and Kingston: McGill–Queen's University Press, 2011), 109.
7 Graham Fraser, *PQ: Rene Lévesque and the Parti Québécois in Power* (Toronto: Macmillan of Canada, 1984), 39.
8 Bruce Ackerman, 'Meritocracy v. Democracy: What to Do about the Lords,' *London Review of Books*, 8 March 1997, http://www.lrb.co.uk/v29/n05/bruce-ackerman/meritocracy-v-democracy/.
9 Elections Canada Online, *Appointment of the Chief Electoral Officer*, http://www.elections.ca/content.aspx?section=abo&dir=ceo/app&document=index&lang=e.
10 Steve Chase, 'Elections Canada Receives 700 Specific Dialling Complaints,' *Globe and Mail*, 16 March 2012, A6; Chase, Renata d'Aliesio, and Daniel LeBlanc, 'House Votes to Give Watchdog More Bite,' *Globe and Mail*, 13 March 2012, A4; Renata d'Aliesio, Steven Chase, and Daniel LeBlanc, 'PM's Ex-Aide Urges "Huge Investigation,"' *Globe and Mail*, 17 March 2012, A3 (emphasis added).
11 Andrew Coyne, 'Robocon Is a Scandal with No Clear Pattern,' *LP*, 1 March 2012, A6.
12 Alexandra Kelso, *Parliamentary Reform at Westminster* (Manchester: Manchester University Press, 2009), 45.
13 Ghita Ionescu and Isabel de Madariaga, *Opposition: Past and Present of a Political Institution* (Harmondsworth: Penguin, 1968), 90 and 95.

14 Bernard Manin, *Principles of Representative Government* (Cambridge: Cambridge University Press, 1997), cited in Kelly Blidook, 'Symbol vs Substance: Theatre, Political Career Paths, and Parliamentary Behaviour in Canada,' Canadian Study of Parliament Group (2012), http://www.studyparliament.ca/English/pdf/KBlidookFinal-e.pdf.

15 John Ibbitson, 'In an Age without Mediators, Many Feel Left Out,' *Globe and Mail*, 12 December 2011, A4.

16 W. Ivor Jennings, *Parliament* (Cambridge: Cambridge University Press, 1939), 508.

Bibliography

Ackerman, Bruce. 'Meritocracy v. Democracy: What to Do about the Lords.' *London Review of Books*, 8 March 1997. http://www.lrb.co.uk/v29/n05/bruce-ackerman/meritocracy-v-democracy/.

Aiken, Gordon. *The Backbencher: The Trials and Tribulations of a Member of Parliament*. Toronto: McClelland and Stewart, 1974.

Allemang, John. 'Layton Stakes His Biggest Bet as Jack of Hearts.' *Globe and Mail*, 28 May 2011, F6.

Amerongen, Gerald. 'Speaker's Ruling: Statement Concerning Status of the Leader of the Official Opposition, March 11, 1983.' *CPR* 8, no. 2 (1983): 44–5.

Amerongen, Gerald. 'Speaker's Ruling: Recognition of the Leader of the Opposition, November 16, 1984.' *CPR* 7, no. 4 (1984): 29

Archer, Keith, Faron Ellis, and Peter Nestoruk. 'Legislators and Their World.' *CPR* 12, no. 2 (Summer 1989): 19–23.

Assembly (Lower Canada). *Journals*, 1809, Appendix and *Lower Canada Statutes*, 51 Geo. III, c.4. Cited in Gary O'Brien, 'Pre-Confederation Parliamentary Procedure: The Evolution of Legislative Practice in the Lower Houses of Central Canada, 1792–1866,' PhD diss., Carleton University, 1988.

Attorney General for Canada v. Attorney General for Ontario and Others [1937], AC 355.

'Backstage at Ottawa.' *Maclean's* 53 (1 May 1940): 51. Quoted in Murray Beck, *Pendulum of Power: Canada's Federal Elections*. Scarborough: Prentice Hall, 1968.

Bailey, Ian. 'Layton Says He'll Be "Driving Hard" to Strengthen Pensions.' *Globe and Mail*, 12 May 2011, A4.

Barnhart, Gordon. 'Tie in Opposition.' *The Table* 46 (1978): 18–22.

Barrie, Doreen, and Roger Gibbins. 'Parliamentary Careers in the Canadian Federal State.' *CJPS* 22, no. 1 (March 1989): 137–45.

Beck, Murray. *Pendulum of Power: Canada's Federal Elections*. Scarborough: Prentice Hall, 1968.

Bélanger, Éric. 'The Rise of Third Parties in the 1993 Canadian Federal Election: Pinard Revisited.' *CJPS* 37, no. 3 (September 2004): 581–94.

Bell, Jeffrey Graham. 'Agents of Parliament: A New Branch of Government?' *CPR* 29, no. 1 (2006): 13–21.

Belliveau, Robert M. *Mr Diefenbaker, Parliamentary Democracy, and the Canadian Bill of Rights*. Unpublished MA thesis, University of Saskatchewan, May 1992.

Benoit, Paul, and Gary Levy. 'Viability of Our Political Institutions Being Questioned.' *HT*, 25 April 2011, 15.

Black, Conrad. *Duplessis*. Toronto: McClelland and Stewart, 1977.

Black, Edwin R. 'Opposition Research: Some Theories and Practice.' *CPA* 15, no. 1 (March 1972): 24–41.

Blaikie, Bill. 'Reflections on the Speaker's Ruling.' *CPR* 17, no. 3 (Autumn 1994): 36.

Blaikie, Bill. 'The Status of Small Parties in the House of Commons.' *CPR* 17, no. 3 (Autumn 1994): 29–32.

Blakeney, Allan. *An Honourable Calling: Political Memoirs*. Toronto: University of Toronto Press, 2008.

Blidook, Kelly. 'Symbol vs Substance: Theatre, Political Career Paths, and Parliamentary Behaviour in Canada.' Canadian Study of Parliament Group, 2011. http://www.studyparliament.ca/English/pdf/KBlidookFinal-e.pdf.

Blondel, Jean. 'Political Opposition in the Contemporary World.' *Government and Opposition* 32, no. 4 (1997): 462–86.

Boswell, Randy. 'Ignatieff Comments on Minority.' *LP*, 20 April 2011, B7.

Bothwell, Robert, and William Kilbourn. *C.D. Howe: A Biography*. Toronto: McClelland and Stewart, 1979.

Boyer, Patrick. *Direct Democracy in Canada: The History and Future of Referendums*. Toronto: Dundurn Press, 1992.

Brett, Judith. 'Parliament, Meetings and Civil Society' (paper presented as a lecture in the Department of the Senate Occasional Lecture Series at Parliament House, Canberra, Australia, 27 July 2001). http://www.aph.gov.au/SENATE/pubs/pops/pop38/c08.pdf (accessed 7 May 2009).

Brown, Robert Craig. *Robert Laird Borden: A Biography*, vol. I, *1854–1914*. Toronto: Macmillan of Canada, 1975.

Brown, Robert Craig. *Robert Laird Borden: A Biography*, vol. II, *1914–1937*. Toronto: Macmillan of Canada, 1980.

Buckingham, W., and G.W. Ross. *The Hon. Alexander Mackenzie*. 5th ed. Toronto, 1892.

Burnet, Jean. *Next-Year Country*. Toronto: University of Toronto Press, 1951.

Campion, Lord. 'Parliament and Democracy.' In *Parliament: A Survey*, ed. Campion et al., 9–36. London: George Allen and Unwin, 1952.

Canada, *Statutes*, 7 Vict., c.3.

Canada. Royal Commission on Bilingualism and Biculturalism. *A Preliminary Report*. Ottawa: Queen's Printer, 1965.

CAR (1928–9): 469–70.

Carr, Cecil. 'Parliament and Pipeline.' *CBR* 35, no. 9 (November 1956): 1100–6.

Cartwright, Sir Richard. *Reminiscences*. Toronto: William Briggs, 1912.

CBC News Online, 'Federal Sponsorship Scandal,' 26 October 2006, http://www.cbc.ca/slash/news/background/groupaction.

Chase, Steven. 'Straight-Talking Fraser Strikes Fear on the Hill.' *Globe and Mail*, 12 February 2004, 4.

Chase, Steven. 'Privacy Watchdog Sounds Alarm on E-Snooping Legislation.' *Globe and Mail*, 28 October 2011, A6.

Chase, Steven. 'Conservative Senators Avoid Charges in Plea Deal.' *Globe and Mail*, 11 November 2011, A4.

Chase, Steve. 'Elections Canada Receives 700 Specific Dialling Complaints.' *Globe and Mail*, 16 March 2012, A6.

Chase, Steven, Renata d'Aliesio, and Daniel LeBlanc. 'House Votes to Give Watchdog More Bite.' *Globe and Mail*, 13 March 2012, A4.

Clark, Campbell, and Daniel Leblanc. 'Fraser Puts Heat on PM.' *Globe and Mail*, 11 February 2004, A1.

Clark, S.D. *Movements of Social Protest in Canada, 1640–1840*. Toronto: University of Toronto Press, 1959.

Cline, Eric. *Making a Difference: Reflections from Political Life*. Saskatoon: Thistledown Press, 2008.

CNF. 'Guillotine Rule Invoked,' 7–20 April 1967, 57.

CNF. 'Opposition Defends Auditor-General,' 1–15 April 1970, 427.

CNF. 'Stanfield Acquiescence Explained,' 16–30 June 1970, 480.

CNF. 'Bilingualism Resolution Approved,' 1 June–15 June 1973, 1026.

CNF. 'United PCs Emerge from Convention,' 16–31 March 1974, 1177.

CNF. 'Parliamentary Rule Changes Proposed,' 1–15 October 1974, 1271.

CNF. 1–15 September 1975, 1443 (from Speech to Kiwanis Club, Toronto).

CNF. 'Clark Would Free Committees,' 1–15 April 1979, 2116.

CNF. 'Rae's Policies Divide Federal NDP,' 16–30 April 1993, 4741.

CNF. 'Bouchard Braves English Canada,' 16–30 September 1993, 4810.

CNF. 'Reform Polls Unity Views,' 1–15 October 1994, 5006.

CNF. 'Bouchard Sounds Battle Call,' 16–30 November 1994, 5030.

CNF. 'Gautier Elected Bloc Leader,' 16–29 February 1996, 5269.

CNF. 'NAC Lobbies MPs,' 16–30 June 1996, 5332.

CNF. 'Manning Uses Quebec Podium,' 1–15 April 1997, 5490.

CNF. 'Reform Plan Scuttled,' 1–15 April 1997, 5473.

CNF. 'Manning Attacked Over Ads,' 16–31 April 1997, 5498.

CNF. 'Manning Accepts Stornoway,' 16–30 June 1997, 5515.

CNF. 'Reform Makes New Waves,' 1–15 June 1999, 4948.

CNF. 'Farmers Stage Ottawa Protest,' 1–31 August 1999, 5919.

Conrad, Margaret. *George Nowlan: Maritime Conservative in National Politics*. Toronto: University of Toronto Press, 1986.

Cook, Ramsay. *Provincial Autonomy, Minority Rights, and the Compact Theory, 1867–1921*. (Royal Commission on Bilingualism and Biculturalism, Study No. 4.) Ottawa: Information Canada, 1969.

Corry, J.A. *Democratic Government and Politics*. Toronto: University of Toronto Press, 1946.

Courtney, John C. *The Selection of National Party Leaders in Canada*. Toronto: Macmillan of Canada, 1973.

Courtney, John C. 'Recognition of Canadian Political Parties in Parliament and Law.' *CJPS* 11, no. 1 (March 1978): 33–60.

Courtney, John C. *Do Conventions Matter? Choosing National Party Leaders in Canada*. Montreal and Kingston: McGill–Queen's University Press, 1995.

Courtney, John C., and David E. Smith. 'Voting in a Provincial General Election and a Federal By-Election: A Constituency Study of Saskatoon City.' *CJEPS* 32, no. 3 (August 1966): 338–53.

Coyne, Andrew. 'Justin Buys into Myth of Quebec Progressivism.' *LP*, 18 February 2012, A11.

Coyne, Andrew. 'Robocon Is a Scandal with No Clear Pattern.' *LP*, 1 March 2012, A6.

Creighton, Donald. *John A. Macdonald: The Young Politician*. Toronto: Macmillan of Canada, 1952.

Creighton, Donald. *Canada's First Century, 1867–1967*. Toronto: Macmillan of Canada, 1970.

d'Aliesio, Renata, Steven Chase, and Daniel LeBlanc. 'PM's Ex-Aide Urges "Huge Investigation."' *Globe and Mail*, 17 March 2012, A3.

DAC. DP, 334, file: Ellen Fairclough, March 1957, 'The Role of the Opposition in Government,' 08763–08770 at 08768 and 08769.

DAC. DP, Diefenbaker to Elmer Diefenbaker, 11 April 1957 and 24 May 1963, vol. 3, 1608–09 and 2933–34.

DAC. DP, 334.1, 08811, file: Material for Questions in the House of Commons, January–May 1957, Sevigny to Diefenbaker, 21 January 1957.

DAC. DP, A526/692, Speech Delivered to Empire Club, Toronto, 21 March 1957. 'The Role of the Opposition in Parliament.'

DAC. DP, MG 01/1X/A/694.1/391.1 (file: Political Parties–Progressive Conservative Party–Leader of the Progressive Conservative Party, 1964), Richard B. Holden to Diefenbaker, 6 February 1964.

DAC. DP, MG01/IX/A/596/334, file: 'The House of Commons – The Opposition, 1964,' 'Government in Canada: The Role of the Opposition,' for publication in magazine 'The Educational ABCs of Canadian Industry.' Letter from editor to JGD, 30 December 1963, 012195–012213 at 012204–5.

DAC. DP, MG01/IX/B/41, file: Pauline L'Orange to Richard Bell, 29 May 1967.

DAC. DP, MG01/1X/B/129, file: Clark, Joe, 1964–5, Van Dusen to Clark, 20 March 1964.

DAC. DP, MG01/1X/B/129, file: Clark, Joe, 1964–5, Diefenbaker to Clark (Draft), 9 February 1965.

DAC. DP, reel M–5561, Report No. 12, *The Social Credit Movement*, 15 October 1955, 21515–671 at 21656 and 21659.

Davey, Keith. *The Rainmaker: A Passion for Politics*. Toronto: Stoddart, 1986.

Dawson, R. MacGregor. *William Lyon Mackenzie King: A Political Biography, 1874–1923*. Toronto: University of Toronto Press, 1958.

Dawson, R. MacGregor. *The Government of Canada*. 5th ed., rev. Norman Ward. Toronto: University of Toronto Press, 1970.

de Souza, Mike, and Amy Minsky. 'Ruling Could Lead to Increased Secrecy.' *LP*, 14 May 2011, A10.

DHOC, 18 August 1920, 547 (John H. Burnham).

DHOC, 20 March 1922, 214. Cited in Kenneth McNaught, *A Prophet in Politics: A Biography of J.S. Woodsworth* (p. 167). Toronto: University of Toronto Press, 2001, 167.

DHOC, 30 May 1938, 3339.

DHOC, 22 March 1954, 3206 and 3232–3.

DHOC, 22 March 1954, 3207 (citing *Edmonton Bulletin*, 16 November 1950).

DHOC, 14 October 1957, 5. Quoted in Robert M. Belliveau, *Mr Diefenbaker, Parliamentary Democracy, and the Canadian Bill of Rights* (p. 79). Unpublished MA thesis, University of Saskatchewan, May 1992.

DHOC (1919, Special Session), 551–3. Cited in Roger Graham, *Arthur Meighen: A Biography*, vol. I, *The Door of Opportunity* (pp. 1, 257). Toronto: Clarke, Irwin and Co., 1960.

DHOC, 2 June 1919, 3014–15. Cited in Roger Graham, *Arthur Meighen: A Biography*, vol. I, *The Door of Opportunity* (pp. 239–40). Toronto: Clarke, Irwin and Co., 1960.

DHOC, 25 May 1965, 1643–6.

DHOC, 20 November 1967, 4460.

DHOC, 12 July 1973, 5553–4.

Diefenbaker, John G. *One Canada: Memoirs of the Rt. Hon. John G. Diefenbaker*, vol. I, *The Crusading Years, 1895–1956*. Toronto: Macmillian of Canada, 1975.

Ditchburn, Jennifer. 'Better Scrutiny of Watchdogs Recommended.' *Globe and Mail*, 4 March 2011, A6.

DLAUC, 23 June 1849, V111.1.1849, 155.

DLAUC, 8 October 1853, X1–11–1852–3, 932.

DLAUC, 4 December 1854, XII.IV.1854–5, 1579.

Docherty, David. 'Representation, Amateurism, and Turnover.' In *Mr Smith Goes to Ottawa: Life in the House of Commons*, 31–59. Vancouver: UBC Press, 1997.

Drewry, G. 'Reform of the Legislative Process: Some Neglected Questions.' *Parliamentary Affairs* 25, no. 4 (1972): 298–9. Quoted in Alexandra Kelso, *Parliamentary Reform at Westminster*. Manchester: Manchester University Press, 2009.

Drury, Ernest Charles. *Farmer Premier: Memoirs of the Honourable E.C. Drury*. Toronto: McClelland and Stewart, 1966.

Dunn, Christopher. 'Executive Dominance in Provincial Legislatures.' *CPR* 13, no. 1 (1990): 11–18.

Edinburgh Review (July 1807), X, no. XX, 413.

Editorial. 'Is Parliament Free?' *Star-Phoenix*, 17 June 1951.

Edmonton Journal, 19 June 1963, 1. Quoted in Lorna Stefanick, 'Alberta's Ombudsman: Following Responsibility in an Era of Outsourcing.' In Hyson, ed., *Provincial and Territorial Ombudsman Offices in Canada* (pp. 27–52 at 28). (Institute of Public Administration of Canada.) Toronto: University of Toronto Press, 2009.

Elections Canada Online. *Appointment of the Chief Electoral Officer*. http://www.elections.ca/content.aspx?section=abo&dir=ceo/app&document=index&lang=e.

English, John. *The Worldly Years: The Life of Lester Pearson*, vol. II., *1949–1972*. Toronto: Alfred A. Knopf Canada, 1992.

Fairclough, Ellen. *Saturday's Child: Memoirs of Canada's First Female Cabinet Minister*. Toronto: University of Toronto Press, 1995.

Fairlie, Henry. *The Life in Politics*. London: Methuen, 1968.

Flanagan, Tom. 'Only Voters Have the Right to Decide on the Coalition.' *Globe and Mail*, 9 January 2009, A13.

Flanagan, Tom. *Harper's Team: Behind the Scenes in the Conservative Rise to Power*. 2nd ed. Montreal and Kingston: McGill–Queen's University Press, 2009.

Flanagan, Tom. 'Some Day, They'll Thank Mr Harper.' *Globe and Mail*, 31 May 2011, A13.

Flanagan, Tom. 'Something Blue: Conservative Organization in an Era of Permanent Campaign.' *Inroads* 28 (Winter–Spring 2011): 90–9.

Flanagan, Tom. 'Political Communication and the "Permanent Campaign."' In *How Canadians Communicate IV: Media and Politics*, eds. David Taras and Christopher Waddell, 129–48. Edmonton: Athabaska University Press, 2012.

Foord, Archibald S. *His Majesty's Opposition, 1714–1830*. Oxford: Clarendon Press, 1964.

Forsey, Eugene. *The Royal Power of Dissolution in the British Commonwealth*. Toronto: Oxford University Press, 1943.

Forsey, Eugene. 'Introductory Note' on the Essay: 'Mr. King and Parliamentary Government,' *CJEPS* 17, no. 4 (November 1951): 451–67.

Forsey, Eugene. 'Never Have So Many Been In So Long.' *Canadian Commentator* 1, no. 5 (May 1957): 1–2.

Forsey, Eugene. 'Canada: Two Nations or One?' *CJEPS* 28, no. 4 (November 1962): 485–501. Reprinted in Forsey, *Freedom and Order: Collected Essays* (Carleton Library No. 73, Toronto: McClelland and Stewart, 1974), 247–69.

Forsey, Eugene. *Freedom and Order: Collected Essays* (Carleton Library No. 73, Toronto: McClelland and Stewart, 1974).

Forsey, Eugene. *A Life on the Fringe: The Memoirs of Eugene Forsey*. Toronto: Oxford University Press, 1990.

Fowke, V.C. *The National Policy and the Wheat Economy*. Toronto: University of Toronto Press, 1957.

Franks, C.E.S. 'The "Problem" of Debate and Question Period.' In *The Canadian House of Commons: Essays in Honour of Norman Ward*, ed. John C. Courtney, 1–19. Calgary: University of Calgary Press, 1985.

Franks, C.E.S. *The Parliament of Canada*. Toronto: University of Toronto Press, 1987.

Fraser, Graham. *PQ: Rene Lévesque and the Parti Québécois in Power*. Toronto: Macmillan of Canada, 1984.

Furi, Megan. 'Officers of Parliament: A Study in Government Adaptation,' MA thesis, University of Saskatchewan, 2002.

Gagnon, Lysiane. 'An Online Petition with a Popular Twist.' *Globe and Mail*, 22 November 2010, A17.

Gagnon, Lysiane. 'Quebeckers' Mental Bloc.' *Globe and Mail*, 16 May 2011, A11.

Galloway, Gloria. 'Watchdogs – or Lapdogs?' *Globe and Mail*, 28 December 2010, A4.

Galloway, Gloria, and Jane Taber. 'Watchdog Scolds Tories for Unilingual Appointments.' *Globe and Mail*, 4 November 2011, A6.

Gardiner Papers. Gardiner to Hon. David A. Croll, 15 June 1957, 66589; Gardiner to Paul Martin, 12 December 1958, 66775–6; Gardiner to Howard Winkler, 9 December 1958, 67498.

Geller-Schwartz, Linda. 'Minority Government Reconsidered.' *JCS* 14, no. 2 (1979): 67–79.

Gibson, Frederick W., ed. *Cabinet Formation and Bicultural Relations: Seven Case Studies.* (Royal Commission on Bilingualism and Biculturalism, Study No. 6.) Ottawa: Queen's Printer, 1970.

Gibson, Frederick W., and Barbara Robertson (ed. and intro.). *Ottawa at War: The Grant Dexter Memoranda, 1939–1945.* Winnipeg: Manitoba Record Society, 1994.

Gibson, Gordon. 'Democratic Reform Should Be This Election's Central Issue.' *Globe and Mail*, 13 April 2011, A17.

Glassford, Larry A. 'Bennett Papers, vol. 950, McRae to Bennett, 23 December 1929.' In *Reaction and Reform: The Politics of the Conservative Party under R.B. Bennett, 1927–1938*, 51–2. Toronto: University of Toronto Press, 1992.

Globe and Mail, 5 March 2011, A13.

Grafstein, J.S. 'The Mystery of the National Liberal Caucus.' Fourth Allan J. MacEachen Lecture in Politics, St Francis Xavier University, 24 September 2001. In James Bickerton, ed., *Reflections on Canadian Politics*, vol. II (pp. 15–33). Antigonish: St Francis University Press, 2008.

Graham, Roger. *Arthur Meighen, A Biography*, vol. I, *The Door of Opportunity*. Toronto: Clarke, Irwin and Co., 1960.

Graham, Roger. *Arthur Meighen: A Biography*, vol. II, *And Fortune Fled*. Toronto: Clarke, Irwin and Co., 1963.

Graham, Roger. *Arthur Meighen, A Biography*, vol. III, *No Surrender*. Toronto: Clarke, Irwin and Co., 1965.

Graham, Roger. *Old Man Ontario: Leslie M. Frost*. Toronto: University of Toronto Press, 1990.

Granatstein, J.L. Manion Papers, vol. 65. Speech to caucus, 13 May 1940 (typed copy).

Granatstein, J.L. *The Politics of Opposition: The Conservative Party of Canada, 1939–1945.* Toronto: University of Toronto Press, 1967.

Gray, Walter. 'Stanfield in First House Vote Joins Liberals to Defeat Motion.' *Toronto Daily Star*, 18 November 1967, 7.

Griffiths, Rudyard, ed. *Dialogue on Democracy.* The Lafontaine–Baldwin Lectures, 2000–5. Toronto: Penguin Canada, 2006.

Halabura, Gerald Michael. *Diefenbaker and Electoral Distribution: Principle and Pragmatism.* Unpublished MA thesis, University of Saskatchewan, 1992.

Halifax Morning Journal, 23 December 1859. Cited in P.B. Waite, ed., *Pre-Confederation,* vol. II (p. 191). Scarborough: Prentice-Hall of Canada, 1965.

Harper v. Canada (Attorney General), [2004] 1 SCR 827.

Hébert, Chantal. *French Kiss: Stephen Harper's Blind Date with Quebec.* Toronto: Alfred A. Knopf Canada, 2007.

Hébert, Chantal. 'Citizens Angry, Engaged, and Ahead of Conventional Parties.' *HT,* 1 November 2010, 1 and 5.

Hébert, Chantal. 'Conservative Monarchist Rebranding of Country Seen as an Ill-Advised Return to Canada's Colonial Past.' *HT,* 20 February 2012, 22.

Heintzman, Ralph. 'The Educational Contract.' *JCS* 14, no. 2 (1979): 1–2, 142–5.

Helms, Ludger. 'Five Ways of Institutionalizing Political Opposition.' *Government and Opposition* 39, no. 1 (Winter 2004): 22–54.

Hewart, Lord. *The New Despotism.* London: E. Benn, 1929.

Himelfarb, Alex. 'We Seem to Have Forgotten the Fact That If We Want Government Services (and We Do), We Need to Pay for Them.' *Globe and Mail,* 15 October 2011, F4.

Hockin, Thomas Alexander. *The Loyal Opposition in Canada: An Introduction to Its Ideal Roles and Their Practical Implementation for Representative and Responsible Government.* Unpublished PhD diss., Harvard University, 1966.

Hodgetts, J.E. *Pioneer Public Service: An Administrative History of the United Canadas, 1841–1867.* Toronto: University of Toronto Press, 1955.

Hoffman, David, and Norman Ward. *Bilingualism and Biculturalism in the Canadian House of Commons.* Documents of the Commission on Bilingualism and Biculturalism. Ottawa: Queen's Printer, 1970.

House of Commons, Canada. *Selected Decisions of Speaker Gilbert Parent, 1994–2001* (2008), '"The House and Its Members," Official Opposition: Designation: Tie in Opposition, February 27, 1996, Debates, 16–20,' 84–93 at 93. http://www.canada.com/ottawacitizen/news/story.html?id=d8cdb413-857e-4ef9-878d-24d1c7b916ea.

'Howe Acting as PM, Fills 11 Other Roles.' *Globe and Mail,* 24 July 1951, 1.

Hurtubise-Loranger, Élise. 'Official Languages and Parliament.' Library of Parliament, Law and Government Division, revised 23 July 2008, PRB 06-28E.

Hyson, Stewart. 'A One-Party Legislature: Where's "Her Majesty's Loyal Opposition": In the Loyalist Province?' *CPR* 11, no. 2 (1988): 22–5.

Hyson, Stewart. 'Determining the Official Opposition in New Brunswick and the House of Commons.' *CPR* 19, no. 3 (1996): 2–6.

Hyson, Stewart, ed. *Provincial and Territorial Ombudsman Offices in Canada.* (Institute of Public Administration of Canada.) Toronto: University of Toronto Press, 2009.

Hyson, Stewart. 'A Primer on Federal Specialty OmbudsOffices.' *CPR* 34, no. 2 (Summer 2011): 34–42.

Ibbitson, John. 'Commons Fully Backs Deployment.' *Globe and Mail*, 22 March 2011, A17.

Ibbitson, John. 'Qualms That Could Keep Harper Up at Night.' *Globe and Mail*, 16 May 2011, A4.

Ibbitson, John. 'In an Age without Mediators, Many Feel Left Out.' *Globe and Mail*, 12 December 2011, A4.

'Interview: George McIlraith.' *CPR* 7, no. 4 (1984): 21–5.

Ionescu, Ghita, and Isabel de Madariaga. *Opposition: Past and Present of a Political Institution.* Harmondsworth: Penguin, 1968.

Irving, J.A. *The Social Credit Movement.* Toronto: University of Toronto Press, 1959.

Jeffrey, Brooke. 'The Parliamentary Budget Officer Two Years Later: A Progress Report.' *CPR* 33, no. 4 (Winter 2010): 37–45.

Jeffrey, Brooke. *Divided Loyalties: The Liberal Party of Canada, 1984–2008.* Toronto: University of Toronto Press, 2010.

Jennings, W. Ivor. *Parliament.* Cambridge: Cambridge University Press, 1939.

Jennings, Sir Ivor. *The Queen's Government.* London: Penguin, 1954.

Jennings, Ivor. *Cabinet Government.* 3rd ed. Cambridge: Cambridge University Press, 1959.

Jerome, James. *Mr Speaker: James Jerome.* Toronto: McClelland and Stewart, 1985.

John A. Macdonald to M.C. Cameron, 3 January 1872. In *Sir Joseph Pope, Correspondence of Sir John A. Macdonald: Selections from the Correspondence of the Rt. Hon. Sir John Alexander Macdonald.* Toronto: Oxford University Press, [n.d.].

Johnson, Neville. 'Opposition in the British Political System.' *Government and Opposition* 32, no. 4 (Autumn 1997): 487–510.

Johnstone, Bruce. 'Farmers Denied the Right to Decide.' *LP*, 17 December 2011, B1.

Johnstone, Bruce. 'Ritz Declares Victory in Battle Over CWB.' *LP*, 17 December 2011, B1.

Juillet, Luc, and Ken Rasmussen. *Defending a Contested Ideal: Merit and the PSC of Canada, 1908–2008.* Ottawa: University of Ottawa Press, 2008.

Kelso, Alexandra. *Parliamentary Reform at Westminster.* Manchester: Manchester University Press, 2009.

Kendle, John. *John Bracken: A Biography*. Toronto: University of Toronto Press, 1979.

Kennedy, Mark. 'Harper Claims Opposition Plans to Form Coalition.' *LP*, 9 October 2010, A12.

Kennedy, Mark. 'Harper Sets Sights on Party Subsidies, Warns of Coalition.' *LP*, 13 January 2011, A7.

Kennedy, Mark. 'PM Says OAS Changes "Being Considered."' *LP*, 4 February 2012, A5.

Kilbourn, William. *Pipeline: Transcanada and the Great Debate, A History of Business and Politics*. Toronto: Clarke, Irwin and Co., 1970.

Kingsley, Jean-Pierre. 'Political Parties Could Be Forced to Return to Big Money Corporate Funding If Per-Vote Subsidies Scrapped.' *HT*, 11 April 2011, 1, 16–7.

Knowles, Stanley. 'The Role of the Opposition in Parliament.' Address to the Empire Club of Canada, Toronto, 21 March 1957, Press Release, Cooperative Commonwealth Federation in DAC, DP, A526/692, 'Stanley Knowles,' 11pp at 7.

Korski, Tom. 'Years Ago, I Tried to Trace the Genesis of Conservative Loathing for the CBC.' *HT*, 16 May 2011, 10.

Kyba, Patrick. 'The Saskatchewan General Election of 1929.' Unpublished MA thesis, University of Saskatchewan, 1964.

Kynaston, David. *Austerity Britain, 1945–1951*. London: Bloomsbury, 2007.

Ladurantaye, Steve. 'No Reprieve for Elizabeth May.' *Globe and Mail*, 1 April 2011, A5.

Langstone, Rosa W. 'Robert Baldwin's Proposals to the Legislative Assembly of Canada, on September, 1841.' Appendix J. In *Responsible Government in Canada*, 221. Toronto: J.M. Dent and Sons, 1931.

Leblanc, Daniel. 'Retiring Fraser Urges Vigilance over Watchdog's Independence.' *Globe and Mail*, 26 May 2011, A10.

Leblanc, Daniel. 'Probe Relying on Ex-Mounties.' *Globe and Mail*, 1 March 2012, A4.

Leblanc, Daniel, and Campbell Clark, 'Harper Threatens Election for Ottawa to "Function."' *Globe and Mail*, 15 August 2008, 1/4.

'Lesage Attacks Trudeau.' *CNF*, 11–31 September 1967.

Levy, Gary. 'Who Killed Parliamentary Government?' Paper Prepared for the Johnson–Shoyama Graduate School of Public Policy Lecture Series, University of Saskatchewan and University of Regina, 11 January 2011.

Lijphart, Arend. 'The Netherlands: The Rules of the Game.' In *Consociational Democracy: Political Accommodation in Segmented Societies*, ed. Kenneth McRae, 136–49. Toronto: McClelland and Stewart, 1974.

Lipset, Seymour Martin. 'Democracy in Alberta.' In *Voting in Canada*, ed. John C. Courtney, 182–5. Scarborough: Prentice-Hall of Canada, 1967. Originally from *The Canadian Forum* 34 (November–December, 1954).

Litt, Paul. *Elusive Destiny: The Political Vocation of John Napier Turner*. Vancouver: UBC Press, 2011.

Lowell, A. Lawrence. *Essays on Government*. Boston: Houghton Mifflin, 1897.

MacDonald, Nicholas A., and James W.J. Bowden. 'No Discretion: On Prorogation and the Governor General.' *CPR* 34, no. 1 (2011): 7–16.

Mackenzie King, W.L. *The Message of the Carillon and Other Addresses*. Toronto: Macmillan Company of Canada, 1928.

MacLaren, Roy. *The Fundamental Things Apply: A Memoir*. Montreal and Kingston: McGill–Queen's University Press, 2011.

MacMillan, Margaret. *Paris, 1919: Six Months That Changed the World*. New York: Random House, 2003.

Macpherson, C.B. *Democracy in Alberta*. Toronto: University of Toronto Press, 1953.

Mallory, J.R. *Social Credit and the Federal Power in Canada*. Toronto: University of Toronto Press, 1954.

Malloy, Kate. 'Public Funding Too High, Political Parties Becoming "Empty Shells."' *HT*, 2 October 2006; http://www.thehilltimes.ca/page/view/.2006.october.2.funding.

Manin, Bernard. *Principles of Representative Government*. Cambridge: Cambridge University Press, 1997. Cited in Kelly Blidook, 'Symbol vs Substance: Theatre, Political Career Paths, and Parliamentary Behaviour in Canada,' Canadian Study of Parliament Group (2012). http://www.studyparliament.ca/English/pdf/KBlidookFinal-e.pdf.

Mann, W.E. *Sect, Cult, and Church in Alberta*. Toronto: University of Toronto Press, 1955.

Manning, Preston. 'Parliament, Not Judges, Must Make the Laws of the Land.' *Globe and Mail*, 16 June 1998, A23.

Manning, Preston. *Think Big: Adventures in Life and Democracy*. Toronto: McClelland and Stewart, 2002.

Manning, Preston. 'How to Remake the National Agenda.' *National Post*, 13 February 2003, A18.

Manning, Preston. 'Democracy in the 21st Century: New Imperatives, Old Restraints.' In *Who Decides? Government in the New Millennium*, ed. Richard M. Bird, 25–35. Toronto: C.D. Howe Institute, 2004.

Manning, Preston. 'New Order Mustn't Threaten Unity, Vision.' *Globe and Mail*, 20 May 2011, A15.

Marchildon, Gregory P. 'Provincial Coalition Governments in Canada: An
Interpretive Survey.' In *Continuity and Change in Canadian Politics: Essays in
Honour of David E. Smith*, ed. Hans J. Michelmann and Cris de Clercy.
Toronto: University of Toronto Press, 2006.

Martin, Geoffrey. 'The Rise and Fall of the New Brunswick CoR Party, 1988–
1995.' *CPR* 18, no. 3 (1995): 19–22.

Martin, Lawrence. *The Antagonist: Lucien Bouchard and the Politics of Delusion.*
Toronto: Viking, 1997.

Martin, Lawrence. *Harperland: The Politics of Control.* Toronto: Viking Canada,
2010.

Mason, Gary. 'Lucky Liberals, NDP Could Be Neck and Neck If Election Held
Now: Poll.' *Globe and Mail*, 20 November 2010, A5.

Mason, Gary. 'Inside the Downfall of Carole James.' *Globe and Mail*, 7 December
2010, A5.

Masters, D.C. *The Winnipeg General Strike.* Toronto: University of Toronto
Press, 1950.

May, Katherine. 'Parliamentary Privilege Used as "Sword" against Citizens,
Political Experts Warn.' *Ottawa Citizen*, 24 April 2008, A1.

May, Kathryn. 'Walsh Was on Guard for Tradition.' *LP*, 11 February 2012, D9.

McArthur, Greg. 'Harper's Ex-Adviser Urges Caution on National Security
Czar.' *Globe and Mail*, 17 August 2010. http://www.theglobeandmail.com/
news/politics/harpers-ex-adviser-urges-caution-on-nation.

McCaig, James. *Studies in Citizenship.* Toronto: The Educational Book Co., 1941.

McConnell, W.H. *Commentary on the British North America Act.* Toronto:
Macmillan of Canada, 1977.

McGregor, Glen. 'Ethics Popular Topic in Ottawa.' *LP*, 4 January 2011, B7.

McHenry, Dean E. 'Formal Recognition of the Leader of the Opposition in
Parliaments of the British Commonwealth.' *PSQ* 69, no. 3 (Sept. 1954): 438–
52. http://dx.doi.org/10.2307/2145279.

McNaught, Kenneth. *A Prophet in Politics: A Biography of J.S. Woodsworth.*
Toronto: University of Toronto Press, 2001.

McRae, Kenneth, ed. *Consociational Democracy: Political Accommodation in
Segmented Societies.* Toronto: McClelland and Stewart.

McTeer, Maureen. *Residences: Homes of Canada's Leaders.* Scarborough: Prentice-
Hall Canada, 1982.

Meighen, Arthur. 'The CBC: A Party Instrument.' In *Unrevised and Unrepented:
Debating Speeches and Others*, 419–34. Toronto: Clarke, Irwin and Co., 1949.

Morton, Desmond. 'A Note on Party Switchers.' *CPR* 29, no. 2 (2006): 4–8.

Morton, W.L. *The Progressive Party in Canada.* Toronto: University of Toronto
Press, 1950.

Munro, John A., and Alex I. Inglis. *Mike: The Memoirs of the Right Honourable Lester B. Pearson.* 3 vols. Toronto: University of Toronto Press, 1975.

National Archives. Eugene Forsey Papers, 60/16, file: Parliamentary Appointments 1981, 1990, 'Officers of Parliament.'

Naumetz, Tim. 'Conservatives "Lay Track" to Attack Media, Real Opposition Party in New Parliament.' *HT*, 13 June 2011, 1 and 6.

New Brunswick and the Commission on Legislative Democracy. *Final Report and Recommendations*, 31 December 2004. http://www.electionsnb.ca/pdf/cld/CLDFinalReport-e.pdf.

Newman, Peter. *When the Gods Changed: The Death of Liberal Canada.* Toronto: Random House, 2011.

Nitoslawski, Jan. 'One-Man Ethics in Government Crusader Conacher to Leave Gig in Ottawa.' *HT*, 7 March 2011, 4.

Nowlan Papers. George Nowlan to Miriam Nowlan, 12 June 1955, Vaughan Memorial Library Archives, Acadia University. Cited in Margaret Conrad, *George Nowlan: Maritime Conservative in National Politics.* Toronto: University of Toronto Press, 1986.

O'Brien, Gary. 'Pre-Confederation Parliamentary Procedure: The Evolution of Legislative Practice in the Lower Houses of Central Canada, 1792–1866.' Unpub. PhD diss., Carleton University, 1988.

Oliver, Craig. *Oliver's Twist.* Toronto: Penguin, 2011.

Oliver, Peter. *G. Howard Ferguson: Ontario Tory.* Toronto: University of Toronto Press, 1977.

Ontario, Confederation for Tomorrow Conference. *Proceedings.* Toronto, 27–30 November 1967.

Orlikow, Lionel. 'The Reform Movement in Manitoba, 1910–1915.' In *Historical Essays on the Prairie Provinces*, ed. Donald Swainson, 215–29. Carleton Library No. 53. Toronto: McClelland and Stewart, 1970.

Page, Donald. 'Streamlining the Procedures of the Canadian House of Commons, 1963–1966.' *CJEPS* 33, no. 1 (February 1967): 27–49.

Pelletier, Yves Yvon J. 'Time Allocation in the House of Commons.' *CPR* 23, no. 4 (2000): 20–8.

Pickersgill, J.W. *My Years with Louis St Laurent: A Political Memoir.* Toronto: University of Toronto Press, 1975.

Pickersgill, J.W. *The Road Back: By a Liberal in Opposition.* Toronto: University of Toronto Press, 1986.

Pond, David. 'The Role of Parliamentary Officers: A Case Study of Two Officers.' *CPR* 33, no. 4 (Winter 2010): 19–26.

Pope, Sir Joseph. *Correspondence of Sir John A. Macdonald: Selections from the Correspondence of the Rt. Hon. Sir John A. Macdonald.* Toronto: Oxford University Press, 1921.

Pothier, Dianne. 'Parties and Free Votes in the Canadian House of Commons: The Case of Capital Punishment.' *JCS* 14, no. 2 (Summer 1979): 80–96.

Potter, Andrew. 'Unbalanced Thoughts.' *LRC*, July–August 2009, 3–4.

Prang, Margaret. *N.W. Rowell: Ontario Nationalist*. Toronto: University of Toronto Press, 1975.

Privy Council Office. *Ethics, Responsibility, Accountability: An Action Plan for Democratic Reform*. Ottawa: February 2004.

'Province Asks Feds to Move Election.' *LP*, 16 December 2011, B10.

Punnett, R.M. *Front-Bench Opposition: The Role of the Leader of the Opposition, the Shadow Cabinet, and Shadow Government in British Politics*. New York: St Martin's Press, 1973.

'Q and A: A Conversation with the Speaker.' *Policy Options* 31, no. 8 (September 2010): 12–16.

'Quebec Alters Opening Ceremony.' *CNF*, 16–28 February 1970, 407–8.

'Quebec Outrage as Tories Celebrate Long-Gun Registry Vote with Cocktail Party.' 15 February 2012. http://news.nationalpost.com/2012/02/15/long-gun-registry-abolished.

Rae, Bob. *From Protest to Power: Personal Reflections on a Life in Politics*. Toronto: Viking Penguin, 1996.

Ranney, Austin. 'Toward a More Responsible Two-Party System: A Commentary.' *APSR* 45, no. 2 (June 1951): 488–99.

Rea, J.E. *T.A. Crerar: A Political Life*. Montreal and Kingston: McGill–Queen's University Press, 1998.

Reid, Escott M. 'The Liberal Party Machine in Saskatchewan before 1929.' *CJEPS* 2 (1936): 27–40.

'Relation of a Member of Parliament to His Constituents: 1.A "Representative or Delegate?"' *Manitoba Free Press*, 2 August 1919. In R. MacGregor Dawson, *Constitutional Issues in Canada, 1900–1931*, 187–8. London: Oxford University Press, 1933.

Review (by Heath Macquarrie) of *Speaking for Myself: Politics and Other Pursuits*, in *CPR* 23, no. 2 (Summer 2000): 37.

Risk, R.C.B. 'Blake and Liberty.' In *Canadian Constitutionalism, 1791–1991*, ed. Janet Ajzenstat, 195–211. Ottawa: Canadian Study of Parliament Group, 1991.

Robertson, James R. 'Political Parties and Parliamentary Recognition.' Library of Parliament, Law and Government Division, rev. August 1996. http://dsp-psd.pwgsc.gc.ca/Collection-R/LoPBdP/bp243-e.htm.

Robinson, John Beverly. *Canada and the Canada Bill*. Toronto: S.R. Publishers, Johnson Reprint Corp., 1967.

Robson, Mia. 'Bill to Kill CWB Monopoly Clears Senate.' *LP*, 16 December 2011, D1.

Rowat, Don. 'Our Referendums Are Not Direct Democracy.' *CPR* 21, no. 3 (1998): 25–7.

Russell, Peter H. *Constitutional Odyssey: Can Canadians Become a Sovereign People?* 3rd ed. Toronto: University of Toronto Press, 2004.

Russell, Peter H., and Lorne Sossin, eds. 'Introduction,' in *Parliamentary Democracy in Crisis*. Toronto: University of Toronto Press, 2009.

Ryckewaert, Laura. 'Parliament's Future MPs Need More Help, Guidance, Direction.' *HT*, 2 May 2011, 18.

SAB, GP, Gardiner to Ken Mayhew, 9 July 1957, 66737–8.

SAB, GP, 'Report from Parliament Hill.' CKCK (Regina), 9 November 1957.

SAB, NWP, A526/117, file: 'Correspondence, 1968,' Minutes of the Meeting of the Leader's Policy Advisory Committee, 26 February 1968; 'Summary of Discussions and Conclusions of the Advisory Committee on the Setting Up of a Policy Research Organization' (author, E.D. Fulton); D.W. Slater and T.H.B. Symons, 'An Outline of Some Topics for Study by the Policy Advisory Committee,' n.d.; E.D. Fulton to Norman Ward, 28 February 1968.

SAB, NWP, A526/175(1), file: Correspondence 1964, Norman Ward to Helen O'Reilly, 17 April 1964.

SAB, NWP, A526/561 (6), Dawson/Ward, House of Commons. 1962–7, 13-page typescript [n.d.] titled 'Divisions.'

SAB, NWP, A526/183 file: Correspondence 1971 (2), Fred Gibson to Norman Ward, 8 September 1971.

SAB, NWP, A526/184(2), file: Correspondence, 1972–6, Ward to Stanfield, 4 November 1974.

SAB, NWP, A526, file: Correspondence, 1974–6, Ward to Otto Lang, 27 September 1976.

SAB, NWP, A526/679, Correspondence 1979–83(1), Ward to Shirley Spafford, [n.d.].

SAB, NWP, A526/692, file: Stanley Knowles, 'The Role of the Opposition in Parliament,' 10.

Samara. 'The Accidental Citizen?' http://www.samaracanada.com/mp_exit_interviews.

Samara. 'It's My Party.' http://www2.samaracanada.com/downloads/ItsMyParty.pdf.

Samara. 'Welcome to Parliament: A Job with No Description.' http://www2.samaracanada.com/downloads/Samara_Report_Welcome_To_Parliament.pdf.

Saywell, John T. *'Just Call Me Mitch': The Life of Mitchell F. Hepburn*. Toronto: University of Toronto Press, 1991.

Schmitz, Gerald. 'Opposition in a Parliamentary System.' Library of Parliament, Political and Social Affairs Division, December 1988. http://dsp-psd.pwgsc.gc.ca/Collection-R/LoPBdP/BP/bp47-e.htm.

Seidle, F. Leslie. 'The Election Expenses Act: The House of Commons and the Parties.' In *The Canadian House of Commons: Essays in Honour of Norman Ward*, ed. John C. Courtney, 113–34. Calgary: University of Calgary Press, 1985.

Seidle, F. Leslie. 'Citizens Speaking for Themselves: New Avenues for Public Involvement.' In *Political Leadership and Representation in Canada: Essays in Honour of John C. Courtney*, ed. Hans J. Michelmann, Donald C. Story, and Jeffery S. Steeves, 81–109. Toronto: University of Toronto Press, 2007.

'Show Time: The Decline of the Canadian Parliament.' The Canadian Collection, Video. Magic Lantern Communication, 1993.

Skelton, Oscar D. *The Life and Letters of Sir Wilfrid Laurier*. Toronto: Oxford University Press, 1921.

Skogstad, Grace. 'The Liberal Party, Insensitivity, and Western Canadian Agriculture: Does the Account Still Stand Up?' In *Continuity and Change in Canadian Politics: Essays in Honour of David E. Smith*, ed. Hans J. Michelmann and Cristine de Clercy, 225–44. Toronto: University of Toronto Press, 2006.

Slater, D.W., and T.H.B. Symons. 'An Outline of Some Topics for Study by the Policy Advisory Committee.' [n.d.].

SLL. Stanley Knowles, 'I Believe in Parliament.' Lecture, Huron College, 19 November 1964, 4.

Smiley, Donald V. *Canada in Question: Federalism in the Seventies*. Toronto: McGraw-Hill Ryerson, 1972.

Smith, David Edward. 'Emergency Government in Canada.' *CHR* 50, no. 4 (December 1969): 429–48.

Smith, David E. *Prairie Liberalism: The Liberal Party in Saskatchewan, 1905–1971*. Toronto: University of Toronto Press, 1975.

Smith, David E. 'Party Government, Representation, and National Integration in Canada.' In *Party Government and Regional Representation in Canada*, ed. Peter Aucoin, 1–68. Toronto: University of Toronto Press in Cooperation with the Royal Commission on the Economic Union and Development Prospects for Canada, 1985.

Smith, David E. 'The Westminster Model in Ottawa: A Study in the Absence of Influence.' *British Journal of Political Science* 15, nos. 1 and 2 (2002): 54–64.

Smith, David E. 'Path Dependency and Saskatchewan Politics.' In *The Heavy Hand of History: Interpreting Saskatchewan's Past*, ed. Gregory P. Marchildon. Regina: Canadian Plains Research Center, 2005.

Smith, David E. *The People's House of Commons: Theories of Democracy in Contention*. Toronto: University of Toronto Press, 2007.

Smith, David E. *Federalism and the Constitution of Canada*. Toronto: University of Toronto Press, 2010.

Smith, David E. 'A Constitution in Some Respects Novel.' In *Federalism and the Constitution of Canada*, 40–61. Toronto: University of Toronto Press, 2010.

Smith, Denis. *Rogue Tory*. Toronto: MacFarlane Walter and Ross, 1995.

Sonier, Loredana Catali. 'New Brunswick's Experiment with a "House of No Nays."' *Parliamentarian* 85, no. 3 (2004): 64–7.

'Speaker's Ruling (Gilbert Parent), The Designation of Party Status.' 16 June 1994, *CPR* 17, no. 3 (Autumn 1994): 33–5.

Steed, Judy. *Ed Broadbent: The Pursuit of Power*. Markham: Viking, 1988.

Stevens, Geoffrey. *Stanfield*. Toronto: McClelland and Stewart, 1973.

Stewart, Gordon T. *The Origins of Canadian Politics: A Comparative Approach*. Vancouver: UBC Press, 1986.

'Stop Knifing Clark, Usually Mild Stanfield Advises Dief.' *Globe and Mail*, 23 September 1977, 10.

'Straight-Talking Fraser Strikes Fear on the Hill.' *Globe and Mail*, 12 February 2004, 4.

Switzman v. Elbling and the Attorney General of Quebec, [1957] SCR 285.

Taber, Jane. 'Tired of "Rabid Partisanship," Liberal MP Quits.' *Globe and Mail*, 11 November 2010, A9.

Taras, David. 'The Past and Future of Political Communication in Canada: An Introduction.' In *How Canadians Communicate IV: Media and Politics*, eds. David Taras and Christopher Waddell. Edmonton: Athabasca University Press, 2012, 1–25.

Taras, David, and Christopher Waddell. 'The 2011 Federal Election and the Transformation of Canadian Politics.' In *How Canadians Communicate IV: Media and Politics*, eds. David Taras and Christopher Waddell. Edmonton: Athabasca University Press, 2012, 71–107.

Taras, David, and Christopher Waddell, eds. *How Canadians Communicate IV: Media and Politics*. Edmonton: Athabasca University Press, 2012.

'The Opposition.' *Parliament and Reform*. Politics Briefing, No. 3. London: Constitutional Reform Centre, 1988.

Thomas, Lewis G. *The Liberal Party in Alberta*. Toronto: University of Toronto Press, 1959.

Thomas, Paul G. 'The Role of House Leaders in the Canadian House of Commons.' *CJPS* 15, no. 1 (March 1982): 125–44.

Thomas, Paul. 'The Past, Present, and Future of Officers of Parliament.' *CPA* 46, no. 3 (2003): 287–314.

Thomson, Carolyn. '"This Place": The Culture of Queen's Park.' In *Inside the Pink Palace: Ontario Legislature Internship Essays*, ed. Graham White, 1–20.

Ontario Legislature Internship Programme / Canadian Political Science Association. Toronto: University of Toronto Press, 1987.

Thomson, Dale C. *Louis St Laurent: Canadian*. Toronto: Macmillan of Canada, 1967.

Topp, Brian. *How We Almost Gave the Tories the Boot (The Inside Story behind the Coalition): A Memoir*. Toronto: Lorimer, 2010.

'Tories Begin Battle Against Coalition.' http://www.cbc.ca/news/canada/story/2008/12/02/harper-coalition.html. Cited in Tom Flanagan, 'Political Communication and the "Permanent Campaign."' In *How Canadians Communicate IV: Media and Politics*, eds. David Taras and Christopher Waddell. Edmonton: Athabaska University Press, 2012.

Toronto Mail and Empire, 6 October 1927. Cited in John Courtney, *The Selection of National Party Leaders in Canada* (p. 76). Toronto: Macmillan of Canada, 1973.

'Toward a More Responsible Two-Party System.' *APSR* 44, no. 3, Pt 2, Supplement (September 1950): 1–14.

Trent University Archives, Frost Papers, letterbook 8, Frost to C.H. Hale, 10 February 1942. Cited in Roger Graham, *Old Man Ontario: Leslie M. Frost*. Toronto: University of Toronto Press, 1990.

Trevelyan, G.M., ed. *The Works of Lord Macaulay* (London 1871), vol. VI. Quoted in Archibald S. Foord, *His Majesty's Opposition, 1714–1830*. Oxford: Clarendon Press, 1962.

Trollope, Anthony. *Phineas Finn*, vol. II. London: Geoffrey Cumberlege: Oxford University Press, 1949.

Underhill, Frank H. *In Search of Canadian Liberalism*. Toronto: Macmillan Company of Canada, 1961.

Valpy, Michael. 'NDP Leader Brought Inspiration and a Message of Hope to a Cynical Age.' *Globe and Mail*, 23 August 2011, S8.

Van Dusen, Tom. *Inside the Tent: Forty-Five Years on Parliament Hill*. Burnstown: General Store Publishing House, 1998.

Van Onselen, Peter. 'Major Party Senators and Electoral Professionalism in Australia.' PhD diss., University of Western Australia, 2006.

Vile, M.J.C. *Constitutionalism and the Separation of Powers*. Oxford: Clarendon Press, 1967.

Walton, Dawn. 'Legislature to Sit for 2 Days, Then Break.' *Globe and Mail*, 21 October 2011, A11.

Ward, John. 'In Memory's Eye: Reflections on Canadian Parliamentarians: Honourable Members-Part 1.' http://www.vindicator.ca/In_Memorys_Eye/3_Honourable_Members_1.html.

Ward, John. 'In Memory's Eye: Reflections on Canadian Parliamentarians: Prime Ministers – Part 1.' http://www.vindicator.ca/In_Memorys_Eye/2_Prime_Ministers.html.

Ward, Norman. 'The Formative Years of the House of Commons, 1867–1901.' *CJEPS* 18, no. 4 (November 1952): 431–51.

Ward, Norman. *The Public Purse: A Study in Canadian Democracy*. Toronto: University of Toronto Press, 1962.

Ward, Norman. *The Canadian House of Commons: Representation*. 2nd ed. Toronto: University of Toronto Press, 1963.

Ward, Norman. 'The Press and Patronage: An Exploratory Operation.' In *The Political Process in Canada: Essays in Honour of R. MacGregor Dawson*, ed. J.H. Aitchison, 3–16. Toronto: University of Toronto Press, 1963.

Ward, Norman, ed. *A Party Politician: The Memoirs of Chubby Power*. Toronto: Macmillan of Canada, 1966.

Ward, Norman. 'A Century of Constituencies.' *CPA* 10, no. 1 (1967): 105–22.

Ward, Norman. 'Hon. James Gardiner and the Liberal Party of Alberta.' *CHR* 56, no. 3 (1975): 303–22.

Ward, Norman, and David Smith. *Jimmy Gardiner: Relentless Liberal*. Toronto: University of Toronto Press, 1990.

Weedmark, Kevin. 'Long Gun Registry Is History: Komarnicki Feels Relief as Gun Bill Passes.' 20 February 2012. http://www.world-spectator.com/news_story.php?id=51.

Weisman, Steven R. (ed. and intro.). *Daniel Patrick Moynihan: A Portrait in Letters of an American Visionary*. New York: Public Affairs, 2010.

Wesley, Jared J. *Code Politics: Campaigns and Cultures on the Canadian Prairies*. Vancouver: UBC Press, 2011.

Wheare, K.C. *Federal Government*. London: Oxford University Press, 1946.

Wheare, K.C. *Federal Government*. 3rd ed. London: Oxford University Press, 1953.

Whitaker, Reginald. *The Government Party: Organizing and Financing the Liberal Party of Canada, 1930–1958*. Toronto: University of Toronto Press, 1977.

Whitaker, Reg. 'Is the Government Party Over?' *Globe and Mail*, 16 May 2011, A11.

Whyte, John D. 'Constitutional Change and Constitutional Durability.' *JPPL* 5 (2011): 419–36.

Williams, John R. *The Conservative Party in Canada: 1920–1949*. Durham: Duke University Press, 1956, cited in John C. Courtney, *Do Conventions Matter? Choosing National Party Leaders in Canada*. Montreal and Kingston: McGill–Queen's University Press, 1995.

Willison, Sir John. *Reminiscences: Political and Personal*. Toronto: McClelland and Stewart, 1919.

Wills, Terrance. 'Tough Debate Looms in House Over Official Opposition.' *The Gazette* (Montreal), 24 February 1996, A9.

Wilson, John. 'In Defence of Parliamentary Opposition.' *CPR* 11, no. 2 (1988): 26–31.

Wingrove, Josh. 'Lone-Wolf Province Getting Back in Fold.' *Globe and Mail*, 5 October 2011, A9.

Winsor, Hugh, and Tu Thanh Ha. 'Manning Set to Have PM Removed.' *Globe and Mail*, 14 December 1995, A4.

Young, Hugo. *One of Us: A Biography of Margaret Thatcher*. London: Macmillan, 1991.

Young, Walter D. *The Anatomy of a Party: The National CCF, 1932–1961*. Toronto: University of Toronto Press, 1969.

Index